# *Know Thyself*

Reverend Albert Gani

Revised and Expanded Edition

KNOW THYSELF
Revised and Expanded Edition


Reverend Albert Gani


Published by: Albert Gani
207 S. Commons Ford Road
Austin, Texas 78733

ISBN 1-882853-16-4


$35.00 Softcover

The painting on the front cover is *Oedipe explique l'énigme du Sphinx* by Ingres Jean-Auguste-Dominique (1780-1867.) ©Photo RMN - R.G. Ojeda, reproduced with the kind permission of the Louvre Museum in Paris.

# *About the Author*

Albert Gani is the author—publisher. His experience includes fourteen years in international trade, and, more importantly, over forty thousand hours of experience, helping people find purpose, self-leadership, their task in life. This faith has taken him from coast to coast in the United States as well as to Europe and Mexico.

He has an uncanny ability to work with people and organizations and help them make major changes in their lives through the application of ethical principles.

Rev. Gani brings to his lectures a keen wit and his extremely versatile knowledge of world history and politics, languages, music, and philosophy, making them informative, thought-provoking and entertaining. He encourages those working with him by using his own crises and struggles as examples of what can be overcome. Perhaps most apparent and inspiring of all his qualities to those whom he has helped is his courageous, ethical and loving stance for the truth, regardless of the outcome.

This book is dedicated to

**J. Curtis Jordan**

whose love for the material led him to devote
countless hours to all the transcribing and
editing, as well as for contributing his
ideas, reactions, support, etc., etc.
He is responsible for making
this book happen at this time.

To

**Judith Clement Gani**

my former wife
who helped me write and typed for me
all of the material written between
1976 and 1980, copyrighted in 1979 and 80,
included in this book.

# *Acknowledgments*

- To my former wife, Judy, who, in the late seventies, lisented to and encouraged my theories of the switch at puberty and the inferior function. She, in 1980, had originally transcribed, edited, and referenced the material of this particular chapter.

- To my wife, Robin, for all of her contributions and leadership.

- To all my friends who encouraged me to write it.

- To all the tens of thousands of people who contributed by revealing who they really are—creatures of God, who, in the final analysis, are unique and cannot be categorized.

# *Table of Contents*

### Section III
### *Crucifixion of the Ego*

### Section IV
### *The Art of Surrender; Yielding*

# *Warning—Disclaimer*

This book is an invitation to spiritual introspection. It is sold with the understanding that it, or anyone involved in publishing or marketing it, make no claims of healing of any kind.

The purpose of this book is to inspire you to a spiritual and ethical life. The author or anyone else involved in publishing or marketing it will not have any liability and desist themselves of any responsibility to any person or group or company for any damage or loss incurred in any way by the contents of this book.

# *Foreword*

Self-study constitutes the fundamental entrance step to any spiritual endeavour. To know yourself means to know how you have shaped your physical, mental, emotional, and spiritual bodies. The descent of the soul into the personality determines it and shapes it. Therefore, spiritual growth, meaning the pursuit of happiness, can only be found through bringing back to consciousness this descent. That will be the only valid way to determine who you are as a person and how you are likely to interact with others.

In this book, I have proceeded from revealed material, progressing into linking various typological theories. From the spiritual angle, you will see how they all merge. You will also see how inadequate and incomplete are the favourite typologies of mundane psychology.

Most importantly, have fun with it.

Albert Gani
October, 1993

# *Foreword to this Revised and Expanded Edition*

All that is changes. Everything is in a state of flux. Arrested terminologies arrest the meaning that created them. Terminologies must change in order to preserve the meaning behind them.

Some new terminologies have already been used in the past. Yet newer ones are used here. All of them have been related to former terminologies that have been used since time immemorial. The endnotes of this book abundantly refer to past methods of defining new concepts.

Anyone who arrogates to himself any new idea is an ignorant fool. All wisdom has always consisted in taking the old one step further into the new. Noone owns any ideas. Everyone has access to them, not only through libraries, but also through inner guidance.

*Know Thyself* is an invitation and an injunction by Socrates. The implications go far beyond philosophy, into religion, ethics and ways of living.

The painting by Ingres on the front cover depicts the power that self-knowledge has to destroy guards and to annihilate the evil that lurks behind them. Indeed, the scales of the Sphinx fall off when Oedipus gives his insight. The lion is now naked and vulnerable to the arrows of truth. By killing the lion/Sphinx, his lower self,[2] Oedipus liberates himself and liberates the city of Thebes at the same time. Your self-knowledge will thus cleanse you and strengthen you, liberating you and those around you. Hopefully this book will show you how to do it.

Albert Gani
July, 2001

# *Introduction*

The first thing we say when we approach **human types** is that it is in no way an exact science and that, therefore, we are talking in relative terms. And what we are going to say concerning character types needs to be taken lightly, as with a grain of salt.

The other consideration to be made is that in the process of self-renewal, or cleansing (which can happen voluntarily or involuntarily through crises or through life circumstances) **human types change**. In fact, the whole purpose of crises or life circumstances, and particularly, the whole purpose of this method is the dissolution of, and therefore, the change of human types.

**The changes are initiated from within. The Life Force, through the Spirit, energizes the soul, pushing the next layer, or type into the personality, destroying or dissolving the one that has been there. This is why only through spirituality or religion can human types make any sense.**

Thus, when the **surface human type is dissolved, it makes room for another human type,** usually its opposite, to come to the surface. The person who is undergoing such a transition will present to the typologist ambivalent or even contradictory messages. The experienced typologist needs to recognize all of this with a sense of wisdom and balance.

Add to this the fact that typology or, to put it better, the formation of a human type, is **nothing but the overemphasis of a particular function, an instinctual function,** a faculty. For example, there are people who are visual rather than tactile. This very much is a typological quality or defect. It does not mean that they have no sense of touch. It merely means that they have chosen to develop sight and to leave touch dormant or, worse, repress the sense of touch. It also means that sight will be used to do the work of touching and that will, of course, create problems both for sight and for touch. The perception of the Universe will be commensurately distorted; as a result, this will bring distorted life circumstances to the individual.

So, **typology is the study of distortion.** It is not the study of Spirit; it is the Spirit's study of personality and soul. Since it is a spiritual study of distortion, Godless psychologists have found themselves lost in it and have ended up with typological systems that have been incomplete.

For instance, **Jung's** characterological structure disregards the Will. Neglecting the Will is impossible when typology is approached from a spiritual point of view. The Will is one of the three Rays of Aspect, one member of the Spiritual Trinity, you cannot miss it. It must be dealt with.

It makes sense, not only to body type theorists, but to us who deal with this from the spiritual point of view, that you create your own reality, and therefore, **you create your body.** Consequently, your body is a **precipitate** of who you are on the more subtle levels. The body type theorists erroneously believe that you are your body to the exclusion of anything else. Their materialism blinds them to the much greater reality of the soul and of the Spirit, which are continuously sending into the personality new aspects that need to be manifested in the person's life. Nevertheless, body type theories have given us excellent insights as to the determination of one's type by the mere examination of his body, his mannerisms, the tightness of his muscles, etc. We include this in our teachings.

Therefore, what I have done is to combine the spiritual typology that we have obtained from various spiritual sources, notably the **Tibetan** in A. A. Bailey's books, with the psychological brilliance—albeit incomplete—of Carl Jung, and the body type insights of body shape and form, found in many disciplines.

xiv

**For the Reader:** We recommend that the Reader take from this manual only what he experiences and what he experientially believes, while putting aside the rest, but keeping an open mind to it. A lot will be said here that may go against your deep religious, sociological, or family beliefs. We do not present it to engage you in a fruitless philosophical or theological debate. Be guided by what you can experience and do not believe anything that you do not experience. Take only what is convincing to you.

We believe that an individual's career goes through many incarnations, in the same manner as he goes through many experiences in one lifetime. The purpose of reincarnation is the continuous education of the soul and the personality. Once the individual has learned all he needs to learn from the sensible [1] world, he will stop reincarnating in it and move on to higher spheres of development, where passing through the doors of birth and death is not necessary.

You may or may not believe in reincarnation. If you do not, the material in this book is still valid. Although we bring into life conditions from past lives, we recreate in this life all of the necessary experiences, misconceptions, reference points required for self-actualization. There is no need to refer to past lives in order to overcome current problems. That knowledge may help to understand the current problem, but it will neither solve it nor heal it. Only the consideration of what has happened in this lifetime will heal those pains. Furthermore, it is possible in this lifetime to heal the pain of this lifetime and of all other past lives. In healing one pain, you heal all others. The healing occurs on the qualitative level, not on the quantitative level.

For example, if out of cruelty in a past life you have been a serial murderer, you do not have to be murdered as many times as you have murdered in order to resolve your karma. In your present life, you may recreate this cruelty on a higher

xv

level, such as the emotional level. The resolution of the cause of this emotional cruelty, and the consequent dissolution of it will free you of all karma associated with this distortion. Here, we find the concept of redemption and forgiveness that is so attractive in Christianity.

I refer, from time to time, to the Tibetan. The Tibetan is the Master Djwhal Khul. He dictated to Alice A. Bailey voluminous and extensive material on esoteric psychology which has enormous validity, not only for the esotericist, but for anyone interested in self-knowledge and knowledge of the Universe. The books are published by Lucis Publishing Company in New York and are widely available.

**Note:** All superscript numerals which follow a particular word or phrase refer to endnotes, to be found in the end of the book. For example, on the previous page, sensible[1] refers to the first endnote.

# Section I

# Necessary Basic Concepts
of Self-Knowledge

# Chapter 1
# *Spirit, Soul and Personality*

Before incarnation the Spirit puts together a soul whose function is to be the kernel, the seed planted in the fertile material body so as to create a human personality. In that seed are contained:

1) Some elements that have not as yet been developed to the point of self-realization or self-actualization.

2) Some harmfulness and regressive aspects coming from past lives, for which the individual has to redeem himself.

3) A task, consisting of service to be rendered to a group or to humanity.

4) Inner support systems, consisting of aspects that have already been transformed in past lives.

## *Personal Case History*
For example, I had abused music in a past life, using it to obtain love, sex, money, approval, position, and power. In my present incarnation, music was put in my soul with the proviso that I could not play it, I could only enjoy listening to it. And, indeed, it has been extremely difficult for me to play any musical instrument. Every time I try to play one I am overcome by incredible impatience and I am led to doing something else. With the support of music and its beauty, I was also given the task of redemption for my dishonesty and theft. Indeed, the misuse of music for material purposes in the

past life constituted theft. I had to experience, in this lifetime, the blatant pain of stealing in order to understand the spiritual implications of it. I had to realize the connection between honesty and integrity, and the capacity to enjoy music—a connection which was absent from my consciousness up to this lifetime.

In the act of overcoming my thievery, I also helped a lot of people. The admission of the theft, cleansing myself with other people's assistance, helped everybody else around me bring up to the surface the little dishonesties weighing on **their** souls. Therefore, in the dissolution of this aspect of my own lower self,[2] I was accomplishing a universal task in helping others dissolve theirs. I was making it a lot easier for everybody else.

Furthermore, in that dissolution, a great deal of guidance and understanding as to the nature of the human personality came to me. It is only after my great money crisis that I understood the switch of interests and personality types at puberty and at menopause, principles that we will deal with in this book.

Also, if it were not for the presence of my appreciation of the beauty of music, I would have found it impossible to go through the excruciating pain of the dissolution of my lower self. Enjoyment of music in my soul made it possible for my personality to do what I did. Last but not least, my past life musical virtuosity has now been transformed into my virtuosity in understanding and putting into words people's problems and helping them make connections. The greedy, yuppy thief who was using his brilliance in business and who was on a collision course with his soul and his Spirit was my personality. As a result of this financial crisis, my personality changed. New elements were released in me for resolution, such as my self-indulgence of food, which did not exist in the past but does exist now. This is my next test. As I solve one problem, another one is presented for resolution. In the process of these resolutions, my progress accelerates and I will reach a point where these problems will no longer exist as problems per se, but will become invitations for creativity. And so it is for every member of the human race. All of this is said to encourage you to study who you really are now, **i.e.,** to become proficient in knowing what is in your Spirit, and what is in your soul, and what is in your personality. What we are attempting to do here is not merely to help people cope—a term that I abhor. What we are trying to do here is to get people to merge with their souls; this will sometimes involve the acceleration of an impending crisis for the sake of greater development and accomplishment of the person's task. The total commitment to the spiritual path[3] involves the dissolution of the rigidified personality—the personality type. This is true no matter what your personality type is, no matter which Ray[4] and which Aspect[5] you have decided to overemphasize. Remember, every single type can degenerate into a distortion, and does. None of them is exempt from this.

All functions exist in each human being and the human type is merely the emphasis of one function to the detriment of the others. Therefore, one can find in diminished degrees the other functions existing in an individual's personality. In a soul is to be found all of the potentials that a person will manifest during a particular incarnation. Therefore, in the soul is to be found all the Rays, since self-actualization is really the point where the personality will manifest the harmonious whole range of Rays.

However, due to the person's idiosyncrasies, task, etc., only part of the soul gets released into the personality at any given time. If all of it were released at once, it would be impossible to take.

Unfortunately, the development of those skills leads the personality (through the line of least resistance[6]) to rest on its laurels. For example, if your soul had released into your personality mathematics and you became a mathematical whiz, and you got a great deal of praise and adulation for your mathematical ability, you would not want to receive the next wave from the soul, which would overshadow mathematics. You would jealously guard your identity, resisting the new identity that is trying to make it through in its raw form, threatening the existing and comfortable status quo.

Here lie **all** of the problems to be encountered by a human being. The resistence against the penetration of the soul into the personality is what creates all the conflicts, inner, and therefore, outer. If the personality learns how to open up and in a flexible manner receive the next waves that need to be integrated, then there are no crises. Highly evolved individuals successfully mesh the incoming energies; however, those not so evolved must struggle, creating all of the problems that we know so very well. (See chapter on *Inferior Functions.*)

## Misconceptions about the Soul

We can see here, therefore, that the soul is not totally good. Our soul is not God in us. Our soul is the seed in which is contained the story of our life as that seed grows and bears fruit. In a soul is to be found everything you need to manifest and resolve in your life.

Therefore, the soul corresponds to the lower self.[7] The soul, obstructed, becomes the lower self. Obstructed potentiality becomes harmfulness. Unimpeded, the soul material releases itself into the personality for the purpose of actualization.

The accomplishment of a person's task is, therefore, the

invasion of the personality by the soul, the blending of the two. The soul and the personality become one. In the Tibetan, this is described as the Third Initiation. It is also the "building of the bridge" (the antakharana, as the Tibetan calls it), between the personality and the soul. The connection between personality and soul also connects soul and Spirit. As the personality steps aside for the soul to come in, the Spirit becomes available to both soul and personality. This is known in conventional religion, when it is said that if you take one step toward God, God takes two steps toward you. You take one step toward making yourself available to your soul, your Spirit will take two steps to make itself available to both your soul and your personality. Guidance is nothing else but what happens when this becomes reality. The only valid, true guidance is the one that comes from the Spirit, the Higher Self [8] as it is otherwise called, which is in touch with other all knowing entities.

## Chapter 2

# *Crystallization and Formation of the Persona; The Personality; The Grandiose Self; The Idealized Self; The Glamours; The Disguise*

---

This is the final crystallization and deceleration of the Divine Life Force. It creates the body, the mannerisms, i.e., what is mundanely called the personality.

In order to hide or disguise the soul, the above mentioned modalities are formed. This concept has been abundantly explored by A. A. Bailey's Tibetan, who called it the mask of the soul.[9] It is also found in ancient Greek drama as *persona*, meaning mask,[10] in C. G. Jung,[11] in Viktor Frankl,[12] in Gareth Knight,[13] in Edgar Cayce,[14] in Yogananda,[15] in Shelley.[16] We also find it in the Zondervan *Life Application Bible.*[17] The concept is found in the Bible as cloak.[18]

This concept has, therefore, existed since time immemorial. It is not anybody's property. Anyone who arrogates it as his is a fool.

The persona, the personality, the grandiose self, the idealized self, the mask is what we put on in order to hide our soul, our lower self, our real self.

Henceforth, in this book, we choose to use Karen Horney's terminology for this aspect of the self, calling it the idealized self.[33]

It is sometimes identified—erroneously so—with the ego. Whenever an idealized self is identified, one can be sure of the existence of harmful material, or stifled potentiality, i.e., a soul/lower self. Attached to it we find harmful intentionality.[19] The idealized self will many times attempt to resemble the Higher Self, thus making it very difficult to differentiate between the two. This is why I have also called the idealized self the *deified self*. Here are some of their differences:

| *Deified/Idealized self* | *Higher Self* |
|---|---|
| Feels sickly sweet. | Feels light and natural. |
| Has harmful attractiveness. | Is long lasting. |
| Exhibits victimization. | Takes responsibility. |
| Exhibits despair. | Goes through sadness. |
| Insists on purism. | Does the best possible. |
| Does not tolerate change. | Welcomes change. |

## Chapter 3

# Rays of Aspect and Attribute; Corresponding Gods and Goddesses Of Mythology

According to the Tibetan and Alice A. Bailey, there are three Rays of Aspect, and Four Rays of Attribute. The Three Rays of Aspect correspond to the Trinity, which is found in Christianity, Hinduism and Buddhism. In Christianity, we have, respectively, Father, Son and Mother (not Holy Ghost); in Hinduism, we have Shiva, Brahma, and Vishnu; in Buddhism, Nirmanakaya, Sambhogakaya, and Dharmakaya, comprising the "triple body" called—amazingly reminiscent of our language—trikaya. The Rays of Aspect are:

1) **Will or Power.** The Ray of the Father, as it is known in the Trinity.

2) **Love and Wisdom.** The Ray of the Son, the Ray of Christ, the Ray of Buddha.

3) **Active Intelligence and Adaptability.** The Ray of Mother, not of the Holy Ghost. The Holy Ghost has been too long a euphemism used by the misogynistic bigots.

Out of the Ray of Active Intelligence and Adaptability come four minor Rays, called Rays of Attribute, as follows:

4) **Harmony through Conflict.**

5) **Concrete Knowledge and Science.**

6) **Idealism and Devotion.**

7) **Order, Ceremony, Good Habits and Magic.**
Each of these Seven Rays constitutes a personality type. Once again, this does not mean that a person who is, let's say, a Ray IV Type, does not have all the other Rays within him. He has them developed to a lesser degree or, as we said before, repressed.

### Gods and Goddesses Associated with the Rays

Gods and goddesses can be associated with the Rays. This indeed would confirm that the idealized self—the personality—is actually a deified self. The idealized/deified self corresponds to and awakens deep archetypal images, reviving them and patterning the individual after them.

Here are some of my thoughts on the matter:

1) **Ray I** can be associated with Zeus, and even Hercules, or Thor.

2) **Ray II** can be associated with Christ-like gods as in Osiris, or in Christ himself.

3) **Ray III** can be associated with Hera, Isis, as well as the Virgin Mary.

4) **Ray IV** can be associated with Vulcan, Hephaistos, the god of blacksmiths, continuously concerned with explosiveness, fire. Vulcan was also involved with a great deal of self-depreciation. Although Venus was married to him as a reward, she had a great deal of contempt for him and was unfaithful to him. This is very reminiscent of the masochistic tendencies to be found in the Emotions Type associated with Ray IV.

5) Particular focus on outward appearance characterizing **Rays V and VII** makes it possible for them to be identified with the models of perfection represented by some of the lesser gods of antiquity. Ray V can be identified with Venus and Apollo. Apollo is the god of the Absolute, of the vertical connection.

6) **Ray VI** can be identified with all prophets and messiahs from Jesus—in contradistinction to the Christ—Joshua, Mohammad, Elijah, etc.

7) **Ray VII** can be identified with Diana/Artemis and Dionysus/Hermes. Dionysus is the god of the relative, of the horizontal connection and is concerned with interactions with humans.

**The goal of life is the unification of all principles. When all gods merge into one, you have within an individual the self-actualized person, the Master.**

As a matter of fact, this is very difficult. For example, the history of humanity up to this point has been one in which humans have had to disconnect from the Dionysian in order to reach spiritual development. Therefore, there has been heretofore a tendency to identify the Apollonian with spiritual development. For the first time, with the Age of Aquarius, the force of spirituality is penetrating the sensible world.[20] This is the divine aspect of Apollo, the Obsessive Penetrator. Therefore, we will increasingly see examples of people who have successfully combined spirituality and sexuality.

With whom do you identify and why? What is the origin of your identification with one aspect or with the other? What is it that you have sacrificed in the process? How can you integrate what you have forgotten and sacrificed? How easy is it to find a role model who has combined the horizontal and the vertical?

Let's talk for a moment about the notion of the Rays of Attribute "coming out of the womb" of the Third Ray of Active Intelligence. The First Son, Ray II, has for a task the bringing to life, or to birth, the Rays of Attribute. This is a beautiful concept that the Tibetan has given us. It shows that through love and wisdom which rule the Universe (God is love), we are able to develop and self-actualize the Rays of

Attribute. Through love, yes, but not without the Father and the Mother, not without Will and not without Reason, Active Intelligence. The birth of the First Son, Ray II, who is the head of the Hierarchy in this solar system, is different from the birth of his brothers, the Rays of Attribute. The initial "impregnation" coming from Ray I to Ray III creates the First Son, bringing the triad to completion. With the presence of the First Son, divinity is at one. Here is where the misconception of virgin birth has distorted the healthy concept of the Trinity.

## Chapter 4
# *The Warping of Sexuality and Its Consequences*

### *The Fallacy of the Virgin Birth*
The feeling of completion achieved at the time of the birth of the first child has triggered many misconceptions, one of which concerns the virgin birth. The first child, who brings to completion the divine triad, does not require a virgin mother. Only if you have harmful feelings about sexuality will you want to believe that the mother has to be virgin, and therefore, "unsoiled," clean. The reality is that nothing is cleaner or more divine in human experience than the experience of sexuality. Since it is the most pleasurable and the closest experience to God, it is also the one that has been the most distorted. It is important to remember, also, that this distortion is not the exclusive possession of Christianity; it exists in many other religions and cultures.

### *Why Sexuality Was Denigrated*
**Since sex is the most pleasurable activity in the human realm, it is also the activity that potentially brings us the closest to God.** Consequently, it becomes the most powerful, and therefore, the most distorted of all activities. The origins of the antipathy for sexuality are to be found in this very fact. Sexuality, being the greatest, the most powerful and the most

pleasurable force becomes the most feared, and therefore, the most distorted. Eventually, it is made to be a representative of evil. So how then could this birth of the Son be explained without resorting to this "dirty process of impregnation and penetration"? That is why the virgin birth was invented, not only by the Christians but by many other dispensations of antiquity.

It is easily understood that the first child in any family creates a sense of completion, since it makes the new mother and father into parents who, hopefully, are responsible and selflessly give. Once born, the Aspect of Love helps in the liberation of the Aspects of Attribute from Mother's womb. The concept of Mother/Matter as merely the element that imprisons humanity, not as the intelligent and adaptable fertile soil without which there is no life, is an unfortunate and denigrating misconception.

## Chapter 5
# *Types, Races and Cultures*

One might ask if typological and/or Ray Types apply across the sexes and to all human races and cultures. The answer is yes, fundamentally. However, from one culture to the next, you will have differences in body types or typologies due to the cultural differences and the karmic heritage of the race.

For example, the black race, being the descendant of the Lemurian, has inherited from that ancient civilization the over-sexed quality. Hence, the overemphasis on the lower part of their body, the great development of the pelvis and the legs in contradistinction to the rest of the body. Another feature of the black race these days is the peculiar emergence of their violence in the inner cities of the United States, and in the countries of Africa. This is due to an overreaction to a condition that existed during Lemurian times. Indeed, the Lemurian race decided as a group to avoid violence at all costs. This decision was taken because of the fact that the previous root race had destroyed itself through violence and warfare. In compensation for the repression of violence at the time of Lemuria, the blacks are now going through an overexpression of it. The Lemurians epitomized the "make love, not war" dictum; their task was to populate the earth. Therefore, their task was really very much centered on sexuality. Eventually the focus on sexuality brought about excesses. Hence, the fact that all of the venereal diseases are really inherited from the Lemurian times.

Nevertheless, all human types can be seen in the black population, as well as in any other population. For example, the inflated bottom, Ray III Type woman, is very much a feature of the black race. So is the Dionysus/Hermes Type male whose emphasis on the pelvis gives us the over-sexed feature in any race.

In the Chinese culture, there is a preponderance of the Ray IV holding pattern. Indeed, the holding creates diminution of their extremities. The Sumo wrestlers are a manifestation of it with their hara—the huge, overgrown belly. Again, if we trace this to the fact that the Chinese are the descendants of the third root race, the Atlanteans, it will make a lot of sense. Indeed, the Atlanteans came in with the task of developing the solar plexus. The solar plexus is the chakra par excellence that typifies the Ray IV Type, the holding in the middle.

If we look at different cultures, we will find a preponderance of one typology over another. For instance, if we differentiate the Latin cultures from the Anglo Saxon cultures, we will find a lot more rigidity and Ray VI Types in the Anglo cultures, and more of the Ray IV and inflated bottom in the Latin cultures. We will also find the peculiar existence of a lot of Ray II Types in the Anglo Saxon cultures. This contradicts the fact that there exists abundance in the Anglo Saxon world. You would think that in an atmosphere of abundance, there would be a smaller percentage of Emaciated Ray II Types. This demonstrates that the creation of the Emaciated Type is not necessarily due solely to lack of food; it is due mainly to lack of love. The Anglo Saxons are not known for their effusive expressions of love, whilst the Latins, on the other hand, are. The Latins are much more prone to nourish their kids with love than are the Anglo Saxons. Hence, the Emaciated Type is to be found more in the

Anglo Saxon population than in the Latin populations. The greater existence, however, of the Ray IV Type of holding in the Latin population is a reflection of the cultural overconcern and overattention given to the child when it comes to food, bowel movement, and so on. The typical Italian mama or Mexican mama creates the existence of the Masochistic holding pattern in their respective populations.

There is an interesting conclusion that arises from all of this, which is the fact that the Protestant religion had greater success in the Anglo Saxon countries than it did in the Latin countries.

The Protestant work ethic is much better suited for the Stiff and Thinking Types, which are more widely found in the Anglo Saxon cultures than in the Latin cultures.

By contrast, the Catholic religion, where progress is either seen as a moot point or denigrated, is much more likely to succeed in an atmosphere of holding where there is a lot more concern with immediate physical nourishment, satiation, satisfaction, contentment, apart from social/financial/material change.

The entire medieval feudal system was not conducive to progress at all:

- Nobility was too busy fighting wars than to educate themselves or to improve their living conditions.
- The clergy considered learning anything technical as superfluous and a deterrent from studying religion and being in a state of meditation and contemplation.
- The third estate could not do anything anyway because they were too poor, too illiterate and too hungry to raise themselves out of their conditions.

One has to wait until the late Middle Ages with the creation of the guilds and the emergence of the bourgeoisie to see any progress on the material level at all. Under these conditions, Martin Luther's Reformation could grow more easily in the Anglo countries than in the Latin countries. The consequences of this are enormous. As we have seen in the past couple of centuries, it is the Anglo countries that have brought about technical progress, that have propagated western civilization all over the globe. Western civilization is really an Anglo civilization, it is not a Latin civilization. It is the English language that is now the international language; everybody does business in English, anyone who travels must learn English, and that is true internationally.

Even if you consider a country such as France, you will find a distinct difference between the northern and the southern parts of the country. The north is a lot more industrial and nordic, and the population, even though still Catholic, is not as Catholic as in the south of France. Typologically, the northern French are much more stiff, and much more Ray II emaciated, whilst in the south of France you have a situation that is much more akin to Italy or Spain, which are Latin, Catholic, more Ray IV Sumo, and less industrially developed. The same syndrome is found in other countries as well.

*Section II*

# *A Description of the Types*

# Chapter 6
# *Introduction*

Having combined three systems into one—Rays, Jungian and body types—I will here, for the sake of clarity, give you a table of correspondences of the various terminologies used, as well as of my own coinages:

| *Ray Types* | *Gods or Deities* | *My New Coinages* |
| --- | --- | --- |
| Ray I, Will | Zeus or Jupiter | Inflated Top |
| Ray II, Love | Osiris or Christ | Emaciated |
| Ray III Female, Intelligence | Hera, Isis, Virgin Mary, Fertility Goddess | Inflated Bottom |
| Ray III Male | I haven't yet found a god with which to identify this type; the closest I can get to this is Einstein | Ray III Male, Inflated Bottom |
| Ray IV | Hephaistos, Vulcan | Sumo |
| Ray V Male | Apollo, Mars | Stiff, Militaristic and Obsessive Penetrator |
| Ray V Female | Venus | Cinderella |

| Ray VI | Jesus, Mohammed, Joshua | Disjointed, Intuitive |
|---|---|---|
| Ray VII Male | Dionysus, Hermes | Femininized Male |
| Ray VII Female | Diana, Artemis | Masculinized Female |

Please keep in mind that no typology is precise. This is merely a guide. It reveals that typology has always existed.

Nor is this complete. No typology is complete. Take, for instance, the case of Athena. She is born, out of her father's head, armed to the teeth. She is the type of woman who is born adult, subservient only to her father. It is tempting to lump her in with Artemis. However, it won't quite do. She is a type of her own, straddled between Hera and Artemis. This is food for thought.

No book is ever complete or perfect. Anyone who claims completeness or perfection is an arrogant fool.

## Chapter 7

# Ray I: The Will Type; Father

## General Characteristics of the Will Type

They will be able to display **physical strength, moral courage,** persistence to the point of stubbornness. They will tend to want to be **truthful to a fault** and will display blind **fearlessness.** They will know how to rule and be good leaders. On the mental level, they will have great capacities to conceptualize, to synthesize and to zero in on resolutions to problems that may baffle the other types. They are great leaders of men.

One thinks here of Napoleon, Caesar and Alexander. Napoleon was able to inspire men into the conquering and the liberation of the entire continent of Europe from the misconceptions of the Middle Ages which were to be found in the old regimes' political systems. He did exactly the same thing in Egypt, for instance, inspiring his troops at the foot of the Great Pyramid and Sphinx when he said, "Men, from the top of this pyramid, forty centuries are looking at you with expectation." There is, in the Will Type, always a sense of greatness, or grandeur which, of course, can degenerate into ego trips, as the rest of Napoleon's life demonstrates.

With Alexander the Great, we can see the manifestation of a great task in the propagation of Greek thought and political systems to the ancient and backward Assyrian and Egyptian Empires. The story of the Gordian Knot is a pointedly significant divine aspect of the Will Type who will not be arrested by the mental or emotional games played by other people.

In the City of Gordia [King Gordius of Phrygia] there existed a knot which was so complicated that it was said that he who could untie it would conquer the world. Alexander, after conquering the city of Gordia, was presented with the knot and was told this story. He drew his sword and with one quick blow slashed through the knot, thus declaring himself the conqueror of the world.

Napoleon, who dragged Pope Pius VII all the way to Paris to have himself crowned emperor, ended up crowning himself and crowning his wife Josephine while saying, "God gave me this crown, beware to you if you ever think of touching it."[21] Caesar's fearlessness to pirates was very well known. While a prisoner, he confronted the pirate chieftain, telling him that he would be sorry some day. Indeed, once ransomed, he proceeded to raise an army and a fleet and rid the Western Mediterranean once and for all of pirates (at least for the duration of the Roman Empire). He also patterned himself after gods, thus allowing an unlimited concept of himself, and also developing a dangerously overinflated ego.

The Will Type will often get the feeling that he has been invested with a divine right and a divine mission. (Here is the connection between the First and the Sixth Rays.) Having a sense of history, they will have a sense of continuity. They will have a deep desire to inhabit father's fortune and to do better than he did.

Madame de Staël, whose salons during the French Revolution greatly influenced the political climate of the time (Napoleon met Josephine at Madame de Staël's salon), was a Will Type. She was a continuous challenge to Napoleon, who felt endangered by her and who banished her from Paris and later from France entirely. Before being exiled, she was behind a few rumblings against the new French Empire. She never relented her opinions and continued to attack Napoleon from wherever she was. The physical characteristics of the Will Type can be clearly seen in the portraits of her found in her biographies.

In the early days of our history, the divine right of kings was beneficial. Indeed, kings were those who had a channel and guidance, and had a clear sense of mission. Their task was to guide primitive humanity and accelerate the development of the race. Later in our history, this degenerated into totalitarianism. The pretense of being given privileges over others was dishonestly used.

An excellent example of this is Louis XIV, called the Sun King. He said things like, "I am the State," totally identifying himself with France; "What I say, France says," i.e., I have total and complete power to make the laws and to break the laws. He came at a time in the second half of the 17th Century when law and order were needed. This explains the initial success of the golden age of French thought, literature, philosophy, science and so forth, which then spilled over into the rest of Europe. To the end of the 18th Century, all of Europe adopted the ways as set by Louis XIV. Ballet, fencing and the rules of etiquette are leftovers from this very powerful Ray I influence of the 17th Century.

An interesting aspect of the Will Type is what Hegel calls "the devouring instinct." If you observe a young child, you will see in him a desire to grasp a hold of an object and change its form, devour it, make it do what he wants. The divine aspect of this is obviously the Instinct of Enquiry combined with the Instinct of Self-Assertion so very often found in the Will Types who come in to change the existing reality. Unfortunately, instead of channeling this very valuable instinct, it is usually crushed, and therefore, distorted. Can you recapture it in your own life? Can you allow yourself to be as curious and vigorous and aggressive as you were when you were an infant, channeling these energies into beneficial tasks for your betterment or the betterment of your group?

### Reactions to the Will Type

All of this is written here to evoke a response from you. How do you react to it? How do you feel about all of these people? Do you see yourself as them, emulating them? Do you recognize your parents in them, do you recognize your bosses or your employees or your children or your wife or your husband here? Do you have contempt for that? Do you envy it? Do you see yourself in it?

See if you can answer all of these questions in writing. Spend time doing it.

So, we can say there are beneficial aspects of the First Ray which include strength, freedom from fear, courage, the ability to synthesize great ideas, and the ability to motivate.

Some harmful aspects are the self-centeredness, the conceit, the ruthlessness in ambition, the coldness, the desire to control, the stubbornness, the fits of anger and rage. Napoleon used to tear his clothes off because he did not have the patience to unbutton himself.

### Physical Description of the Ray I Type

This Type, when overdone, gives you the macho, overpowering, overbearing, caricature of the male in our society. For example, if you examine the body builders, you will find them to be Will Types or desperately trying to become Will Types. What characterizes the Will Type on the physical level is an inflated top. It is as if someone had squeezed their pelvis and all of the energy has been pushed into the upper part of their body, particularly their head. In some cases, the Will Type can be identified merely by having a big head, the rest of the body being small. Often you will find them to have short legs, even weak ones. Bulging eyes will also give that typology away. You will feel as if the eyes are trying to overpower or convince you, mesmerize you. The weak pelvis indicates deficiency. Therefore, in spite of their pretense of being great lovers, Will Types will struggle with issues of impotency or frigidity.

The majority of them will be found to have a "break" across their lower back. When they bend over, instead of having a harmonious curve in the spine, there will be an interruption in it. This not only triggers back problems, but also interrupts the flow of energy into the pelvis, creating sexual impotency or lack of sensitivity in the pelvis, numbness in the pelvis and legs.

### *Origins and Causes of the Will Type*
The early history of the Will Type is the history of a broken child. Parents or authority figures have humiliated him, broken his spirit. You can see here the reason for the break in his spine. The child, faced with irrational violence from parents and from authority figures, comes to the following conclusions:

- In order to survive I must comply.
- All authority is irrational.
- Some day I will grow up and I will show them. I will be just like them and I will own the world. I will make my own rules.
- There is no justice in the Universe. Justice is a travesty. I must train myself never to trust authority or anyone around me.
- The only way, therefore, to succeed, is through cheating, pretending to be law abiding while actually breaking the law, or by blatantly breaking the law without pretense.

Most Will Types have been prematurely toilet trained. In addition to this, their sexuality has been seen not only as bad but has also been the trigger for punishment. They have been caught masturbating or in sexual interactions with other children and severely punished, physically or emotionally.

By the way, the impact of a severe beating is very comparable to the impact of a severe tongue lashing, scolding through words. The intensity of a fit of anger from a parent has the same effect as a severe beating; it is seen just as irrationally and just as all powerfully. The conclusion in the child receiving such treatment must be: "I am not about to give up what gives me all of this pleasure. So I am going to find ways of doing it under wraps. I will even go so far as to pretend that I agree with your position. I will denounce those who masturbate or who indulge in sexual pleasures while I surreptitiously go on with mine. In order to survive I have to lie." Such behaviour explains the hypocrisy found in the famous evangelical leaders of our time who are repeatedly caught molesting, indulging in prostitution, harassing members of their congregation. The following Sunday, they will condemn sexuality from the pulpit and denounce others for doing what they actually do under wraps.

The unfortunate thing about this is that, to some extent, it works. The child, and later the adult, find pleasure in acting out in a clandestine and dishonest manner. Once this pleasure is found, the adult will not let it go. So, in order to justify the continuation of pleasure in the only manner they know—dishonestly—they will continue to want to believe that authority is bad, that the Universe is cruel, and therefore, they will seek, consciously or unconsciously, justifications for this, i.e., irrational authorities, punishment by the law, etc. They will continuously recreate the harmful reality of their childhood so as to continuously recreate the experience of pleasure under wraps. Looked at from this point of view, we can see that the great gangsters are really little children who are taking their revenge for having been prematurely trained to go to the bathroom or whose sexual development had been arrested.

### Description of the Will Type on the Emotional Level

The Will Type will have a great guard against feeling or experiencing. Feeling and experiencing take you over; this is abhorrent to the Will Type. He does not trust being taken over by anything, including his own feelings. Challenging this through pleasure will convert him. If he experiences the pleasure of feeling, the pleasure in sensing, in touching, he will be converted. If he will allow that to happen to him and to take him over, his life will be transformed because he will no longer have to impose his own laws on the Universe; he will let himself be transported by the laws of the Universe. Sexually, the Will Type will have reluctance to be touched. He will want to touch the other but he will not want to be touched. Again, that is because he does not want to feel or to experience something that does not originate with him, anything he does not control.

An example is to be found in Catherine II of Russia, Catherine the Great, who used her husband and her lovers to prop her up as ruler of Russia and builder of a very strong empire. Paintings of Catherine the Great reveal the change of her typology from an Emaciated Type, to An inflated top (Will) and Masochistic (Emotions/Ray IV) Types in her later life.

### Compliant Aspect of the Will Type

There is an aspect of Will Type that is compliant. On the one hand, the Will Type relies on power and strength to get his way. However, on the other hand, he will respond to power and strength. He will obey, he will submit to a strong authority's wishes and directives. As irrational and powerful as his parents seemed in his childhood, they created in him a sense of responsibility. The young Will Type believes that he has to rescue his parents, that he has to save them from their out-of-control destructiveness and cruelty, so he becomes the perennial good boy. "Mama, look at me; see how good I am," he says while strutting around displaying the strength in his upper body while, and at the same time, squeezing and denying the lower part.

There are two reasons for the enhancing of the upper part of the body while denying the lower:

1) On the individual level, the Will Type has been cruelly punished, emotionally or physically, for wetting his pants or moving his bowels at inappropriate times. Toilet training in Will Types occurs unreasonably early. The punishment could also be as a result of being caught in sexual interactions with other children. These reasons obviously create a great deal of denigration of anything that exists below the waist, making these parts of the body diminished and debilitated.

2) There is a societal denigration of the pelvis (the legs being extensions, the denigration of the pelvis creates a diminution of the legs automatically). Excretion, along with sexuality, have been seen throughout the ages as inferior, unlovable, unacceptable activities. This sense of unlovability and unacceptability is very powerfully developed in the Will Type since it is supported by his personal experience with his parents.

Then, of course, to compensate for this, we have the development of a "good boy" behavioural pattern, accompanied by a secret life of sexual acting out of some form or another. Looking at recent events that have occurred in some of the churches, we can see this syndrome manifesting most clearly. Indeed, if one considers Jimmy Swaggart and Jim Bakker, one sees two Will Types who exhibit a lot of these characteristics:

1) Good boys.
2) Compliant.
3) Secret sexual life.
4) Denigration of sexual life.
5) Dishonesty.
6) To compensate for all of this is a forcing current and a judgmental attitude inflicted on those who are their subordinates or followers.

### Dishonesty

There is another aspect of the Will Type which is extremely important and yet very seldom mentioned. That is dishonesty. The very fact that he believes that he can create laws, means that he can break them. The Will Type who is disconnected from love and active intelligence will break laws, and therefore, will become a sociopath. That sociopathological state is very much an aspect of the Will Type. Napoleon, when asked how it was that he always won at cards, replied, "It's very simple, I cheat."

My history of theft is a direct result of my delusion of believing that I was all powerful. The Will Type will use any means at his disposal to get his way. He will use his intelligence, and/or his emotions, depending upon what suits him. He will lean on his seductiveness, on his charm to convince others to do his bidding.

The very fact that the Will Type will resort to dishonesty in order to get his way means that he does not trust in the flow of the Universe. Therefore, the Will Type is very insecure. His insecurity resides in his pelvis and his legs. He will, therefore, create issues of betraying and being betrayed. He will insist on being supported but at the same time will not trust those who support him. He is in essence like an empire with clay feet, or a bull continuously charging, but who is vulnerable when banderillas are stuck right below his guards, i.e., where his shoulder blades are.

Example, Napoleon placed his brothers and sisters on the thrones of practically every kingdom of Europe, then proceeded to mistrust them and to render them ineffectual; this brought about his doom. The same can be seen in other dictators. The pattern of nepotism which is universal with the Will Type is a manifestation of their demand to be supported and encouraged—because they feel insecure. They then proceed not to trust, and therefore, to castrate those on whom they had originally conferred power.

An excellent example of a woman Will Type is Tseu-Hi, last Empress of China, grandmother to Pui-Yi who later because Emperor of Manchuria and who was the subject of the film, "The Last Emperor." Tseu-Hi antagonized just about everybody and then underestimated their strength, including the great western empires such as the English and the French. This megalomaniacal underestimation of enemies is very much a Will Type characteristic. It can be seen in the lives of Will Types such as Napoleon, Caesar and so forth. Their demise has always been brought about by the overestimation of their own strength. And so it was with Tseu-Hi, whose Chinese empire was annihilated by a coalition of western forces led by the British. She very foolishly thought she could vanquish her enemies with the antiquated Chinese forces at her disposal.

In the history of a Will Type, we will find eras of compliance, of collapse and capitulation, of total yielding. We can even find simultaneously areas where they will be tyrannical and dictatorial, and others where they will be compliant and capitulating. Hitler was a tyrant to others, forcing everybody to submit, eliminating people through his final solution. In the bedroom, he was totally compliant, having his mistress and other women defecate on him. In like manner, is the Nazi mindset known as the "bicycle syndrome," wherein the person submits by bending to those who are above him, as on a bicycle, while kicking those who are below through pedaling.

We can see here a familiar pattern developing: being overrespectful to the point of sycophancy to strangers while demeaning, rejecting and denigrating those who are familiar. This is very much a common distortion of the Will Type—seductiveness and desire for possession of others, and the rejecting of them once he has got them. Here is highlighted the promiscuous aspect of the Will Type who is continuously engaged in conquest, in possessiveness, always demanding more. And, of course, we know that below this is a huge insecurity. The continuous conquest of others is an attempt at overcompensating for this deep sense of debilitation and insecurity on the sexual level.

The Will Type will always want to be Number One. You will find him as the greatest law upholder or the greatest law breaker. He will not rest until he reaches the apex, the first one in his profession, and he will be extremely unhappy if he is not or if he is brought back down again.

One notable example is Cleopatra, who put her sexuality to the service of her ambition. Indeed, she seduced first Caesar, with whom she had a child, Caesarian, and then Anthony and convinced both of them to build empires with her. One might think Cleopatra was more a Venus Type (who also is prone to put her sexuality to the service of her ambitions). The difference is that a Venus Type is a Cinderella; she will submit to the man whom she has conquered through her sexuality. A Will Type will not submit. A Will Type will use the man in question for her own ends. She will use her sexuality, she will use her thinking, her emotions, whatever it takes to achieve her goals. This is what Cleopatra did.

There is an aspect of Will which also involves the destroyer of form. Destruction is not necessarily harmful. In fact, without destruction there can be no construction. The Ray of Will must destroy first before the Ray of Love can come in and build anew. Think of the concept of discrimination from the divine point of view. Everyone needs to discriminate, to say yes and also to say no. This ability to say no, to "repulse" what is undesirable, or to destroy what is superfluous is very much an aspect of the First Ray. The advent of First Ray energy always involves destruction of old form. Check this out in history, but also check this out individually in your life. This will then give you confidence in the beneficial effects of the Law of Repulse. You will be more willing to destroy that in your life which has been built on wrong premises.

### Healing

If the Will Type learns how to love and to acquire reason, he becomes a great leader. He can then motivate people for better and not for worse. His successes will be unparalleled, his courage limitless. He can learn to conquer his own insecurities by facing them. This brings us to a fundamental prerequisite for growth of the Will Type: he must face his insecurities; in the facing of his insecurities he will find his capacity to love and to give. Through the acknowledgment and the owning up to his insecurities he will find the meaning of his place in the Universe, of the existence of forces that are greater than he. And he will learn how to tolerate being lived by those forces; he will learn to be receptive, the real meaning of yielding.

### How to Deal with the Will Type

There is a general misunderstanding and condemnation of the Will Type because there is in psychotherapy and in religion a glamour of love and wisdom. Anything that is expressed through love and/or wisdom is good; therefore, anything that has to do with the Will is bad. This unfortunate identification is very deeply ingrained in our psyche, our collective unconscious. For instance, the devil is seen as a Will Type. Immediately that makes the good guy, the loving and wise person, into a weak, ineffectual, namby-pamby victim. Hence, the two misconceived equations:

A) *loving = weak = good;* and

B) *will = strong = bad.*

It is extremely important, as individuals and as groups, that we dissolve these misconceptions about the Will. The only way to do it is through the painstaking task of purifying ourselves of them and by learning how to deal with Will Types around us.

First of all, it is a misconception to believe that the only way to deal with a Will Type is to appease him. How can you appease a bull on the rampage? You either have to stop him or to kill him. This very much applies to the Will Type who has gone out of control. It is senseless to think of being able to appease Hitler or Idi Amin or Napoleon or Saddam Hussein. They are totally out of control and they have to be stopped.

So we have to differentiate between the Will Type who is willing to cleanse, as opposed to the Will Type who is not. The difficulty that the Will Type will have in a method of cleansing or renewal is the facing of his insecurities. He needs to be convinced that's the way to go. Let us here suggest a modus operandi, a procedure:

1) Allow the Will Type to express through words, through emotions, with his body, with his feelings, and with his thoughts, all of his wants, no matter how outrageous they seem to be. During this time, be receptive, as receptive as you possibly can be. Think of yourself as a toreador, making it possible for the bull to expend his energy. It will not last too long. The Will Type is someone who has limited amounts of energy. He pretends that his energies are limitless, but in

reality (unlike the Stiff Type, for example) his energies are limited. Soon he will weaken, he will slow down, being beckoned by an inner desire to collapse.

2) As he is doing this—the vociferous expression of his demands—introduce in the form of questions expressed in a low tone of voice and mildly, new ideas, alternatives to his demands. As you do this he may protest, even attack you personally for it. See if you can disengage from taking these attacks personally and continue your toreador work as the tantrum goes on.

3) There will come a point when he is ready for the coup de grace, i.e., what he needs to hear. You will feel it because he is out of steam, he is ready to yield. Do not attempt to deliver it until he has exhausted himself. If, as you are delivering the coup de grace, you see him coming back again, disengage and continue the toreador stratagem. The coup is delivered pointedly but in a disengaged manner. Do not engage a Will Type. Deliver what he needs as if you were a mailman, with healthy detachment. Convince him through deduction that there is a better way. Use his own arguments against him. Example: "Isn't it true that you want success? Isn't it true that you've tried to obtain success through dishonest means? Has it worked? Isn't it better to obtain it through truth? You are now ready to create success in a permanent, secure way with very strong foundations, if you will face your insecurities." Or, "How would you feel if what you did to this person were done to you?"

4) The Will Type, similar to the Intuitive Type, has a great fear of disintegration. The difference between the two is that the fear in the Will Type is covert, while in the Intuitive Type it is out there in the open and acts as a guard. If you can successfully reassure the Will Type that he will not disintegrate when he reveals his insecurities, or his lies, or his dishonesties, you have got it made. Remember that he needs

reassurance, he needs support and if he feels reassured and supported by you he will trust you. If he trusts you, he will do anything you tell him to do. He will become stubbornly faithful to you.

### *Illusory Self-Images of the Will Type*

1) "I am physically the strongest;" or, "he who is the strongest physically is the best."

2) "I am the most important and the most powerful."

3) "Everything is dependent upon me." This is a distortion of the Law of Personal Responsibility.

4) "I am the only one who counts." "Success is the most important thing in life."

5) "The best place to be is in the position of ruler or dictator and I don't care who gets hurt in the process."

6) "I have the best ideas when it comes to political solutions."

7) "I have the greatest insight when it comes to law."

8) "I have the right to make or break laws."

9) "I am the King." This is a very powerful self-image in the Will Type which should be explored as such. The Will Type, in order to recognize it, should say to himself several times, "I am the King," and see what it feels like and see how this is and has applied to his life.

10) "I love destruction." This is the idealization of the necessity to destroy in order to build anew. The best example is the one of the Arab General Amr who in 642 A.D., after the conquest of Alexandria, burned the city's great library to the ground. When asked why he did it, he replied, "There is no need for any other book but the Koran." This combination of the harmful attributes of the First and the Sixth Rays destroyed the greatest accumulation of knowledge in the world to that date.

11) "I am alone at the top." Here we have a combination

of isolation and victimization. The notion of "it is lonely at the top" is highly overdone by the Will Type. He lords it over others—and suffers from it.

12) "My will be done over yours." Here there is a deification of the Will Type's way, imposed upon others for his own satisfaction, whether they be individuals or groups.

## Chapter 8

# *Ray II: Love/Wisdom; The Son*

It is very tempting to believe that Ray II is a Ray of emotions or emotionality or expressiveness. Actually, Ray II is the Ray of Consciousness, the Ray of "pure reason," as Immanuel Kant would have said. Indeed, love is impossible without reason, and reason is impossible without love. Pure reason is love, pure love is reason. Therefore, the love/wisdom person corresponds to the body Emaciated Type who is basically a Thinking Type. Another temptation is to identify the Thinking Type with Ray III. Here again a mistake is made. Ray III, as we shall see, especially contains an adaptability quality which is not to be found in Ray II. For a long time, I have struggled with this, and I have come to the conclusion that what we are giving you here is closest to the truth.

Let's remember, this is the Ray that links the masculine to the feminine. It is the Ray of balance. People in it will be concerned with balance. A lot of their immobility, their negation of action, is really an attempt at finding balance. Unfortunately, negating action degenerates into numbness rather than the healthy tension of a scale at rest, which is really the aspect of love. Upsetting the apple cart—confrontation—is seen as the ultimate evil. Controversy is feared as the great enemy. We can see here the connection between the Second

Ray and the Seventh Ray of Order and Ceremony, wherein everything must be in order and nothing must disturb the crystallized order of things.

### Physical Description of the Ray II Type

The Ray II Type will be concerned with economy of effort. Therefore, his body will be thin, sometimes small, sometimes elongated. It is as if he has stretched himself out of experience. There will not be lack of homogeneity—the disjointed quality found in the Sixth Ray Intuitive—but there will be sometimes an overelongated neck or a lack of energy in the extremities.

Aside from being a physical Type by itself, the Ray II quality of deficiency—orality—exists in other Types: tendencies towards economy of effort, deficiency, issues of need, issues of minimalizing life. Later in this book, you will find in Ray VII Types that have sunken chests. This means that they include the Emaciated Type in their character makeup. It does not mean, however, that they are Emaciated Types, per se. The behaviour pattern of someone who has an overall Emaciated Type is to be clearly distinguished from the behaviour of someone whose emaciated quality is localized and who combines other features in his typology.

### Origins and Causes of the Ray II Type

According to the body type theory, this type of person has not been given enough in childhood. The deficiency is not only to be found on the physical level but also on the emotional level. This person has not received enough nurturing on either level. He has not been given enough food and he has not been given enough love and attention. He craves nurturing, to be fed—hence the name of this type, Emaciated. He believes that there is not enough to go around, and therefore, he must economize. He must make do with as little as he possibly can.

This belief forms between the age of one year to twenty months. It is sometimes erroneously believed that the lack of or the interruption of breast feeding will create this type. Actually it may, but then again it is not necessarily the only cause of it. Take the example of the child who has been physically nourished, even breast fed, but not emotionally nourished or spiritually nourished. It is as if the mother, in feeding the child, is taking from him, is using the child to get love from him, not to give love to him. This climate of emotional deficiency is the cause of this condition, not breast feeding or lack thereof. On the other hand, many who have not been breast fed, or who have had their breast feeding interrupted (myself), have not developed these characteristics of deficiency. So much for the glamour of breast feeding.

### *Description of the Ray II Type on the Emotional Level*

As a result of this early history, there is in this type a great issue with needing, being needed, giving, being given to, etc. For example, inside they have an enormous need to be nurtured, to be given to; however, they consider that experiencing this need would be the worst possible fate. Consequently, they very tightly cover it up, overcompensate by exaggerating self-sufficiency: "I do not need you." In fact, they will take it so far as to create situations where they are needed, where they nurture, where they give, with the result, of course, that they grow more and more frustrated and they do not know why.

Furthermore, since the overgiving in this type is so very often superposed, it does not nurture the person or the people who receive it. The receivers remain frustrated, and their demands on the Emaciated Type increase accordingly. In response to this, the Love/Wisdom Type will find it impossible to say no, being afraid of not being loved which would be the ultimate, the worst possible fate, since it is the disconnection, the cutoff from possible nourishment coming from other people, particularly those who "need" them. Therefore, they will have in their lives issues of abandonment, fear of, and therefore, creation of abandonment.

Independence and autonomy are a great problem for these people. Most of them find a way somehow to be autonomous and independent so as not to express need of anybody or to anybody. Inside, however, they are plagued with constant worries about having enough or not.

Under stress they will resort to thinking. Since they will not want to rely on their body, on their experience, or on their feelings, there will be an overload in the brain and an overreliance on the mind.

Because love is magnetic and contagious, these people will have an incredible number of friends and acquaintances. They are the ones who seem to have no enemies. Their answering machine is full of calls every day when they come home from work. Everyone is trying to contact them and be close to them and take counsel from them. Since they are incapable or unwilling to discriminate, i.e., to say no, they will find themselves flooded with human contact and depleted by it. This is a Second Ray tendency: to always include, not exclude; to build, never to destroy; to accumulate, never to discard.

Mother Teresa was a Ray II Love/Wisdom Type. First of all, physically, you can see that there was a great deal of deficiency. She was very thin and she was diminutive. Second, her entire mode of operation, her entire lifestyle, was a slow and measured one that took everything equitably, step- by-step and was basically focused on the issue of need and of food. I believe that her focus on feeding all of those hungry people was healing her deficiencies and her lacks. Because she was not nourished as a baby she overcompensated by nourishing, which was the perfect solution and resolution of the typological defect. The question is, did she let other people nourish her; to what extent was she open to receiving help and nourishment from others? My hunch is that she did not and was not. And here is highlighted the defect of this type of personality: the unwillingness to be fed or to receive out of fear that they might get used to it and that it might dry up. Please understand that I have the utmost respect for Mother Teresa and her great and continuous giving; what I have said about her rests on this respect.

### *Healing*

Although Mother Theresa's giving represents a pseudo-solution, in the last analysis it is not such a bad one since the adult, by giving, nourishes himself. The adult who expects forever to be given what he has not received in childhood never resolves his problems. Resolution can come only through selfless giving. It seems to me to be beautifully paradoxical that we would resolve what has been missing in our childhood by giving to others those very same things, i.e., seeing that they are satisfied where we were frustrated.

Sexually, Ray II, uses physical contact with others for emotional nurturing rather than for sex. Sex is a secondary issue for them. This Love/Wisdom Type will be secretive when it comes to their emotions. First, they will think of the best way to share some feeling they have for you, and then they will present it when it is safe to do so. Confronted with great outbursts of emotions they will retrench into a thinking modality and will display weakness and victimization. There is in these people a tendency to be passive, to be too complacent in understanding rather than to take action.

The lack of movement aspect in them brings up a petrified state which, significantly, is fear. Not only is fear a great issue, but they do not mind expressing the fact that they are afraid or that they are unduly sensitive. In fact, they idealize these harmful traits. Since love is the greatest force in the Universe, its distortion, fear, is the greatest distortion to be found in the Universe as well. Let us not forget, there is nothing vainglorious about fear; fear is really the most perniciously destructive lower self manifestation that exists.

The Second Ray person sees his brother, the First Ray, sometimes as the arch enemy, the arch devil, the one who will destroy what he has so painstakingly built. This misconception has led to the knee-jerk harmful reactions to the Destroyer.

This is also a type that favours laziness. Once again we find here the aspect of economy of effort. A philosopher comes to mind: Immanuel Kant, the author of *Critique of Pure Reason*, never traveled more than 100 miles from his home during his entire life. We can see here the economy of effort. His *Critique* is nothing else but a brilliant demonstration of the fact that love is inseparable from reason. Love is reason, pure reason; and pure reason is love. There is no love that does not make sense, even if at first we are not aware of the causal connections that trigger it.

Such is the quality of work to be found in this type. You cannot rush them. Given time and space they will produce work of great quality and insight. Rushed and under pressure they will react defensively, using their thinking modality as a weapon of guard.

All in all, there is a general sense of calm and a divine emanation from them. Even the body type theorists recognize this and they describe it sometimes as a peculiar and difficult to understand continuously good attitude in the Emaciated Type. Well, it is easily understood if you recognize that the Emaciated Type is the Love/Wisdom Type. He is helpful, he is loving, he is wise. That's his fundamental nature.

Another aspect of this Ray is their faithfulness. They are faithful to a fault. Once they love you they will adhere to you through thick and thin. It will be very difficult to disengage from them. The reduction of this is to be found in the representative of the Second Ray in the animal kingdom, the dog.

Ray II people have a highly developed capacity to feel and understand the wonder and magnificence of creation. In spite of their deficiency, or perhaps because of it, they have a sense of the glory of the Universe, the glory of creation, the glory of God. This quality is to be found in some of the great medieval cathedrals or some of the great works of music that celebrate the Christ and the glory of God. Anything grand, magnificent, and ostentatious will be found to be very attractive to this person. The combination of the longing for nurturing and the capacity to build, the Great Geometrician, results in this *Gloria* aspect, as I call it, in the Second Ray of Love and Wisdom.

Remember the connection between the Second and the Fifth Rays. The Second Ray of Love and Wisdom is the Ray of the Teacher but also the Ray of the Geometrician and the Builder. Here we can see that the Second Ray has an enormous capacity for concrete knowledge which he needs in order to build (Ray V is the Ray of Science and Concrete Knowledge). He is continuously building; he is continuously amassing things around him either for self-protection or for the glory of creating.

### Contradiction

We have spoken about the overgiving of the Ray II Type, characterizing it as unsatisfying. We also spoke about the selfless giving of someone like Mother Teresa as being the healing agent for this Type. There seems to be a contradiction here. What is the difference between the two?

The difference is to be found in the fact that the former is a pseudo-giving, while the latter is a real giving.

## Pseudo-Giving

This is done for the purpose of approval, to over-compensate for a deep lack within one's self. It is usually experienced by other people who receive that giving as too much, as heavy, as embarrassing, or as guilt producing; it has a program to it; there is an ulterior motive behind it. The recipient of this type of giving will find himself urgently trying to reciprocate.

## Real Giving

Here we have giving done in a relaxed way. It does not have any ulterior motive and does not expect anything in return; it is done for its own sake, the way an adult gives to a child, not expecting anything back from the child. This type of giving is a function of the adult. An adult needs to give. Giving from the adult heals the adult and heals those who receive that giving.

The difference between this giving and the former is that this one will be experienced as light and joyful and graceful. There will be no guilt attached to it. The person receiving it will not feel any compulsion to reciprocate. Only gratitude will come when this type of giving is received by someone. This type of giving will nourish. The former type of giving will deplete.

## How to Deal with the Love/Wisdom Type

First and foremost, remember not to engage him in a thinking battle. You will lose. You will be manipulated by him since he can outthink you and outsmart you. Instead of engaging him intellectually, see if you can make definitive statements to him which he will appreciate and which will then disengage you from him. This, of course, presumes that you know what you are talking about, that you are secure in what you are presenting to him. If you are not, it is best to say, "I don't know," and categorically end the agonizing engagement on the mental level.

Do not expect a Thinking Type to agree with you. She will not. She will only agree with you partially. If you ask her, "Do you agree with me?," she will say, "Yes, but." So, in communications with her, you have to be very autonomous and very careful of not depending on her approval. She will try to engage you by endlessly asking "yeah buts"— yes, but this, yes, but that. She will always find the antithesis to your thesis and press that point. She enjoys this because it gives her a sense of power over you—the only power she believes she can have, the only way for her to establish her jealously guarded autonomy.

Do not expect them to open up and reveal their true feelings right off the bat. Slowly, as you gain their confidence and as you are experienced as a giving and loving person they will respond to you. They are not good motivators. Unless they are modified by the acquisition of some Ray I characteristics they will not be able to lead or inspire others because they do not have the energy; they are too busy nurturing themselves and filling their own gaps.

Since there is this problem of deficiency, you will have a sense of your energy being drained when you communicate with them. An extraordinary percentage of them wear glasses. This is because their eyes are inwardly directed, as it were. Instead of penetrating outer reality with their eyes, they actually suck in outer reality with them. This is contrary to the Will Type who is found sometimes to have bulging eyes and who penetrates with his eyes. The Thinker, the Love/Wisdom Type, will do exactly the opposite. He will drain your energy with them. I call that "vacuum cleaner" eyes. The way to deal with this is to look within yourself for the endless source of energy and not expect them to give it to you.

Do not emotionally confront this Type. See to it that whatever emotions you have are not directed at them. Then present the problem, with your feelings if need be, to them in a demagnetized way. You can say, for instance, "I am angry at you," but you cannot express that anger at them if you want them to respond openly. It is best to spend your anger elsewhere and come to them with the clear statement, "I am angry at you because..."

There will be found with this type a great deal of stubbornness. But instead of expressing it actively, it will be stubbornness of the withholder who will refuse to cooperate. One thinks here of Gandhi's nonviolent resistance. If you look at pictures of Gandhi throughout his life, you will see that he personifies this Love/Wisdom Emaciated Type.

In the workplace, this type will be great at analyzing. Present him with a problem and leave him alone with it; he will give you extremely clear and concise options and possibilities. Then it will be your job to synthesize, to decide. They are not good at seeing the whole; they will want to see differences rather than common denominators. We can see the divine aspect of this in Descartes' "Method." Descartes suggested that any insoluble problem can be divided into soluble parts. He advised that we take a problem and divide it into manageable parts, to continue this division until we can solve the little parts. This is very much a Ray II Love/Wisdom behaviour. This is in contradistinction to the capacity to see great ideas and motivate great numbers of men, as found in the First Ray.

### Illusory Self-Images of the Ray II Type

This type loves the idea of being loved. He will compromise his integrity for that sake. We can also find here the reasons for his great social success and popularity. He will tend to see himself as a very wise person, being conceited about this wisdom and substituting this wisdom for right action when it is needed. He would much rather be wise than to act. He will love to portray himself as a very responsible, self-sacrificing, altruistic person. But a lot of it is more for show than for cause. His desire to be loved and to be popular will preclude his ability for tough love. He will be just as unable to give as to receive confrontation.

He will idealize self-pity and the martyr in himself. We can see here why fear is not only not resisted but welcomed, idealized, seen as good. The person who is afraid is seen as closer to being "holy" or "good" than a person who is courageous, who is seen as "bad."

There will be in this person an idealization of self-satisfaction. He will see himself as not needing anything, and therefore, as self-satisfied. As a guard against feeling his perennially unfulfilled need, he will glorify that state of lack and of lack of fulfillment.

## Chapter 9
# Ray III: Active Intelligence and Adaptability; Mother

---

### *Physical Description of the Female Ray III Type*

There is a misconception in body type theory which puts the "inflated bottom" woman in the category of the Will Type. They say that an inflated top is for men what an inflated bottom is for women. And therefore, you can find two types of women in the Will category: one is the inflated top woman, and the other is the inflated bottom woman. Actually, this is a misconception. Once again, they have discounted the Seven Rays and they have not really studied the history of the woman and of the Mother Goddess.

Indeed, some of the early representations of the female sexual ideal are not at all the nubile, almost androgynous type that we have today. Instead, we have pictures of women with huge pelvises, enormous buttocks and upper legs. In some cultures they can still be seen. Even these days, if you travel in Latin, Arab, or African countries, you will find this type of inflated bottom woman. You will also find men who are very attracted to this type of manifestation.

This is not by any means a Will Type. On the contrary, it is adaptability in its most significant manifestation. In the woman, it is the negation of the upward part of the body as if in yielding to the incoming Initiating Will that impregnates her, as it were. The huge pelvis signifies the great capacity for receiving the impetus coming from the Will, and thus allowing creation to come about. An excellent book to read on the subject is called *The Great Mother,* by Eric Neumann. This inflated bottom of energy will occasion an emaciation of the chest and the breasts. In some cases, big breasts are to be found in this type of woman in spite of the fact that they have very sunken chests and almost no shoulders.

### *Physical Description of the Male Ray III Type*
The male Ray III is unkempt. He does not really care about the way he appears. He is, by definition, abstract in his focus.

He is characterized physically with an inflated bottom. He will form heaviness around the pelvis and deficiency in the chest and often in the head and face. This is very similar to the Ray III female. It is odd that he has never been recognized by all the diplomated typologists, all the M.D.'s, psychologists, psychiatrists, with their PhD's. They went so far as to talk about the Ray III female, erroneously calling her a female Will Type, demonstrating that they neither understood male nor female Ray III.

It is interesting to note that Carl Jung didn't understand the Will Type, and that the Reichians didn't understand Ray III; Carl Jung didn't understand Father, and the Reichians didn't understand Mother.

Only through the focus on types from the divine point of view does he become visible. He is all around you. See him sitting at his computer, unmoving, descending into his pelvis an accumulation of energy.

He thinks, schemes, plots, incites others to do work for him, presenting himself as a helpless victim.

Indeed, he is the male correspondent to the great goddess

of fertility, Eric Neumann's great father, as it were.

### Description of the Female Ray III Type
### on the Emotional/Mental Level

Here we have a woman who has a very definite set of ideas about life. A great amount of maturity is to be found in her, often prematurely. We can find a tendency to want to be older faster. There is in her a love of wisdom and of old age—gerontophilous. It is as if she wants to skip her twenties and thirties, and quickly make it to the age of 45. She is very adaptable, though with a closed heart, which is demonstrated by her tremendous resistance to being penetrated, particularly by a strong man. These women will either fiercely guard against intimacy with a strong man, or falsely comply to it, making themselves into martyrs. They will have an exaggerated sense of their attractiveness as women, accusing any man with the slightest manifestation of good feelings, of being sexually attracted to them. They see the masculinity of men as dirty, harmful, something to be demeaned, simplified, or two-dimensionalized. They love the concept of the Immaculate Conception. The idea of being impregnated by God without having to yield to the penetration on the physical level by a man is very dear to them. In fact, I call this tendency in them the "emasculate conception," because it is very much a desire to emasculate the man or to reduce him into a little boy.

This is the Ray of the matriarchal, androgynous Amazon. She uses men to be fertilized and then she discards them or disposes of them. Perhaps, this is why the body type theorists have made the mistake of seeing her as the female Will Type. The deficiency in the upper part of her body explains this heartless condition, this indifference, disconnection from feelings and total involvement in what is purposeful, useful or what makes sense. Self-forgetfulness is a characteristic of this type—abstract thinking. This could be confused with the Ray IV characteristic, but actually it is different.

### *Description of the Male Ray III Type*
### *on the Emotional/Mental Level*

The Ray III male is epitomized by Einstein who became more and more unconcerned with his physical appearance as he grew older and who was totally devoted to his thinking, mathematical thinking, mathematical discovery. They tend to see the world as irrelevant to their thinking. They will not be rebellious about it; they will adapt to the conditions of the world, so as to have everyone leave them alone so they can do some more thinking. Everything is subordinated to thinking.

Laziness is very much a part of the Ray III. Laziness of the body, laziness in terms of movement and even of feelings, in contradistinction to overactivity in the mind and in the brain.

Here are some additional thoughts about the Ray III Male. Since I consider this to be an extremely important discovery, I will describe a few individuals of this type that I have personally known:

- A fellow student of mine, in Paris, whom I will call Isaac Bok. He appeared to be a peasant, wearing shabby, unattractive clothes. His pelvis was inflated, even at that age (he must have been about 18-19). He wore a continuous smile on his face and tried to please everybody. At the same time, he displayed mathematical brilliance. He was soft spoken and distant in spite of his smile. He was physically lazy and awkward, prone to respiratory problems. He attracted a great deal of derision and cruelty with his victimization.
- A person to whom I was a teacher. The inflated bottom was not as apparent because he hid it well. However, with him also, were:

—The continuous smile.
—The subservient/compliant attitude.
—The soft spoken way.
—The distance in spite of the smile.
—The physical laziness and awkwardness.
—The collapsed chest, prone to respiratory problems.

### How the Female Unkempt Ray III Type Behaves

This type of woman will tend to give you work to do, make you work for her, issue orders—another apparent connection to the Will Type. However, unlike the Will Type, the orders are not going to be direct. They will be given in a subtle and manipulative way through indirect suggestions.

Madame Curie is a Ray III Type. She devoted her life to her task, the discovery of radium, to the point that she herself died from radium poisoning. She refused to patent her discoveries, making them a gift to the world, which is another form of ultimate adaptability and receptivity in action. This is again a manifestation of the total honesty and integrity to be found in these people.

### How the Male Ray III Type Behaves

Ray III is unkempt because he does not care about what he looks like; he is so involved with inner processes of thinking that his physical appearance is a non-issue for him. This, too, can be differentiated from the Second Ray Thinking Type. The Second Ray is not unkempt, he is aware of outer level realities with which he deals with economy of effort. The Ray III Type is not concerned with economy of effort, it is not an issue for him; he is concerned with abstract thinking and that is all.

Even if we consider the immense laziness of the Third Ray Type and compare it to the laziness of the Fourth Ray, we find the following differences:

• The Fourth Ray Type broods emotionally in his laziness,

the Third Ray Type is lost in his thinking during his laziness.
- The Second Ray laziness has for motive economy of effort.
- The Third Ray laziness is not real laziness, it is merely that movement is a non-issue for him, movement occurs in his mind or his brain, not in his body.
- The Fourth Ray laziness is a consequence of lack of self-respect.
- Sixth Ray laziness is motivated by desire for disconnection.

The male Ray III's intense involvement with thinking gives him a fantastic power of concentration. He can think all day without ever stopping, he loves it. Here is his sincerity; he will not even think of dishonesty, that is not at all an issue for him —not consciously, anyway. (Unconsciously, we are all dishonest since by definition we hide things.) He has great difficulty finishing tasks. Since his goal is basically to think things out, to conceptualize but not to concretize, he will start projects and not finish them. He is very bad at completing tasks.

Unless modified by the existence of Fifth or Seventh Ray tendencies there will be a tremendous propensity for inaccuracy. It would seem as if overthinking would bring more clarity. In reality, the exaggeration of any attribute or aspect is its own killer. Overthinking brings confusion, not clarity, because it is the product of a continuous obsession of contradictory inner thoughts. Ray III is afraid to have a clear thought because that would lead to action, which he abhors.

Having so very much developed their intellect, they also have developed intellectual conceit. This manifests in an attitude of rebellion. It is as if they are out to destroy existing systems of knowledge, status quo, etc. However rational

Descartes was, his philosophy contradicted the existing philosophies, challenged them. This is different from the First Ray violence or even the Sixth Ray wrecking ball. This is a statement of contradiction, a very powerful **no** that is expressed through the discoveries of the mind.

Take for instance, Einstein's Theory of Relativity. He demonstrated that if you are traveling on a train and you are looking outside the window, it is indeed the landscape that is moving, not you. You, as a fixed point in the universe, are not only experiencing as an optical illusion the movement of the landscape, but what heretofore was thought to be an optical illusion, turns out to be a reality. The landscape **is** moving. After all, everything moves in the universe, so the only question is, which do you consider to be the fixed point?

As a Ray III Male, Einstein was lazy and enjoyed stasis. Isn't it interesting that he came up with this "I am a fixed point; everything else moves around me" theory?

The other so very well-known theory, $E = M/C^2$, demonstrates that the speed of an object in space reduces the number of atoms and molecules in that object. There is actually a disappearance of mass, not weight, in a moving object.

Here we find another typological connection. The inflated bottom feature in Ray III's constitutes repressed and accumulated sexual potentiality. They believe that it is dynamite, that they are sexually irresistible. This very much corresponds to the explosive power of matter demonstrated by the $E = M/C^2$ theory.

These two mind-blowing theories defy conventional reason, and yet they are based on mathematical demonstration.

The mind-boggling implication of Einstein's theories makes sense from the spiritual point of view. Spiritually, we know that the deceleration of energy is what creates matter. The worlds of matter are vibratory worlds of a particular frequency. An increase in the rate of vibration takes matter out of a particular manifestation—in this case the sensible—and transposes it into another. So, from the sensible point of view, the atoms and molecules have indeed disappeared and have been transformed into energy— burnt, you might say.

In our realm of existence, the sensible world is a wonderful way of testing out ideas. Precipitating ideas on the level of concrete knowledge and science (Ray V) tests their validity. The Third Ray man is not interested in that. He is interested in pursuing the ideas for their own sake. Einstein was not interested in following through with the applications of his ideas, nor was Descartes, who did some work in analytical geometry but never really pushed it to the point of application.

Jung could be said to be a Third Ray Type; he made valiant attempts at continuously and perpetually proving scientifically what he had found through the process of thinking; he was also contemptuous of the scientific method, preferring the introspective type of approach. He would spend extended periods of time in isolation and without modern amenities in a house that he built with his own hands far out in the countryside. This is a recurring theme in the Thinking Type. Descartes had to isolate himself in a little cabin with a wood stove for an extended period of time in order to break through his *cogito ergo sum,* "I think, therefore, I am."

Rene Descartes, who wrote his *Discourse on the Method*, was called "the sleeping philosopher" because he spent his days in bed. He wrote in bed, he did his best thinking in bed. He slept every day until noon. At the end of his life, he was employed by Queen Christina of Sweden. One cold winter day he walked over to see her, caught a chill, fell ill and died of pneumonia in a very short time. One can see how vulnerable to colds Descartes was; he was also very anxious about exposure. This is indeed an issue for this type—overprotection and overconcern about exposure (physical or emotional).

### *Origins and Causes of the Ray III Type*

The formation of this type is the result of the presence of a crushing parent of the opposite sex. The parent imposed his will over the child, threatened the child in the heart with his cruelty, and also overexcited the child sexually, either consciously or unconsciously. The presence of a macho Will Type father will create this condition in a little girl. The presence of a controlling, androgynous mother will create this condition in the boy.

There need not be a physical influence such as the one I described. The existence of it on an emotional level is enough to create this condition. It is as if there is a castration on the heart and mind levels, and therefore, an encouragement of pelvic abilities. It is a peculiar dichotomy to say that although this type is extremely intelligent, the person is intellectually castrated. However, this is exactly what has happened.

The presence of the inflated top dominant parent who continuously challenges his child with his mind and his emotions, creates a combination of self-depreciation of the child's own mental abilities and, at the same time, a desire to gain the parent's approval through the development of the mind. The child also wants to spite the parent by becoming better than he is. So, although we find the ultimate femininity in this type, we also find a contempt for femininity, in both genders.

There are similarities with the Ray VII Type since they both have deficiencies in the top of the body and proficiencies at the pelvis. Mixed with their sexuality towards their parent is a rebelliousness and a great amount of hostility. Ray III Types have this problem in a lot more pronounced manner than the Ray VII Types.

I have observed that, later in life, many Ray VII Types become Ray III. It usually happens after the menopausal switch, i.e., around their forties or even fifties. The oversexed Ray VII reverses himself. Having abused sexuality, having disconnected it from loving—deficiency in the chest—sexuality becomes laden with guilt, decelerates and collapses into fat in the pelvis and the upper thighs. The person now, instead of enjoying sexuality, cuts it off, blaming the opposite sex for what religion calls "concupiscence," i.e., contemptible incontinence.

In this state, the Ray III female is into "emasculate conception." She has rejected the male. Here, we find the multitude of inflated bottom females in Latin countries. They all are devoted Catholics, worshiping the virgin Mary and the virgin birth, thus excluding both God and Jesus, the two males of the family.

This syndrome and type is also found in other countries and cultures such as the Moslem, the Hindu, the Buddhist and so forth. The inflated bottom manifestation in the female is linked with the freezing of sexuality. The fat is a protection against it.

The appearance of this in the forties and fifties of a woman's age, often corresponds to the time of death of the husband. Indeed, the husband, having married younger women, dies in his sixties while the women are still 40. The freezing of sexuality reinforces their collapse into mourning and victimization which then become a way of life, facilitating laziness and the line of least resistance.

The corresponding aspects in the male gives you the overweight and overfed Bishops and Cardinals, whose sexuality has been stifled and who, at 45 or so, have become completely disconnected with it, freezing it into fat around their pelvis and stomach.

Indeed, one does not have to look for them only at the

Vatican, or at the Catholic Church. One also finds them as middle-aged owners of stores in the Turkish Grand Bazaar, or in Cairo, or in Alexandria where I was born.

There is a wonderful representative of this Ray III Type in the movie, *Casablanca*. Sidney Greenstreet plays a wonderful café owner, complacent in his fat, continuously smiling and scheming, highly intelligent—the perfect Ray III male!

Sidney Greenstreet does it again in the *Maltese Falcon* in which he plays the very knowledgeable, widely traveled art dealer, charming everyone with his mind.

### *How to Deal with the Ray III Type*

If you are a Will Type, you will develop a love-hate relationship with this person. You will find yourself either irresistibly attracted to or irresistibly repelled by the Ray III Type . The way out of this is to stop trying to control him/her. This type is impossible to control. It is impossible to get on top of him/her even though you will be lured into trying.

This is reminiscent of the story of the capture of the girdle of Hippolyte by Hercules. Hippolyte, in hesitating to give Hercules Venus' girdle (meaning her pelvis), triggered Hercules' wrath and he killed her. Here we find the manifestation of irresistible attraction and violence that exists in this kind of relationship. We are also reminded here of Carmen and the murderous rage that she was able to incite in Don Jose.

So do not try to control the Ray III Type, do not try to penetrate their guard. Deal with this type as an equal. The word "equal" is extremely important. Issues of fairness and equality are vital this type. Within this climate, Ray III will blossom, will open their heart. The woman will develop breasts, and will joyously participate in life. Without this, the old pet peeves will be perpetuated ad infinitum et ad nauseam.

If you are a Thinking Type, watch out, because Ray III

will want to devour you, make you into a son or daughter and totally control you. There will be no problem in you confronting the Third Ray person or in you establishing your independence or autonomy, even in your showing some leadership towards them. Ray III will not be afraid of you; your energy does not threaten them. In fact, they will have protective feelings towards you, and will accept whatever it is that you will say to them.

If you are an Emotions Type, Ray IV, relax and become a lot more receptive than you are or you will find yourself at loggerheads with Ray III, a little bit similarly to what the Will Type encounters, but not exactly. The Third Ray will feel less threatened by displays of emotion than by imposition of somebody else's will. A certain amount of emotional expression, however, may be beneficial. The Emotions Type will have to feel through it. It is difficult to write a script in this case.

If you are an Intuitive/Ray VI Type, you have to be even more careful than if you are a Thinking Type, because Ray III will completely devour you and disintegrate you, making you their own; and you will have a desire to give in to them, and have them take care of you; this will totally debilitate you. The Third Ray is the epitome of grounding while the Ray VI is the epitome of lack of grounding.

This type will be capable of relationships with many different types. Ray III may have a violent, passionate relationship with a Will Type followed by a sedate relationship with a Love Type, followed by a very possessive and destructive relationship with a Ray VI Type in which he/she completely dominates and takes over the life of the Intuitive Type. If you are a Stiff Type, you need to be more receptive than active in your rigidity. That is why the type of Stiff called the Dionysus/Hermes male will have great success in attracting this type of woman (as well as the Diana/ Artemis woman which is nothing else than a less developed Active Intelligence Type. We will see this in a later chapter.).

An example of this type of relationship is to be found in Bill and Hillary Clinton. Hillary Clinton is a Ray III inflated bottom type; she is well-grounded, well-controlled, very intelligent, obviously more intelligent than her husband. He is a combination of Dionysus/Hermes and Will, perhaps more Passive Feminine than Will. He allows himself to be swayed by her. Here we see his attraction to the Mother Aspect.

### Illusory Self-Images of the Female Ray III Type

1) "I am irresistibly sexually attractive but I will not openly admit it."

2) "I don't need subterfuges to be irresistibly attractive, I am naturally. I don't need to move, become, change."

3) "All men have sexual feelings for me, I have no sexual feelings for them."

4) "Men's sexual feelings are dirty, women's sexual feelings are loving."

5) "Men are inferior to women; women's capacity for knowledge and effectiveness and common sense is a lot greater."

6) "The fact that women can give birth makes them superior to men."

7) "If women do not become active and aggressive, they will automatically be victimized by men."

All of the feminists' ideologies are to be found in this category, since she represents Woman, the Mother, Matter.

### Illusory Self-Images of the Male Ray III Type

Here we find the idealization of computers—God in the machine or God in the computer. The Ray III male, and the female to a large degree, consider themselves to be spiders at the center, controlling webs in which they trap their victims or the people they would like to manipulate, gradually weakening them until they can come in for the kill.

Another illusion of this person is that of being too busy, too busy to do anything, always too busy to take care of himself, to take care of outer level matters. They are too busy, of course, because they have elevated their thinking and their intelligence above everything else. Nothing is more important than the formulation of their own ideas. This then creates a particular type of selfishness: "I think, therefore, I am" brings us to "It is what I think that counts, not what needs to be produced, done, etc."

1) I am irresistibly sexually attractive to mother (or a Mother Type) but I will not openly admit it.

2) "I don't need subterfuges to be irresistibly attractive, I am naturally. I don't need to move, become, change."

3) "All women have sexual feelings for me, I have no sexual feelings for them."

4) "Women's sexual feelings are dirty, men's sexual feelings are loving."

5) "Men are inferior to women; women's capacity for knowledge and effectiveness and common sense is a lot greater."

6) "The fact that women can give birth makes them superior to men."

7) "If men do not become active and aggressive, they will automatically be victimized by women."

## Chapter 10

# Ray IV: Harmony Through Conflict; The Emotions (Sumo) Type

---

## Physical Description of the Ray IV Type

This type will be in most ways the exact opposite of the Second Ray Type. He will be prone to be physical, to have a great deal of energy, to be overweight. If he is an extrovert, he will be explosive, the life of the party, entertaining, and perhaps gregarious or bad tempered. If he is an introvert, he will tend to give the impression of being a time bomb that is about to explode. A dear friend of ours who epitomizes this type is called by us "The Furnace." Their extremities will tend to be small, since their energy is not projected to the outside; it stays held inside. Little energy going to the extremities creates small hands and feet. The body will tend to be squat and compact with short and fat necks.

As mentioned when we studied Ray II, there are types that will display a holding pattern in a particular area of their body, not overall. We need to distinguish between the person who has an overall holding pattern and who is a true Emotions Type in contradistinction to the person who has a localized, overgrown pelvis, which is a feature that is found in the Ray III woman and sometimes in the Ray VII Diana/ Artemis female, and in the Dionysus/Hermes male. See the chapters on those types.

## Origins and Causes of the Ray IV Type

According to body type theory, the formation of this type comes at about twenty months. Contrary to the Ray II Type, this type has been overfed and has received an overabundance of love and affection. There was a continuous concern about intake of food and evacuation of food. Parents were overly interested in both orifices—literally!—making both of them centers of pleasure. It is as if this type of person has been compressed between his mouth and his anus. Everything else becomes unimportant; only what is between those two extremities matters.

The overprotectiveness and overconcern with physical matters in this type has its origin in that relationship with mother and food. The parents made sure that the individual remained a baby and enjoyed it, which of course precluded sexual development. Castration is the obvious result of this. One thinks here of the castrati and of the fact that they all had a tendency to become overweight and to enjoy food. The existence of this condition in the world of music confirms the connection between this type and music and art.

## Description of the Ray IV Type
## on the Emotional Level

For them, the *cogito* would be, "I feel, therefore, I am." They will resort to what they feel, what their gut tells them to do and will proceed from there. Nevertheless, this is not an "irrational" type in that they are capable of telling you why they feel the way they do. Therefore, they are good thinkers in spite of the fact they are Emotions Types. Here is the connection then, between the Second and the Fourth Ray—the capacity for consciousness.

It is very interesting to note that the Tibetan asserts that Ray IV is really a lot more concerned with mathematical symmetry and precision than he is with the artist. The Tibetan does say that the artist can be found on any Ray and it is not the exclusive property of Ray IV, as is erroneously portrayed in many other typological studies.

Along the same lines there will be a peculiar propensity for spiritual awareness. This peculiarity is similar to the Second Ray's propensity for positivity. For the Fourth Ray, contact with the spirit world, soul contact, the good feelings generated from meditation are all avidly sought.

Nothing is equitable about this type. Everything is exaggerated and overdone, whether it is the overexpression or the collapse into apathy. It is the Ray of Drama. There is also in this type a deep and violent contempt for restriction, for form, for administration. Faced with restriction, they will have one of two reactions: they will explode, trying to completely wipe it out, or, they will scheme and plot and become dishonest, trying to bypass the laws and regulations in a way similar to the Will Type, though not as virulently or generically. Under stress they will violently react against confrontation, particularly if it is done with the quality of economy of energy as displayed by the Ray II Type. They will rev themselves into a frenzy. It is fascinating to see what happens in interactions between those two. The less energy displayed by the Ray II Type, the more violent and angry will get the Ray IV Type, which will make the Ray II Type withdraw even more, and we are on to a dangerous, and downward spiral.

This is the Ray of Colour, the Ray of the Artist. The resolution of conflict brings harmony. It is important to understand that it is not conflict that leads to creativity but the resolution of it. If this type understands this, he will stop glorifying conflict and save himself a great deal of unnecessary pain. There will be an obsession to make things right and to glamourize the conflict that makes things right. Here, a good example is Churchill, who was obviously a Ray IV Type and who put all of his energy and all of his identity into WWII. There is emptiness in his life before WWII and after WWII. Only during wars does Churchill become effective. He was First Lord of the Admiralty during WWI and Prime Minister during WWII.

Perhaps the fundamental feature of this type is conflict. To illustrate this, we fortunately have an historical person who epitomizes this type: Ludwig von Beethoven. He was musical, obviously, and that then is very much a qualification of this type. He was compact and seemed to be holding his energy in like a time bomb. But also his life was full of conflict. He was deaf for the best part of his composing years; he was lonely and yet capable of incredibly intricate, powerful, as well as delicate feelings of love in every conceivable sense—from the divine to the filial to the romantic. He was playful as well as somber. He was loud, as well as subtle. In fact, very often one can find in a single composition all of the above mentioned conflicts, sometimes existing in the same musical sentence.

An historical example can be found in Maria Teresa, Empress of Austria (mother to Marie Antoinette, Queen of France who was beheaded during the Revolution). Maria Teresa is the epitome of the complaining victim. She was victimized by stiff Frederick the Great of Prussia, who ruthlessly and shamelessly invaded territories that belonged to the Austrian Empire. Here is a perfect example of the typical Apollo, the Obsessive Penetrator, father-oriented bad boy who does harm to a poor, masochistic, complaining and victimized mother, penetrating her territory and appropriating it. Interestingly enough, the Maria Teresa Thaler is a currency that has remained popular to the present time. The thaler is particularly popular in Arab lands whose inhabitants consider the picture of Maria Teresa's abundant physique a wonderful mother figure.

From the divine point of view, this type will have a great

deal of energy and will be capable of producing an enormous amount of work. If you employ this type, he will be happy and feel flattered if you give him a lot of work to do. He will approach work as he approaches a good meal.

An example of this type is Louis XIV's minister, Colbert, who used to rub his hands in the morning as he first sat down at his desk and considered what needed to be done during the day. People who knew him described him as somebody who was joyously ready to devour an appetizing leg of mutton. They will be jolly, motivating and charismatic. They will enjoy physical contact. Do not be afraid of touching them; they love it. Physical contact with them will promote their confidence. They will have, also, a tremendous capacity for caring and for empathy, continuously being concerned about other people, caring for them, feeding them, asking about their health, almost living other peoples' lives for them. They will be empathetic to a fault.

Here are the harmful aspects of the Emotions Type. They will complain. They will have a propensity for playing back a great deal of tapes from the past. They are continuously whining. These people have a propensity for anxiety. They will be caught up in endless bouts of anxiety or fear which will alternate with bouts of incredible rage and cruelty. They will have a penchant for gossip. They will create conflict, they will look for conflict. If you get into a fight with a Ray IV Type, do not stop; they love a good fight, so give it to them. Regardless of the outcome, they will respect you for it and it will be an opportunity for you to be a channel of expression for their overblown and held-in energies.

In spite of their propensity for food, they will find it very difficult to be good to themselves, as in buying a new car or having a nice home or buying an object that will give them pleasure. The overindulgence in food will make them feel so guilty and self-depreciated that they will deny themselves everything else.

It is important to remember that in spite of the fact that there will be a great deal of expression of emotions coming from them, these people are still holding. They have so much energy that no matter how much is spent they will still be holding some back. It seems they are an endless source of energy, as in Beethoven continuously obsessing over his compositions, not only writing new ones but correcting and recorrecting old ones, writing on the walls when he would get inspired, and so on.

This overabundance of energy will be particularly difficult to understand for three types:

1) The Love/Wisdom Type, Ray II.
2) The Stiff Types, Rays V and VII
3) The Intuitive Type, Ray VI.

These types are incapable of holding any energy. Keeping a secret, holding back an expression of something is virtually impossible for the Rays II, V, VI and VII. For the Ray IV Type, it is a way of life, that is the way they live. They hold, they hold forever. In Ray I, the holding becomes dishonesty; in Ray III, it becomes manipulation and seduction.

They will also tend to collapse as severely as they had been overactive in a previous stage, so their lives, or their week, or their day will be a succession of overactivity and overpassivity —one after the other. They will be capable, for instance, of staying for extended periods of time being a couch potato, eating and watching TV. Then they will jump up and go into a binge of work lasting 16 to 18 hours.

Another harmful aspect of the Emotions Type is their disorder and their morass. Their desk will continuously be disorderly, they will look disheveled. Here we see the enormous self-contempt and self-depreciation that exist in this type. They have a very low opinion of themselves. It will be very difficult for this type to accept compliments. They will always feel embarrassed and try to change the subject or compliment you back. Having worshiped harmfulness for so long, it is a reversal for them to see anything good about themselves.

When it was suggested by members of the Parliament that Churchill become Prime Minister, it was very difficult for him to believe it, even though it was an obvious choice after Chamberlain's shameful compromise.

Their held-in energy also creates problems of impotency, of frigidity, and of sexual yielding; they confuse the latter with compliance. Therefore, there is an enormous conflict within them. On the one hand, there is a great deal of desire for sexual contact fueled by the overdone emotions. On the other hand, there is a holding back from sexual contact, a holding in, an implosion of the sexual energy. Not only does that lead to impotency/frigidity, but it also leads to pornographic concerns, voyeurism, sex devoid of love.

These people will be caught in issues of dependence versus independence. Having been hovered over by their parents, particularly on the physical level, they will tend to mistake any expression of love directed towards them as an intrusion of their independence and as an attempt to get them to comply. They will make the other person submit through their love and at the same time be afraid that people who love them will make them submit. It is as if the goal in their life, good or harmful, is to be free, without obligations, without ties; this is a reaction to the hovering over that they endured during their childhood.

### How to Deal with the Ray IV Type

As we said before, physical contact is an excellent idea. Take him on physically, or emotionally, if he is so inclined. He will love it. He will not harm you because he is very caring and very loving, and you will gain his confidence if he feels you are giving an honest fight.

If you are their boss or supervisor, see that they have a lot of work to do and then leave them alone to do it. When giving them instructions, it must come from a firm and energetic place and not from a depleted one. Give them a minimum of restrictions but let them boast about their achievements to you. However, if they get into one of their whining litanies, it is extremely important to very firmly and rationally point that out and then disengage. There is a point when these people get so harmful that you must disengage from them.

Allow them physical and emotional expression of their feelings. Once that is done, you can start the process of dissecting the problems and finding resolutions to them. It is impossible to resolve the problems as long as this person is still caught up in a pattern of holding. You have not gotten to the bottom of it unless and until they are spent physically. This may take quite a few weeks, sometimes months. Do not lose patience. The time spent clearing decades and perhaps centuries of accumulated issues, loaded with all kinds of conflicting energies, is time well spent. Once that is done, you can begin reasoning with an Emotions Type.

When speaking about a problem which may have absolutely nothing to do with you, they will try to hook you in, provoke you to taking sides. They will talk to you as if you are the one they are blaming. Make sure that you disengage from this by empathizing in a neutral way with statements such as "I can see why you would feel this way," or "I understand what you are saying." Give them exercises to do, such as pretending their antagonist is sitting over there—far away from you, of course—and have them relate to this person as if they were actually there, telling him all that has been left unsaid.

Another method that I find extremely helpful in working

with these people when they seem to be caught up in their tendency to complain is to:

1) Empathize with them, but do not stay in that empathetic state too long.

2) Quickly switch into talking about your complaints; you start bemoaning about your life, tell them how miserable you are.

What will miraculously happen is that no longer will they complain about themselves but they will start caring about you. Since they will be giving for a change, they will feel a lot better about themselves and stop grumbling. Here, sharing is actually a giving.

It will not be difficult for these people to admit their harmful volition. They love harmfulness; they relish it. You have to be careful here about allowing it to become victimization. There is a fundamental difference between approaching harmfulness from the point of view of a victim and approaching it from the point of view of self-responsibility. They will be prone to give you the victim line. See if you can get them to the point where they will take responsibility for their love of harmfulness. It is not that far away, although it may seem to be in the beginning.

In communications with their counselor, they will feel a great deal of shame which is a cover for guilt about their sexuality, about their eating habits, and so on. The hardest part is going to be to get them to let it all hang out, as it were. Once that is done, the rest will be easy. If they will merely express what is inside, the rest will then fall right into place.

### *Illusory Self-Images of the Ray IV Type*

Their abhorrence of precision and limits will make them idealize vagueness in their artistic expression. We find here the lack of precision of the Romantic painters who abandoned the classical proportions. We find here Beethoven painstakingly correcting and recorrecting what he had written at first, since it was so disorderly.

## Chapter 11
# Rays V and VII:
# Concrete Knowledge and Science;
# Order, Good Habits,
# Ceremony and Magic;
# The Stiff Types

### General Comments on the Ray V and VII Types

They both are representatives of Jung's Sensate Type, and of the body Stiff Types. In body type theory we find four subtypes of them: the Diana/Artemis, the Dionysus/Hermes, the Venus and the Apollo.

Another common denominator of all these types is their opposition to the Intuitive/Disjointed Ray VI. As much as the Intuitive Ray VI is concerned with inner level realities and concerns, the Sensate/Stiff Types, Rays V and VII, will be concerned with outer lever realities. They will pride themselves on being realists because they are so very much focused on sensate reality. They will be concerned with the bottom line. They will be overconcerned with their physical appearance, to the point of narcissism. Consequently, they will represent the standards of beauty in our society. They will wear the clothes that are required or that will please the societal norms; they will keep their bodies trim and lean.

Other common denominators pertaining to all of them are:

They are withholders. They will have great difficulty loving and opening their hearts. It is as if they operate freely but within very specifically defined—on the outer level, of course—norms.

Here we are reminded of the French classical period of the 17th Century, of the baroque, and to some extent the Rococo styles of architecture and of music that ensued. If one considers the rule of the three unities in dramaturgy, (time, place, plot), for example, they very much represent that rigid control within which great creativity is possible.

*Qu'en un jour, en un lieu, un seul fait accompli*
*Tienne jusqu' à la fin le théâtre rempli.*
—Boileau

Indeed, plays had to be written to fit within a 24 hour span of time; they had to take place in one setting without change of scenery, and have only one plot. Verses were subjected to the same strict scrutiny. Notwithstanding his great creativity, Bach rigidly respected the limits imposed by the norms of his time period. The rules of etiquette as we still practice them today and probably will for the foreseeable future were devised during that time. Most of this was toppled and overturned by the Romantic, Impressionist, Cubist, and Nihilist periods that followed. Nevertheless, the strong influence of that era still is with us on a daily basis. This gives you an idea of how persistent can a Sensate/Stiff model be.

Here I would like to make a comment that I feel very strongly about. The body type theorists have erroneously stated that this type is more developed than the other types because, in their terms, this type has achieved the "genital" stage. They contend that only the Stiff Type or the Stiff part of ourselves has reached the questionable distinction of experiencing the Oedipal problems.

For the sake of clarification, the Oedipal problems is the desire of a son to kill his father and have sex with his mother, or take his mother as a wife, as in Sophocles' play.

The worshiping of the Stiff Types by the body type theorists is a manifestation of the inherent distortion of that theory. Indeed, the entire theory is based on the fact that you are your body. There is a soulless aspect to this theory no matter how many times they say otherwise. When you have decided that you **are** the outer level reality, it is obvious that you are harbouring an idealized self that corresponds to the Stiff Type. You are in love with the Stiff Type and prop it up as being superior to all other types. Obviously, this will lead you to the incredible distortions reached by the body type theorists.

With body type theorists, you get the sense that nothing is ever achieved in the world except by Stiffs, and that, in fact, there are a lot of people who believe this way. In response, I would have them look at the achievements of Will Types, of Ray VI Types, of Emaciated Types, or Masochist Types. I would also have them ponder on the fact that in every single one of these types there have been manifestations of the Oedipal complex to a pretty extended degree.

In reality, there is nothing vainglorious about the Stiff Type. They may have their outer life together, or tend to, but that neither necessarily means spiritual development, nor does it necessarily mean self-actualization, it simply means encrustation in the sensible world. The person who is yuppily successful may be much further away from self-realization than the hobo who is searching for himself and is still in the wanderer phase of his life. Here is where we find Christ's preference for thieves, prostitutes and outlaws over the seemingly law-abiding Stiff fallacies. Many people who seem to have their life together do not even know how miserable they actually are. Others, who have broken the societal boundaries, destroying what many consider to be very precious, are much freer and closer to self-actualization and self-realization.

## Subcategories of Rays V and VII
Before we distinguish the differences between Rays V and VII, let us study the four subcategories by themselves:

| Ray | Male | Female |
|-----|------|--------|
| V | Obsessive Penetrator Apollo | Venus/Hysterical |
| VII | Femininized Male Dionysus/Hermes | Masculinized Woman Diana/Artemis |

### Physical Description of the Female Ray V Type
She is called the Venus Type. Here you have the exquisitely symmetrical, hourglass shape of Venus of the Golden Age of Greece, or Marilyn Monroe, or Sophia Loren, or Elizabeth Taylor.

### Physical Description of the Male Ray V Type
He is called the Apollo, the Obsessive Penetrator Type. Here we have the great heros of the forties and fifties, the Errol Flynns, the Humphrey Bogarts, Rock Hudson (although he has a touch of Will in him), Cary Grant, Clint Eastwood (even though he is not a forties or fifties star). Similarly to the Venus Type, you have a pretty homogeneous development of the entire body. It is harmoniously balanced throughout. The extreme idealization of the Apollo, Obsessive Penetrator Type, brings to mind the elite Fascist Youth or the elite University Debating Societies in England or in the United States.

### *Origins and Causes of the Male Ray V Type*

The origin of the Apollonian type is father-centered. Here, at the time of the formation of the ego structure, this person was very much impressed with and tried to emulate father characteristics of masculine perfection, i.e., idealized his father and idealized his father in himself. He made his all of the mass freezes that in our society characterize the male. He made himself desirable as a male and he knows it. He is proud of it and he competes with other males for supremacy. This has been done consciously and deliberately, at the time of the formation of the ego structure starting about age two and a half.

### *Origins and Causes of the Female Ray V Type*

Here we have the admiration, idealization and emulation of the feminine—the beautiful mother who is sexually desirable but also compliant to the male, while expecting to be taken care of by him. This Venus Type has absorbed all of the societal characteristics of a female as we "conventionally" know them to be. This she did consciously and deliberately, particularly around the formation of the ego structure starting about age two.

### *How the Male Ray V Type Behaves*

The Apollo, Obsessive Penetrator, behaves in a competitive, stiff way. He is full of himself, he always strives to be Number One. He may exhibit some flexibility but nevertheless, what is first and foremost on his mind is achievement.

He has an uncanny inability to love. For him, opening his heart is just about impossible. This is true for all Ray V and Ray VII people. If there is anything that binds them in common it is their inability to love.

The Apollo, Obsessive Penetrator Type will be obsessed

with justice—but justice without mercy; blind justice. He will have a "love them or leave them" attitude with women even though he may make sure to marry the right kind of person. He will for instance, have the right type of person at home taking care of the kids and so forth, probably a Venus Type, and then he may have affairs with other Venus Types or Diana Types on the side.

This type is so concerned with control that a lot of them have great difficulties reaching orgasm. They can stay erect for a long time but they often cannot orgasm. They will idealize and rationalize that as a staying power, a sexual prowess.

They will be obsessed with organization, everything has to be organized and hierarchical. They will not be able to tolerate anybody violating set norms or behaviour. They will very much adhere to the Theory X type of management (MacGregor) whereby people are motivated by carrot and stick policies, always on the outer level, either by threats or by outer level rewards, material rewards. They will not believe in giving freedom to their subordinates and letting their subordinates develop their own desire to contribute and to motivate themselves.

The Apollo Type will tend to have his life in order and to have a great deal of precision and exact knowledge about things. They are good at everything they do except loving. As a psychotherapist, he would be technically correct, he would be analytically correct, but he would not care for his patients. As an engineer he would be precise but he would not really love what he is building; he would be able to adapt to what his clients ask him to do very well even though he may secretly harbour contempt for them. As a lawyer, he would try to expunge his opponents in court with very precise details. He would know the rules of the game and play them. Everything he does is done within the rules, including cheating. He will find a way to justify everything he does, even cruelty.

### Relations to Ray I

Although all of this reminds us a lot of Ray I. The difference is that Ray I:

A) Is able to open his heart for the purposes of his will; Apollo is not.

B) Ray I is a lot less resilient than the Ray V male; he will crack and collapse sooner.

C) Ray I will have problems with having an erection, let alone sustaining it; the Ray V male will have no problem having an erection and sustaining it, he will have a problem with the orgasm (losing control).

D) Ray I is a lot closer to surrender and/or disintegration than is the Apollo. It is not that it is easier for Ray I to surrender. It is only that Ray I is closer to surrendering. In one way the Ray V male is more flexible than Ray I in that he is able to recognize his deficiencies and fill them from the point of view of knowledge or adaptability. In another way, Ray I is more flexible than the Apollo Type in that he is a lot closer to collapsing and surrendering, albeit unwillingly.

### How the Female Ray V Type Behaves

She is the type of person who will want to adapt, not only to what society expects of her, but also to what her husband expects of her. She will want to be an extension of her husband and to perfectly please him at any cost. Through her sexuality she is convinced that she can conquer the world, and she proceeds to try to do it. She will tend to sell her sexuality and her heart to the man who represents the most desirable party, socially and/or economically. She is continuously trying to prove her power through sexuality. The Venus female is as open to sexuality as is the Dionysus/Hermes male. She has no problem with her femininity. Her capacity for orgasms is phenomenal.

A typical behavioural pattern of this type is that she will be attracted to and fall in love with a man who seems to have all of the attributes she would want in a husband—being a good provider, having money and position, being a "professional" with a diploma. Then she meets someone else who is superior to her husband in his profession or position or power. She will proceed to be attracted to the more powerful person, wanting to leave her husband for him. Basically, we have here the Cinderella Complex repeated over and over again. There is a compulsion to be continuously rescued by a powerful man—the prince in shining armor. The power of the Venus woman is that she can make these men rescue her. In the process of doing so, of course, these women neglect their own task, their own call to become someone in their own right (an aspect that they gave up in childhood when they decided to emulate their mother and the feminine principle).

Why are they called Hysterical? The term was originated by Freud and Breuer. It depicts the somatization of a desire to be rescued. For example, in the case of Anna O, her false pregnancy was her unconscious self attempt to have her therapist, and therefore, rescuing prince Breuer, sweep her off her feet and marry her. This, itself, was a recreation of a repressed childhood attraction to her father who thoroughly disappointed her by dying on a prostitute's bed in Naples.

The term Hysterical describes extreme reactions of disintegration of a woman's character. For example, if this Venus Type is challenged, criticized or disappointed she will degenerate into fits of crying and shouting and great dramatization of her emotions. However, sorry ladies, this is not genuine disintegration. If you compare it, for example, to the disintegration of a Ray VI Intuitive Type, the Ray VI disintegration is real and dangerous, whereas the Venus disintegration is false and not to be believed. It is a ploy, a first line of guard, another way of getting rescued.

The Cinderella Complex also implies a desire for

defeatism. Indeed, the more victimized is Cinderella—the deeper she is in the cinders, the ashes—the more likely she is to be rescued by the Prince and the sweeter is her victory over her mother and her sisters. We can also see here the way in which this type will enlist others, usually men, to fight their battles for them. They will make themselves weak, i.e., attracting defeat into their lives, while demanding to be rescued by a male.

Obviously, the shows of weakness, the fits of crying and dramatization get quite a bit of mileage from the heroic Apollo Type and the Will Type. They will rush to the rescue, justifying their masculinity. This is a mistake, since it rewards harmful behaviour. It may temporarily stop the Venus person from what she's doing, but not for long. Count on the fact that she will be back at it.

Now, you might think that this is not true for Venus who exhibits so much emotionality and seems to be so irrational on the outer level. Nevertheless, it is true. The emotionality is a smokescreen for cunning, to get her way. The Apollo Type is also capable of incredible temper tantrums when he does not get what he wants.

Marilyn Monroe's life of hysterics with a succession of powerful and brilliant men did not work and led to her death. I find it hard to believe that she committed suicide. I prefer to believe some of the theories that have come up recently whereby she was killed either by the Mafia or by some Kennedy henchmen or by both parties in collusion with one another. Here is how an Venus woman can become dangerous to the men who rescue her.

There is no end to a Venus woman's desire for power over men. She will extricate secrets from them; she will then use those secrets to blackmail them. She will find out in her coy and apparently innocent manner what are the buttons of the men with whom she is involved. She will then proceed to press them all, taking full advantage of her power. When a man no longer suits her, she will simply go to another. This will throw men, particularly the Apollo and the Will Types that she attracts, into fits of violent rage, which has proved throughout history to be murderously dangerous. Examples: Henry VIII, Othello, Helen of Troy, Menelaus and Paris.

Ava Gardner was a Venus Type who was beaten by Howard Hughes and by George C. Scott, according to her autobiography. She drove both men crazy and they put her in the hospital a couple of times. She returned the favour to Howard Hughes. This is proof positive of this type's capacity for inciting violence in men. She will attract them, she will use them and then she will reject them.

### *How to Deal With The Ray V Type*

This type requires very strict rules of behaviour, very concrete rules established at the beginning of the relationship or at the beginning of every project undertaken with them. Sometimes, however, this is not possible, and you find you must deal with intangibles. As long as you can quantify the imponderables, the unknown, by precipitating them into the sensible world, thus making them understood to this type in his own language, you have no problem. Difficulties begin as soon as it comes to something that they cannot control through the certainty of "the material level." If that occurs, it is extremely important to be very firm and arbitrary about what you want and to tell him "that's the way it is; end of discussion."

Unlike Ray VI, here you can confront all you want. You can safely attack the character, you can compete, you can beat them at their own game. They may not like it, but they will not leave; they will respect you and they will continue learning from you. If you break them, they will very quickly form themselves back all over again. Not to worry. Do not buy their games, do not buy the tantrums, and do not buy the hysterical madness; it is not madness, it is a game.

Secretly they will be grateful to you for breaking them because at last they can collapse. The reason why this type cannot reach orgasm is because they cannot relax. Relaxing is similar to orgasm to them and their rigidity is unconsciously a desire expressed by them to be broken. This is true for the men but not the women. The women can have hundreds of orgasms without breaking. The capacity for Venus to have multiple orgasms corresponds to the capacity for Apollo, Obsessive Penetrator Type to stay erect and be unable to come for a long time. So, you can imagine the kind of relationship that exists between these two types; the endless bouts of sexuality intermittently interrupted by endless bouts of tantrums. Apollo and Venus make a very passionate, but obsessive couple.

### *Illusory Self-Images Of The Ray V Type*

This type will believe that they are right, holding a very narrow point of view and refusing to look at anything else. They will even pride themselves in that. In that sense— narrow-mindedness—they resemble the Sixth Ray person. however, their bigotry is based on concrete knowledge, not intuition or abstractions.

This type will thoroughly convince himself or herself that form is the only thing that is important, materialism is the only thing that counts and that they can do away with everything else. They will also be convinced that through concrete knowledge, they will get what they want.

### *Ray VII*
### *Order, Ceremony, Good Habits and Magic*

This Ray corresponds to the Dionysus/Hermes male and the Diana/Artemis female. From the Jungian point of view, we are still dealing here with the Sensate, so everything we have said about Sensate characteristics in general applies here as well.

However, there are differences. From the physical point of view, there is a diminution of the function of the heart. compensated for by a strong jaw and a strong pelvis. This, interestingly enough, creates opposite characteristics in the male and in the female. The male of this body type will be passive, will be an eternal adolescent, will glorify lack of decision making. The female, on the other hand, will exhibit exactly the opposite. She will know exactly what to do, she will be very decisive about what needs to be done and when. She will tend to have a successful professional life at the expense of her home life and of her motherhood.

What is interesting about Ray VII and its sub-types is that in spite of the fact that they represent order and ceremony, they also seem to show up in romantic, counterculture periods of our history. More than any other type, this one epitomizes Romanticism. Indeed, in times when the father principle is not around, there seems to be a reversal of roles wherein the woman will take charge and the man will become obsessed with matters of introspection and self-search.

Throughout history, romantic periods have followed periods of great activity, such as great wars. The romantic times that came after the Napoleonic Wars gave us this whole self-concern with overexpressive emotions, overdone colours, overblown inner conflicts and a deep sense of failure and of self-contempt. It was based on the feeling that it would be impossible to achieve what their parents had achieved in the previous era. It is the glorification of *nostalgie de la boue* (nostalgia of the mud, as the French call it); the glory of suffering, the glorification of pain, the radical chicism of the sixties, the torn blue jeans for which you paid a fortune, the *nouveau pauvre*, the glorification of poverty.

If one considers, for instance, George Sand, the famous French writer and poet of the first half of the 19$^{th}$ Century who wore pants, smoked cigars and was savagely promiscuous, one sees exhibited in the female all of the male characteristics of machismo, except that in the times of romanticism they are glorified.

Chopin was one of the many lovers that George Sand took in her days. He was a Dionysus/Hermes male. His music exhibits both the fastidious characteristic of rigorous precision and the apparent disorder that elicits a state of world weariness when we listen to it. On the one hand, they tend to be fastidious and superorderly, on the other hand they are revolutionaries favouring counter culture.

The sunken chest was even idealized during that period. Consumption was not only accepted, but fashionable, as in the story of Camille (*La Traviata*). Chopin, and Alfred de Musset were both consumptive and were both George Sand's lovers. Beau Brummell dying of consumption, Lord Byron dying early; all point to the Dionysus/Hermes's same morbid fascination.

A specific issue that affects the Diana/Artemis (female) and the Dionysus/Hermes (male) is the disconnection between the heart and the pelvis. These people can have sex without feelings. A great deal of contempt is associated with sexuality. One of the most difficult things for a Stiff to do is to surrender and to totally commit, whether to a partner or to a creed or to an idea. They are the perennial experts at hedging so as to take best advantage of both sides of the fence.

### *Physical Description of the Male Ray VII Type*
He is called the Dionysus/Hermes Type. Physically, he will resemble the Diana/Artemis female. He has a sunken chest and powerful pelvis and legs with a protruding jaw. We have Mick Jagger, Elvis Presley, James Dean, Bill Clinton, Woody Allen.

### *Physical Description of The Female Ray VII Type*
She is called the Diana/Artemis Type. This type has deficiency in the chest but a strong head and pelvis, often with a protruding jaw which is homologous to the overdeveloped pelvis (both pelvis and jaws are receptacles with hinges; the overdevelopment of one corresponds to the overdevelopment of the other). Here we have Lauren Bacall, Angie Dickinson. Lauren Bacall is the epitome of the Diana/Artemis Type since she married a father figure, Humphrey Bogart, at the end of his life, quite similarly to Electra.

### *Origins and Causes of the Male Ray VII Type*
He has been close to mother. She sexually aroused him, either directly or indirectly. There need not be abuse on the physical level in order for sexual arousal to occur. A seductive mother, a mother who desires being desired, or a mother who is sexually frustrated with her husband will consciously or unconsciously transpose on to her male child sexual feelings that he cannot handle. The mother will enjoy this since she can, for a change, control her little man a lot better than she can control her big one. The response of the child is to be very sexually charged, which explains the preponderance of the pelvis and the legs as well as the protruding jaw in this type at the expense of the collapsed chest.

Once again, the formation of this type occurs at the formation of the ego, which is between ages two and a half and three and a half.

### *Origins and Causes of the Female Ray VII Type*
Here we have the same syndrome except that she was close to father; she was sexually aroused by father, whether consciously or unconsciously. Once again, the same thing applies. A father can sexually arouse his daughter in many different ways. One does not have to do it by abusing her or

by consciously seducing her; the mere unconscious transposition of his sexual feelings for his wife or other women onto his little adoring woman is enough to magnetize the situation in the child's pelvis. She now wants to be daddy's buddy. She wants to participate in games with him. She develops characteristics that are similar to his. She admires him. She has contempt for women. She has contempt, for example, for Venus (check out the causes of the War of Troy, Venus versus Athena and Artemis for Paris' allegiance). We are talking here about the formation of the Amazon, the denial of the feminine, the denial of the breasts.

### How the Ray VII Types Behave

It is important to remember that the Dionysus/Hermes male and the Diana/Artemis female are idealizations in their own right. In spite of the fact that we preponderantly live in a patriarchal system, matriarchy is alive and well and showing itself during periods of romanticism. The study of history will reveal that periods of romanticism have alternated with periods of aggressive father type behaviour.

Example: 1920s and thirties, romanticism, lack of responsibility, were the Dionysus/Hermes and Diana/Artemis Types. In the 1940s and fifties, the father aspect emerges, with war. The return of the importance and dominance of the provider, comes back to the fore and the Venus Female increasingly stays home to have babies and to cook. This culminates in the McCarthy era in the United States, the Korean War and the domination of patriarchy. The sixties and seventies show a return to Dionysus/Hermes male and Diana/Artemis female type behaviour; the antihero becomes the hero, the adolescent male is the sex symbol, as is the powerful androgynous type female. In the eighties and nineties we return to the father aspect, the Apollo, the yuppy type fatherhood, establishing the balance.

### Dionysus/Hermes Type

He behaves like an adolescent, a perennial, perpetual adolescent. He shuffles, he does not make decisions. He loves not making decisions. He loves getting other people to make decisions for him. He wants to be indecisive. He wants to remain an adolescent not knowing what he will be when he grows up. He loves rebelliousness. He especially loves rebelliousness through the silent treatment.

In the Camille story, we have Camille (or Violetta in "La Traviata"), a strong woman— strong, albeit, consumptive, i.e., denying her lungs and her heart—being attracted to a beautiful young man (Alfredo) who has nothing to say for himself and whose decisions are entirely made by his father and Camille. The fate of the Dionysus/Hermes lover is decided by Camille, who is Diana/Artemis, and by the lover's father, a Apollo.

He will attract women through passivity; he will not court them. And so it is in other areas in his life, passively waiting for things to come to him, waiting for the other person to make a mistake. In that sense, he will be very reluctant to compete.

The Dionysus/Hermes male is generally not promiscuous. He is usually faithful, even though often jilted. One of the great misconceptions about the Dionysus/Hermes male is that he has problems with impotence. In fact, the Dionysus/Hermes male is probably the greatest and most potent lover of all male types, no matter what others pretend. Indeed, he has got an incredible amount of energy in the pelvis, and his sexuality is not marred by the ego trips that so upset the Apollo and Will Types. The Apollo Type, for all of his pretense of prowess, has the problem of very often being unable to achieve orgasm. The Dionysus/Hermes male does not have that problem. The Will Type male is, very often, impotent; not so the Dionysus/Hermes male. The Will and the Apollo Types see the Dionysus/Hermes male as less a man than they. Little do they know that the Dionysus/Hermes male is deep down very comfortable with his masculinity and his expression of it; his problem of identity lies only on the surface.

This type will continuously be creating and living contradictions. For example, the diminution of the chest means a cutting off from love, whilst the augmenting of the pelvis means an overdevelopment of sexuality. When it comes to loving, it is the same here as with the other Stiff Types; there is an inability to allow himself to love. Thus, in their lives, these people will find themselves creating conflict between love and sexuality. They will continuously go from one sexual partner to another, being dissatisfied and never knowing why. The reason why is that their heart is closed. The key to the healing of this type is opening their heart.

This contrast is also to be found in the many examples that we have given above. For instance, the Dionysus/Hermes male's extraordinary sexual prowess in contradistinction to his femininity. The Diana/Artemis female's inability to reach orgasm in contradistinction to her voracious promiscuity.

This type will love to be the underdog and love to protect the underdog. They are the heros of "counterculture." Of course, we can only judge this from the point of view of a patriarchal society such as ours. I would be willing to bet that in the days of the matriarchal society, the Venus and the Apollo were the ones who were the counter culture, while the Diana/Artemis female and the Dionysus/Hermes male were the acceptable norms.

Oedipus started off by being an Apollo, Obsessive Penetrator Type male. Indeed, he challenges and kills his father and marries his Venus Type mother. Later, when he finds out the truth, he blinds himself, debilitates himself, and sinks into a Femininized Male, Dionysus/Hermes modality,[22] being controlled by and led around as a wanderer by his Diana/Artemis daughter, Antigone. Both types in this Ray will idealize their body.

### *Diana/Artemis Type*

By contrast, the Diana/Artemis female will tend to be promiscuous. She will have great difficulty reaching an orgasm, similarly to the Apollo male. These women will prefer masturbating themselves or being masturbated by others. The incidence of orgasms through intercourse is very limited.

Here we have the penis envy syndrome; they would have much rather been born male than female. They resent their role as females. They will try to control their male partners and be in charge. They will either be attracted to younger, better controllable males or older, better controllable males. In any case, they will be attracted to the Dionysus/Hermes male which will compensate for their type. Some of them will also be attracted to the Ray VI Intuitive male who they can control and who then proceeds to inordinately worship them. This explains the overdeveloped pelvis and the underdeveloped chest. The denial of femininity and the overemphasis aspect of the personality creates this aggressive behaviour.

The syndrome of the younger woman marrying and taking care of the older man is very much a manifestation of this. Just as the Venus Type was put up as a role model during the forties and fifties, the Diana/Artemis Type was very much the role model of the sixties and seventies, the era of the controlling, androgynous mother—androgynous because she combines aspects of both sexes, denying the feminine and inhabiting the masculine.

Promiscuity is to be found here, as well as in the Apollo Type man. This person will have a great deal of problems committing to one relationship, in contradistinction to the Venus, who commits to one and then proceeds to another after a while. With the Diana/Artemis Type, the existence of more than one sexual partner is not unusual. It is reminiscent of the promiscuity of the Apollo Type, with the little black book full of all the different people that they can date at any particular time. If a study were to be made of a Diana/Artemis's little black book, what one would find in it is a great percentage of Dionysus/Hermes males or of Ray VI Intuitive Types or even of collapsed Will Types in their old age. It would be very difficult for a Diana/Artemis female to sustain a relationship with a Apollo male; they would continuously want to penetrate and humiliate each other.

Unlike the Venus Type with her endless capacity to have orgasms, the Diana/Artemis Type will have difficulty reaching orgasm. In that particular sense, she will resemble the Apollo Type. She will use sex to get close to men. The localized sexual arousal in the pelvis makes it very difficult for her to totally surrender to an orgasm. Many of these women will not care much for sex, going through extended periods of time without it. Diana was a virgin goddess, she had a contempt for sex. She was a good huntress, though, focused on achievement, outer level achievement, conquests, action, profession, just like her father. We find here the penis envy. All this happens during the formation of the ego between the ages of two and a half and three and a half.

If there is anybody who epitomizes a Diana/Artemis, it is Eleanor of Aquitaine. Here are some of the facts about her. She was very close to her father and to her grandfather, both of whom were strong, patriarchal figures. She adopted just about all of their traits, disregarding the customs of the 12th Century. She was instrumental in constructing the rules of chivalrous conduct whereby the man behaved as the servant of the woman and the woman was seen as superior to the man. Hers is the epitome of the story of penis envy. She would much rather have been a man. She behaved like a man.

Needless to say that did not go over very well with the

existing authorities, particularly with St. Bernard de Clairveaux. Her divorce from Louis VII of France (an obvious Ray VI Type devoted to his church a lot more than to his sexy wife) and her subsequent marriage to Henry II Plantagenet displayed the typical Diana/Artemis concern with career. I doubt that she ever fell in love with anyone. She did not love Louis VII. She adopted the promiscuous lifestyle of her father, more to please him than because of her sexual appetite. She was not in love with Henry II Plantagenet, although she bore him many sons; being a breeder for Henry II was what she was supposed to do, and she did the job exceedingly well, working to make his house more powerful than the house of his suzerain, Louis VII of France.

Even her emasculating behaviour with Richard the Lion Heart fit the description of the Diana/Artemis woman. Richard the Lion Heart adored his mother, imitating her to the hilt, becoming her in essence. He disappointed her by being homosexual. Perhaps this is the way that he found to rebel against her on a very, very, deeply unconscious level.

The total devotion of her sexuality, her beauty, her knowledge, her body, her inheritance for the sake of her career is very much a Diana/Artemis trait. The statues that are available of her seem to confirm that she also had this type of body. She was trim, she never got fat. In spite of her numerous pregnancies, she took care of herself physically and she lived to the unconscionable (for that period of time) age of 82.

In contradistinction to the Venus Type, this type will develop her career and will insist on doing so. Her approach to motherhood is as an achievement, not so much an instinctual need. She will tend to be cut off and contemptuous of her motherhood instincts, choosing to overemphasize the instinct of achievement and self-assertion. This, of course, will bring on the condition in which the job itself will become the baby. The divine aspect of this is, obviously, the caring that she will give her profession. The harmful aspect of this is the extraordinary possessiveness, jealousy and competitiveness with which she will approach that profession.

### *Description of the Male Ray VII Type on the Emotional Level*

We find continuous indecision which he emotionalizes. There is here an all pervasive sense of anxiety, of not knowing what the solution is, and thereby attracting other people, particularly Diana/Artemis females, to save him, to tell him what to do. To these resolutions he will respond with "yeah buts," yes but this, yes but that, and will blame whomever suggested them for anything that does not work out.

There is also an inability to love, to open his heart. He will use women to do his bidding, or even to pay his way in some instances, and once he has gotten what he wants, he will drop them and go on to another. Here one can see a parallel with the Venus Type. The link, of course, is that they are both close to mother.

If this type gets angry it is going to be a defeatist anger rather than the anger of the Apollo or of the Will Type. These two types want results from their anger; they want to overcome others through their anger. The defeatist anger of the Dionysus/Hermes will have for purpose the attraction of somebody stronger to do their bidding.

### *Description of the Female Ray VII Type on the Emotional Level*

Just as the Venus Type was attached to and tried to emulate mother, the Diana/Artemis Type tries to get close to and emulate father. Father was very much the dominant figure of her childhood. He was close to her physically and she at an early age developed sexual feelings for him. In fact, a great deal of the issues of nourishment from mother—the need for mother—has been repressed and transferred to father. This then results in the squeezing of the energy in the heart and in the breast, both of which become diminished, and the consequent overdevelopment of the pelvis—sexual feelings for father—and the homologous controlling and protruding jaw.

The destruction of the father aspect in the world of the Diana/Artemis female triggers the transsexualism and permissiveness and lawlessness that usually occur in the romanticized periods of history such as the first half of the nineteenth century in Europe, the twenties and thirties, and in the sixties and seventies.

The compulsion for professional achievement and success triggers crises of conflict in the life of the Diana/Artemis female. There comes a point in her life when she realizes that there is one big area in her life where there are no achievements, i.e., children. She then proceeds to consider the business of making babies. She will go out and choose a man who is the best suited to produce babies with her. Whether or not she marries is secondary; the marriage is perfunctory.

One here remembers Vanessa Redgrave who, after having met Franco Nero, decided that he would be a great father for a child with her and proceeded to have one without ever marrying him or even having a loving relationship with him. Therefore, the men are seen as sexual objects to be used for pleasure or progeny. Here again, we see in the Diana/Artemis the distortion of machismo, except that it is being exhibited by a woman and not by a man. Machismo is, therefore, not an exclusive property of the male sex. This type is a female Don Juan or James Bond.

In the world of the Diana/Artemis female, strong men are bad and weak men are good. In fact, there are no strong men, no fathers; men have been reduced to little boys. There are androgynous mothers and little boys; everyone else—little girls and strong fathers—are excluded. Conversely, in the Venus female, there are no little boys and mothers; there are only little girls to be rescued and fathers.

Mythologically one thinks of Thetis, Achilles' mother who rescued her son by seducing Vulcan into making him a new armor. Earlier Thetis, upon giving birth to Achilles, goes to Hades with him and plunges her son into the River Styx in order to make him invulnerable. Here is the overprotective, hovering and emasculating quality of a Diana/Artemis mother over her children.

Let us differentiate this type from the Jewish or Latin mother. The Jewish or Latin mother belongs to the Ray IV or Ray III Types. She is overconcerned with issues of food, issues of excretion, issues of physical sensations, pleasure and pain, and is overprotective in that sense of her children. This is different with a Diana/Artemis Type whose concern is not so much for food but for the child having a perfect education or benefitting from perfect conditions.

Female Ray VII Types tend to become Ray III, either past menopause, or as a result of widowhood, or of betrayal on the part of their husband or mate. For more information about this see *Origins and Causes of the Ray III Type* above (page 60).

### How to Deal with the Ray VII Type

Here again, do not be afraid to give specific directives and make the rules of the game and the rules of your relationship with them very clear from the start, no matter what that relationship is. When confronted, instead of the hysterical response of Ray V Types, you will get a "be careful" response, as if they were fragile. Do not buy it. Go straight through. They, too, need to be broken. They merely appear to be fragile, but they actually are not. You can assert yourself, you can confront them, and you can also break them, and once again, they will be grateful for the breaking. The destruction of their rigidity will make room for the final flow of love, giving, and a reconnection with the will of reality. There is a similarity between the Dionysus/Hermes Type and the Venus Type, in that both of them were close to mother. They both represent receptive types, adopting characteristics that are identified with the feminine in our culture. At the same time there is a similarity between the Apollo Type and the Diana/Artemis Type in that they were both close to the father. They exhibit active, aggressive characteristics that are attributed in our society to the male. This, of course, enlightens us as to how to deal with them in terms of, perhaps, being more directive with the receptive types and more Socratic with the active types. Nevertheless, in all four types, one can he assertive and firm when the need arises. When you do this and are firm, you take away from them their rigidity and give them, finally, the opportunity to relax which will release the loving characteristics.

At some point, the Stiff Types get tired of their rigidity. That is true for the four of them. These points significantly are to be found just before or during the great crises, adolescence and menopause. In those times, the Stiff will consciously or unconsciously look for somebody or something to rely on, so as to be able to collapse and finally relax.

This explains why so many competent people totally abandon their profession to join cults or spiritual organizations where they occupy themselves in tasks that are well below their capacities. I am thinking, for example, of a couple that I knew who were both Stiff Types—she Venus, he Apollo—who were Ph.D. physicists working at NASA. They both abandoned their profession, joined a commune and took menial jobs in that community. They did this because they were tired of being Stiff Types and they wanted somebody to tell them what to do. Keep in mind that this is not leaving their rigidity because these people are still looking for rules to obey, only this time given to them by some outer level authority, instead of imposing them for themselves in their own lives. The final realization has not as yet been made. The final realization is the existence of a soul.

### *Illusory Self-Images of the Ray VII Type*

They will want to give the impression that they have magical powers, that there are mysterious magical things that they can do for you. They will believe in superstition, and they will try to threaten you with it. This type will be prone to want things to come about all by themselves. In the Diana/Artemis female, there will be a demand that this happen. In the Dionysus/Hermes male, there will be a self-imposed debilitation, based on his illusion that the weaker he is, the more likely it is that he will be magically saved.

There will be an overemphasis on being fastidious, orderly to the point of superstition. Professionally, he may be a failure and even glorify it, nevertheless, he is very orderly about it. The pride of being disheveled is one way that this will manifest. He is studiously disheveled. During the sixties this was called radical chic, the carefully torn blue jeans, the studiously worn out clothes. They see themselves as the guardians, the custodians of a particular form or of a particular trend, whether it be a rebellious one or an establishmentarian one. They will insist that everything be just so without disturbing the order in which it was done in the past.

They will think of themselves as irresistibly attractive sexually, and they will want you to think so, too. They will keep you at arm's length, accusing you explicitly or implicitly of sexualizing your interaction with them: "you are attracted to me, not me to you, so I must protect myself from your sexual feelings." Actually, they are the ones who are charged and this is merely a projection of their own sexuality on you and fear of their own sexuality. They have spent so much time and energy convincing themselves that they are sexually attractive, that they have problems seeing reality, which is that they may not be as attractive as all of that. This extends beyond the sexual arena into other areas of their lives, where they will have a distorted self-image.

## Chapter 12
# Ray VI:
# Idealism and Devotion;
# The Intuitive Type

---

### Physical Description of the Ray VI Type

They are the ones whose body parts seem to be disconnected from one another. You will find a small body with long arms that end with huge hands and feet, or you will have a small head with an enormous chest, or perhaps a small chest with enormously elongated legs and feet that seem to belong to someone else. Another physical characteristic is the disparity between the left and the right sides. Their left profile will be distinctively different from their right, with, perhaps, a left eye bigger than a right eye. All of these are indications of an Intuitive Type. Another indication of this type is the facial deadpan—the blank expression that seems to say "no one is at home."

### Origins and Causes of The Ray VI Type

This condition seems to have been formed between zero and six months of age. There are two fundamental causes which have had the same effect. These same causes can be recreated through severe crises later in life:

1) Shattering violence, either from the parents, from a traumatic experience, or from repeated traumatic experiences

in early life. The fear is so great that the person disconnects, goes out to lunch, goes into a catatonic state.

2) More subtle is a continuous double message coming from parents or parent substitutes: on the one hand, the parent seems to love the child and, on the other, he seems to reject him. A good example is a parent's verbalizing love for the child while actually paying attention to something else. There are two messages here: a) I love you and I care for you, and b) I actually do not care at all, I care for something or somebody else. The child's deep and generic desire for love will thus be traumatized. The response from the child will be to go into that catatonic, out to lunch state.

Either of these causes will produce a shattering of the personality or of the guards—of anything that has any hope of crystallizing. The person develops a taste for disconnection, for going out to lunch, for going inside, and a fear and abhorrence of whatever is on the outside. He feels more confident in religious or philosophical matters than anything that has to do with the senses; he would not enjoy science or visual arts, for instance.

Major changes in an individual's life will propel him into a Ray VI modality of behaviour. Take, for instance, adolescence. All adolescents seem to be Ray VIs. They all have issues of time and space. All of their bodies look like they are not quite finished, and have parts that seem disconnected from one another. The lanky aspect of the adolescent is to be found here. The way in which an adolescent will drape himself over a chair, their repeated "I don't know" answers to whatever it is that you ask them, their deadpan expression are Ray VI characteristics. Adolescence is a shattering crisis. The release of the forces of adulthood and of sexuality from the soul into the personality shatters the heretofore rigidified substances of childhood.

Late childhood is a kind of old age. The latency period

between ages seven and ten makes children look old and set in their ways. All of a sudden adolescence springs upon them and they are disconnected; they don't know what they are doing, they have identity problems (very much a Sixth Ray characteristic), they want to commit suicide, also a Ray VI problem. They are disconnected from the sensible world. More often than not, they do not know what they are wearing or why they are wearing it. They do things to their hair which are very strange. When Bill Cosby accuses his children of being brain damaged, this disconnection is what he is referring to.

Whenever a severe crisis occurs it will recreate these aspects in an individual. The harmful aspects of the crisis are obvious. The divine ones are that, just as adolescence does, they will release new, and heretofore, untried potentials.

### How the Ray VI Type Behaves

The fundamental characteristic of this type is their disconnection from the sensible world. Therefore, they are concerned with anything that has to do with inner life. All inner thoughts, events, dreams, meditations, reflections, abstractions are of prime importance. These are the people who have ultra religious experiences, who are very concerned with philosophical matters and who, at the same time, forget about the concrete world. In fact, they will have great contempt for all those who do have any interest in the sensible world.

The Intuitive Type will tend to forget about time, losing tract of it to a surprising degree. For instance, I remember asking an Intuitive what he had done over a long weekend. He replied "nothing," and he meant it. He actually did not do anything. He was lying on his bed being disconnected, forgetting to eat, forgetting to do anything most of the time, just lying there being disassociated from reality. Meditation is for them the easiest thing to do; it is their line of least resistance.

Self-denial is also easy for them. This explains why a lot of religious types practice so much self-denial. Typologically, it makes sense. They enjoy it. It is not denial at all for them; it is actually pleasurable.

The Sixth Ray Type will be prone to superstition and prejudice. The over concern with protection and the great anxiety of not having any boundaries will make him want to attach himself to little physical symbols of safety. Fetishism is to be found here, as well as all of the tendencies in the Catholic Church to pray to icons, to go through the incredibly intricate gestures of the ceremonials. It is always amazing to me to see the Pope with his miters, double crowns and scepters along with the little idiosyncracies that show themselves at the altar. All of this is the product of the Sixth Ray which has been dominant during the past two thousand years, ruling the Age of Pisces that is now ending.

These people are very ethical, very grounded in spirituality, very perceptive, very capable of performing with incredible degrees of excellence tasks that are specific. They possess an uncanny ability to intuit what somebody else is thinking or feeling, etc. Therefore, strangely enough, they will make good administrators and builders.

The reason for their great perceptive ability is the fact that their guards have been shattered. This makes them open to extrasensory perception. They cannot rationally explain what happens; they will just tell you that it exists. They will even be surprised and annoyed if you ask them why. The question why is immaterial to them.

Under stress will come out the harmful aspects of the Intuitive. To begin with, they will refuse to put up with stress. They will react to it by asking for space. They will fuss over any discomfort, any cross remark, or any remark they believe is cross. Their response to stress will be extremely quick. They will not hold any of their reactions the way the Fourth Ray does. They will try to immediately strike back by making counter accusations.

The other reaction they will have is to disconnect totally and go "out to lunch." The silent treatment that is so characteristic of defensive behaviour is mostly attributable to the Ray VI Type. In their silent treatment and in their disconnection they will exhibit what seems to be an incredible dumbness, which contradicts the fact that they are very intelligent.

They will also have a lack of capacity to account for time or space. They will have an uncanny ability to lose things. As a protection against this, they will become obsessively meticulous, reviewing over and over again things that need to be done. For instance they will worry about whether or not they locked the front door, whether they took their keys with them, etc. A friend of ours of this type continuously carries with him little note cards on which he obsessively and continuously writes reminders of appointments, what he is likely to forget, etc. Given a particular task, they will be found to be agonizingly slow, tracing and retracing what they have done to make sure they did it right. In most cases, this slowness is their way of expressing hostility and rebellion.

Their propensity for cruelty is a peculiar aspect of people on this Ray. Since they are disconnected from the sensible world, they will tend to be cruel to anything that lives, anything that has a body. The specific cruelty of this type is to the opposite sex. Since they dislike intimacy, there will be an antagonistic attitude towards the opposite sex, and hurt them mentally or even physically. This is to be found both in men and women. The cruelty as well as the fear of intimacy are characteristics of this type. Also, this type will be prone to be cruel to animals, being totally insensitive to pain inflicted on them, finding excuses to harm them physically.

Finally, this cruelty will take more subtle forms: the withholding of feelings and the enjoyment of withholding, making people or animals squirm. It is extremely important to understand that this is a direct result of their disconnection from the sensible world and of their unwillingness to experience anything in the body.

An excellent example of this has been given to us by Peter O'Toole in *Lawrence of Arabia.* In one scene of this movie, Lawrence extinguishes a match with his bare fingers without exhibiting any reaction to the pain it must have caused him. One of his colleagues tries to do the same thing and says, "Ouch! It damn well hurts. What's the trick?", to which Lawrence responds, "The trick is not minding that it hurts." In a later scene in the desert, Lawrence exhibits his extraordinary capacity to go without water and his competitiveness with Arabs who had been raised and had been used to not need much water.

Another excellent portrayal of Ray VI by Peter O'Toole is to be found in his General Tanz in *The Night of The Generals*, a film version of the excellent novel by Hanz Helmut Kirst. Here, the rigid facade—Ray V—is betrayed in private by the murderous, disconnected, drunk Ray VI. The abhorrence of being touched is also brilliantly portrayed in this film.

Most Ray VI Types will not go to such extremes, but they will tend to punish themselves physically and to get others to suffer physically under the banner of idealism, or spirituality, or faith, or self-control, etc. All of this is not actually idealistic at all, but a demonstration of their line of least resistance. Having disconnected from their body, they really do not feel anything. They believe that others do not feel anything either. Unconsciously, they want to recapture connection with that feeling part of themselves from which they disconnected. So, they get others to feel, harmfully; thus, they demonstrate that feeling something is a harmful experience, and therefore, they justify to themselves the "fact" that feeling is painful and that they should disconnect from it.

Another example of a Ray VI Type is Joan of Arc, also called the Maid of Orleans, i.e., the Virgin of Orleans (*pucelle* in French). Early in life she heard voices that convinced her that her mission was to liberate France from British occupation. She tirelessly brought her message to Charles VII, King of France, in spite of many obstacles: she had no title of nobility, she was a mere peasant, she was a woman (it was inconceivable then—it still is now—that a woman could become a hero who militarily liberates a country from occupying forces that heretofore had been found to be indestructible—the British). She was finally captured by the British and burned at the stake. Her example, however, was so powerful and her impetus so great that the momentum created was enough to eventually throw the British out of France. Every aspect of her behaviour—her disconnection from sexuality by remaining a virgin, her hearing voices, her sense of indefatigable mission, her stubborn pursuit of her goal at incredible physical costs—are all characteristics of Sixth Ray behaviour.

### Description of The Ray VI Type on The Emotional Level

This type, being involved with inner matters, will by second nature gravitate towards spirituality. He will choose to become a monk, or a priest, or a fanatical and ascetic campaigner in whatever field of endeavor he chooses. For example, Jerry Brown, the presidential candidate who was very much into self-denial, is a Ray VI Type. Some of the things he said made a lot of sense, but some of the others were really off the wall. His aversion to the market place was very much this type's aversion for the sensible world.

A wonderful example of this is to be found in Italian history. Savonarola, who kicked out the Medici of Florence in the late 15th Century and established an ascetic regime, typifies the reaction of an Intuitive to a Sensate (Rays V and VII) situation. The Medici were very much into sensible Sensate reality: wealth, art, material possessions, marrying off their daughters into the nobility of Europe. In the few years, under Savonarola, all of this was wiped out and a regime of religious asceticism ruled Florence.

Another example of this is the Iranian revolution of 1978-79, in which the sensate (Rays V and VII) Shah of Iran, who was very much focused on Western industrialism, wealth, material comfort, and militarism, was violently replaced by the Ray VI Intuitive Ayatollah Khomeini whose only concern was the inner life and Moslem fundamentalism.

The entire history of the Arabs, as a matter of fact, is the spreading of the Sixth Ray dispensation and its destructive effects on the existing empires. Indeed, the Byzantine Empire and the Persian Empire were both very much concerned with outer level representations: art, incredible indulgence in sexuality, and dissipation in food and drink. The Arabs wiped all of this out as they invaded the countries that had been occupied by the Byzantines and the Persians. Their focus on the inner life precluded for them the representation of anything alive. It is forbidden in the Moslem religion to paint, to sculpt, and, in a more modern fashion, to photograph anything alive. The result of this, of course, has been the creation of the exquisitely complicated arabesque decoration on buildings, and calligraphy of the Koran. All of the senses were then focused into these art forms.

The destruction of outer knowledge in favour of the inner can also be seen in the example of the Arab General Amr, as related in the *Illusory Self-Images of the Will Type* #10, (page 39).

Here, we see the connection between Ray I and VI, also found in the example of the Ayatollah Khomeini.

It is interesting to note that Western civilization has a

Sixth Ray idealization and devotion history in the Dark Ages. The last 500 years have come as a reaction to the preceding 1000 years of medieval darkness. The period from 500 to 1500 A.D. is the characteristic expression of the Sixth Ray. From 1500 to the present is really a coming out of it, a swing from the disconnection of Ray VI into the rigidity of materialism.

Renaissance, as well as 17th and 18th Century reason, are a reaction to Christianity and not an adherence to it. It is the reaction to Christianity. It is this reaction that created the Industrial Age. A proof of this is demonstrated by Alain Peyrefitte, a modern French writer and sociologist. He shows that the countries that adopted the Protestant religions were much quicker to develop industrially than the countries that remained Catholic. Indeed, France, Italy and Spain were to remain backwards when compared to England, Holland and Germany in terms of industrial development. This is very simply due to the fact that Protestant religions accepted change and the new work ethic, while the Catholic religion remained steeped in medieval feudalism. Medieval feudalism contended that there should never be any change, that the nobility should wage war, that the clergy should take care of spiritual matters, and that the third estate should till the land.

There was no room for the bourgeoisie. The bourgeoisie emerged in spite of Catholicism and along side Protestantism. The coming out of the Middle Ages (Sixth Ray) into Renaissance and industrial development is a disengagement from the Sixth Ray dispensation and a reemergence of the other, more Sensate functions of the Fifth and Seventh Rays.

However, in spite of this reaction to Sixth Ray idealism in the past 500 years we also have counter reactions to it, such as the Counter-Reformation, Savonarola, Arab fundamentalism, the Pilgrims. Another counter reaction is to be found in the disintegration of the great colonial empires of the

19<sup>th</sup> Century into fanatical narrow-minded nationalism. The resurgence of fundamentalism, both Christian and Moslem, in the 1980s and most particularly in the 1990s is, in my opinion, the last gasp of the Sixth Ray. It is reminiscent of the ferocious battle that a dying beast will give. Those philosophies have shriveled to irrelevance in spite of throngs of people still attending the churches, mosques, synagogues, and temples and still claiming to adhere to those Sixth Ray dispensations. One can easily feel the emptiness and the insecurity found in the "believers." Their increased fanaticism is proof positive of their underlying insecurity.

The late and great renewal experienced by old time religions has not come from within the religions themselves. It comes from New Age ideas that they have borrowed and modified to suit themselves.

The Christian-based New Age teachings are New Age teachings. Many hypocritical teachers have tried to bastardize the teachings of the New Age in order to ingratiate themselves with the established churches. They will fail since they will hit the wall of embittered narrow-mindedness displayed by the Sixth Ray dispensation in the conventional churches. This is already happening. The conventional churches are denouncing the attempts of some New Agers to infiltrate their ranks; they call them false prophets—and they are right. The bastardization of New Age teaching is the hypocritical denial of the new dispensations. Instead of specifically defining the differences between the new and the old, they are muddying the water for personal gain and personal power.

Mark 2:22:

> *And no man putteth new wine into old bottles: else the new wine doth burst the bottles, and the wine is spilled, and the bottles will be marred: but new wine must be put into new bottles.*

## How to Deal With The Ray VI

First and foremost, do not touch them. Respect their sense of space and their sense of time by giving them the time and the space they need. Become aware of the comfort distance that exists between you and them. If you really tune in, you will know what that is; you will know when you have come too close to them—physically or emotionally or intellectually. Allow great periods of silence to exist. You may, for instance, find yourself saying something to them and having to wait a minute or two for them to respond. This minute or two may be endless for you, particularly if you are a Will Type, or an Emotions Type, or even a Stiff Type. For them, it is nothing. They may need more than that in order to come to their decision.

Given time and space they will be tamed to trust you and at that point will do whatever you want them to do. They will become the best employees, the best followers, the best at whatever task you give them because they are not only highly intelligent but also devoid of defensiveness.

They will not make good leaders. It is not a good idea to put them in positions of responsibility where initiative is needed. In many ways, they are the opposite of the Will Type, but only in a sense; on the other hand they are very close to the Will Type in their one-pointed fanaticism, in their insistence on the truth, their fearless abandonment of themselves into a cause, as examples.

If you need to confront them you must do it with a great deal of care, making sure your energy does not invade theirs, You can say whatever you want as long as you say it in a laid back fashion, leaning back in a chair, making sure that your energy is receding and that the upper part of your body is way back. Once the confrontation is given, allow them the necessary time and space to make their decision or to respond at their leisure.

It is extremely important, also, to tolerate the fact that they will say or do things that seem to come out of the middle of nowhere. For instance, you may be talking about a certain subject and they will respond to you by talking about something entirely different. It is important to give them room to do this and then gently come back to the original subject. It would also be helpful if you could find a link between what you were talking about and their response. This will ground them and make them feel very secure. It may also propel them into a sense of gratitude and joy, since they so very much love intuitive connections.

If this type is your employee, he will need precise parameters so as to limit his disconnection. Given a task to do, he will perform it with amazing degrees of excellence and efficiency, if it is very well defined. This is reminiscent of the Second Ray who also likes this type of straightforward directive.

### *Illusory Self-Images of The Ray VI Type*

This person will consider himself loyal to "T." He will want to make all the people he likes into angels and all the ones he dislikes into devils. He will see himself as an angel one minute and the next as a devil, depending upon whether he approves or disapproves of what he does or even more so of what he thinks or feels. This is different from the Emotions Type, Ray IV, in that it there is no holding. Everything is given free access, free passage in and out of the person's system.

There will he an idealization, a fanaticism of the narrow vision. I had a discussion with a Ray VI minister of a church and I asked him "Can't you have a little bit of an open mind about this?" His response was "No, I don't have an open mind; I am a bigot." And he took great pride in it.

Exclusive love, as in "you and me against the world," is

very much a way of life for people in this category. This is, of course, the fundamental cause of fanaticism. "My country, right or wrong," is another out picturing of the idealism of this type, who will defend to the death something in which Ray VI believes, whether it is right or it is wrong. There will also be an idealization of what does not make sense. The less it makes sense the more it is going to he attractive to the Intuitive who is continuously looking for the inner self, for what is inexplicable through cause and effect.

The theologian Tertullian is a very good example of this. He said, "I believe it because it does not make sense." The grain of truth here, of course, is that sometimes you intuitively know without having time to figure out, what do to, what not to do, what to feel, what to think. However, it does not mean that what you have intuited makes no sense; it merely means that you are not at the present time in touch with the causal connection that brought you to think that way.

The distortion of this type will totally negate the existence of a causal connection, and will see the pursuit of the causal connection as heretical, to be avoided, evil. If we are to consider Eric Berne's typology, this type would be described as "I'm not OK, you're not OK." Indeed, they will spend a great deal of time and energy demonstrating to themselves and to others that nothing is worth pursuing, that life has absolutely no meaning whatsoever, that there is no causal connection. They glamourize nihilism and they take great pleasure in destroying causality and enjoying its destruction. Here, we see Hume's wrecking ball.

The wrecking ball is the name given in philosophy to Hume's destruction of any causal connection, or of the scientific method. For example, Hume would say that just because the sun has risen every morning for the past X billions of years does not mean that it is going to happen tomorrow. This empiricism has been abused by a lot of Ray VI Types who have used it to break laws and inflict a great deal of damage. Here we have an interesting connection with the destructive aspect of the First Ray, The Destroyer. However, unlike the will-directed and systematic destruction coming from the First Ray, this is a scattered and explosive one that does not seem to have any rhyme, reason, or focus.

It is also interesting to note that empiricism has become a materialistic philosophy, though in reality it is a Sixth Ray negation of anything on the material level. The materialistic implications of Hume's wreaking ball—empiricism—have created the entire focus on the physical to be found in late 19$^{th}$ Century industrialism. It is the ruthlessness of the robber barons, it is also the attitude of idealistic communism in the early part of the 20$^{th}$ Century. This materialistic extreme in the Sixth Ray is paradoxically arrived at by the disconnection from material reality. The more you try to disconnect from an aspect or attribute, the more likely you are to find yourself in the midst of its worst possible manifestation, exactly what you tried to avoid in the first place by disconnecting. Resist not evil means do not disconnect or run away from anything, do not deny.

*Section III*

*Crucifixion of the Ego*

## Chapter 13
# Freezes Hinder Happiness
# and the Experience of God

Plato originates the idea that before birth we knew the Absolute. The **shock of birth**[23] created amnesia in us. Now we have a vague longing and recollection of this knowledge. These are our innate ideas and they explain reincarnation.

These innate ideas are frozen in our soul. We come in with them, reproducing them in our present life.

These have been called images by Patanjali, Carl Jung, Alice A. Bailey, Augustine, Abelard, Aristotle, Epicurus, Hobbes, La Mettrie, William James, Sabatier, and Edgar Cayce, to name a few.

In Plato, the concept is abundantly explored in his *Allegory of the Cave*. In addition, here is a quote from his *Symposium*:

> *Remember how in that communion only beholding beauty with the eye of the mind, you will be able to bring forth **not images of beauty, but realities,** for he has hold not of an image, but of a reality and bringing forth and nourishing true virtue to become the friend of God and be immortal if mortal may.*

Therefore, anyone who arrogates the concept of images as if it were his own or their own private property is an ignorant fool.

I prefer the word **freezes**, rather than images. We form these freezes in a Pavlovian way. We condition ourselves to erroneously associate love with rejection, for example, in the same way as a dog associates the sound of a bell with food, causing him to instantly salivate. For the past 30 years, I have represented these wrong associations as follows:

> Love = Rejection

This is a freeze, a wrong association. These wrong associations slip below the level of consciousness and rule one's life in accordance to the beliefs engendered. The sum total of a person's freezes is his lower self. See *The Lower Self* in the chapter entitled *The Many Selves.*

So, before entering the body, the soul experiences a state of total at-onement with God. In that state, total fulfillment is enjoyed. There is no distance between cause and effect. There is no sensible world to separate cause from effect. The entity experiences perfection (Ray III), omnipotence (Ray I), and Eternal Life (Ray II).

Birth, therefore, comes as a shock, a propulsion of the soul into the sensible world. It is the most painful experience in the life of an individual. It is much more painful than death. All of a sudden, the entity experiences itself in its state of total powerlessness. In that state, expression is also impossible. Only through shrills of crying can the newly born entity draw attention. In fact, the first shrills are not even thought of in that particular context. They are uttered merely as a result of the incredibly painful situation of disconnection. It experiences itself as a bundle of abject needs with no hope for any fulfillment whatsoever.

Enter the parents, who partially assuage the pain, and the child concludes:

- No one will ever be able to fulfill my wishes the way God did before my birth.
- The world is not perfect.
- My mother and father are not perfect.
- They are not always there for me.
- I have to settle for a compromise.

None of these conclusions are wrong. Indeed, the world that the entity finds itself in is imperfect. Parents are not God. Never will total fulfillment be experienced in the confinement of the sensible world, the way it was experienced in the infinite reality that preceded birth. There is no problem up to now. The problem starts when **freezes,** wrong associations are formed. They freeze the energy flow because they are distortions.

There is a Spiritual Law which says that distortions interrupt and crystallize the flow of the Cosmic Life Force. For example:

- Crying brings me attention;  the more I cry, the more I get attention.
- Being helpless draws rescuers to me;  the more I am helpless, then the more will I likely be saved; here we see the birth of the most insidious of all guards, the one Karen Horney calls the **compliant solution,**[24] a palliative, not a resolution.
- Since I am not totally fulfilled, Mother isn't giving, therefore:

  | all women = withholding |
  | --- |

- Later, if I am disciplined by Father, I may arrive at the wrong association:

```
discipline = cruel
men = discipline
therefore:
men = cruel
```

This does not mean that we are perceiving the reality about our parents. Mother can be a very giving person. However, since I have experienced frustration, I choose to draw the conclusion that she is not giving. **I want to see Mother as ungiving; somehow it alleviates the pain of my frustration. The reality of our parents is now falsified.** Projecting onto them these freezes reduces them to a limited and unrealistic picture. Later, if we rid ourselves of those freezes, we discover other facets of our parents which always surprise us.

**Since initially they were for us the world, later, we will project onto the world the same freezes. The world will appear as cruel, or withholding, or ungiving, as if perceived through the petrified stained glass that we have put between us and our parents. Also, we will want to maintain this freeze of the world under the illusion that this will protect us from our pain of lack of fulfillment.**

The formation of a freeze is, therefore, in a distorted way the result of seeking pleasure through avoiding pain. I avoid the pain of my lack of fulfillment by deciding that it is their fault. Since I never want to reexperience this original excruciating pain, **I will condition myself to maintaining this freeze. I will make myself continue to believe . . .** [fill in the blank].

This is the stimulus-response, Pavlovian mechanism with which we condition ourselves. It is very primitive and very irrational. There are, of course, many other consequences of this particular freeze formation. There are also many other types of freeze formations. Each one of us has his own style of his own story. Here is another:

### Formation of Freezes

A child is just born and has two parents, Parent A and Parent B. Parent A is perceived as always there, caring, loving, giving, feeding. The child does not long for that parent's love or care—he has it, and therefore, he takes it for granted.

Parent B, however, is perceived as not always there, as less giving than Parent A, as detached. Therefore, Parent B becomes the object of curiosity, in other words, **desirable.** Since the child desires Parent B and since Parent B is detached:

```
detached = desirable
```

This is a freeze that this person will carry with him. "In order to be desirable, I have to be detached, or simply absent." I, therefore, grow up always wanting to leave, thinking that I am desirable this way, or I play hard to get, or I tease, etc. Detachment, non-loving, is absurdly seen as desirable, which, of course, will result in great pain and suffering later in this person's life.

Detached, or absent, is the opposite of loving. In no way is it magnetic. It may work for a while with some people who hook in, but its life is finite. Eventually, detached will meet equal detachment and will result in utter loneliness, frustration, and pain.

Meanwhile, since Parent A was loving and present, but not desirable, another set of equal and opposite wrong associations are formed. We call them **anti-freezes:**

| love<br>commitment<br>presence<br>service<br>selfless giving | equals | worthlessness<br>not being<br>desirable<br>being taken<br>for granted |
|---|---|---|

An anti-freeze is of course itself a freeze, being the reverse of the coin of another freeze. (By the way, Plato seems to have been afflicted by that freeze. He believed that the loving person is inferior to the loved one.)

This same person will find himself disappointed or put off or turned off by someone who loves him. Only when a person is detached, will he become desirable. The minute a desired, detached person turns around and loves them, they will lose interest and leave.

Perhaps we can take a moment to look at the patterns of our lives. Does the above remind you of anything? Have you in your life taken love for granted, destroying very valid relationships only to regret what you have done later once the person has finally decided that he has given you enough and it is time to withdraw?

### Properties of Freezes

1) **They are mechanisms,** conditioned responses, addictions.

2) Since they distort reality, **they block and/or distort the light.** They act as a stained-glass blocking or distorting the influx of Divine Light. There is no such thing as a "divine freeze." Where there is no freeze, there is no block, and therefore, the light flows through unimpeded, without needing explanation.

3) **They are unconscious.** The deeper they are, the more they are powerful and the greater their role in our lives.

4) **They are units of consciousness,** albeit distorted,

capable of drawing to them other units of consciousness. For example, if I have an freeze that says, *all women are weak*, and I also have a relatively healthy attitude wherein I see women as loving, the freeze, *women are weak* will distort the notion of *women are loving* and will become *loving is weak.* So, we have this progression: *women are weak; women are loving;* (therefore) *loving is weak.* Here, we see the "pacman" nature of freezes, devouring all that stands in its way, enslaving divine units in our consciousness in order to ensure its survival.

5) **They are units of energy.** If I have within myself a unit of consciousness that says loving is weak, I will **feel** weak when I love, and I will **act** accordingly, or I will feel contempt and act in a rejecting fashion.

6) **Freezes always breed duality.** If I form an freeze, *love equals weak*, I will also form an equal and opposite freeze, *not loving equals strong*; or *cruelty is strong*. Here, we see the nature of evil which is the continuous splitting of itself. Here, we also see how you become your own enemy. At times of your life, you will be loving and weak, despising those who are strong, seeing them as not loving. You will then, after a crisis, flip down into the other side of yourself and become strong and cruel. Now you will despise as weak those who are loving. These continuous vicious circles[25] will eventually bring more and more crises, leading to your realization that the freeze is not really protecting you from any pain, but is in reality bringing you a lot more pain. You will realize that it is better to finally allow yourself to experience the original pain of lack of fulfillment. **The very same pleasure principle that led you to protect yourself against pain through the formation of these freezes will now lead you to abandon them.** We, therefore, arrive at another property of freezes:

7) **Freezes are finite.** They are doomed to die since the very instinct that gave them birth—the seeking of pleasure or

survival, etc.—will kill them. Here we see how evil is finite while good is infinite. If I think, feel, and act in accordance to *strength is cruel*, I will develop guilt; I will debilitate myself; I will end up feeling good, but feeling weak. Then I will feel frustrated about weakness and goodness. I will rebel and be propelled back to strength and cruelty. Never will I build on firm ground. By contrast, if I see loving as strong and cruelty as weakness, nothing can stop me. I am not manufacturing guilt, and I have no reason for rebelling. Only good can come. I am embarked on an ever-growing, infinite, benign circle. Evil is finite; good is infinite.

8) **Freezes have a Survival Instinct**. Being units of consciousness, they will fight for their survival. We have seen in 4) how they will continuously seek expansion, living on divine energy, drawing light into darkness. When light shines upon them, they fight to the death, knowing that they cannot survive out in the open and that their reason for existence will be questioned, which will then lead to their final extinction. All of this is reminiscent of vampire movies, which are nothing else but the out picturing and personalization of what we are saying here. **The greater the defensiveness in you or in somebody else, the more it is obvious that an freeze has been discovered and is fighting for its survival.**

9) **Freezes will justify themselves by attracting circumstances that will confirm their distorted reality.** For instance, if I have wanted to believe that love is seen as weak, I will attract situations to prove it. I will even distort reality to believe it.

10) **Freezes repel all experiences, situations, and people that pose a threat to them or question their veracity.** I will be blind to situations that will prove to me that love is strong. I will reject anyone or anything that will remind me of this. I will negate people around me who are loving and strong. This, of course, will not endear me to anybody, which will reinforce

my belief that the world is harmful, that indeed loving is weak and cruelty is strong.

### Consequences of Freezes On the Spiritual Level

**A) The more we have freezes, the more we will create gods in accordance with them.** For instance, one of the consequences of the freeze of *love is weak; cruelty is strong* is the perpetual misconception of a weak Christ who was crucified. Christ's strength and absolute fearlessness is forgotten about, blocked. Therefore, contact with Him becomes impossible or warped. Only by freeing ourselves of these distortions, only by removing the stained-glass, can the clean white light finally penetrate. It will then become obvious that He was always there, and we had perpetually blocked Him through our wrong associations. **Freezes block the light, the presence of God.**

**B) The more we have freezes, the less we will not be able to experience the blessings of God's love.** For example, people pray for God's mercy. In the meantime, God's mercy is always there, merely blocked by our own evil, our own misconceptions. Remove the misconceptions and you will find mercy immediately. You will also find guiltless pleasure, the ecstasy of at-onement with God and His love. **Freezes block love and pleasure.**

**C) It is obvious that you will not be able to know your task, nor will you want to accomplish it if you have not dissolved your freezes.** Your potentials will remain dormant, hidden behind the pseudo-protection of the freezes. Freezes thwart action and accomplishment.

Obviously, C) is the Father, B) is the Son, and A) is the Mother (not the Holy Ghost).

Anyone who does not know his spiritual mission must realize that, at this point in their life, it consists in finding and thawing their freezes.

### Consequences of Freezes On the Emotional Level

**Freezes will attract wrong people.** Even if you attract the right ones, freezes will see to it that the right people respond to you in the wrong way. Freezes will also attract wrong thinking; wrong emotional responses will result in the areas of religion, politics, etc.

### Consequences of Freezes On the Material Level

**Freezes will distort your physical body.** Your body has been formed in accordance with your freezes. The body is a physical manifestation of all that is good or harmful in our soul. Life circumstances are also manifestations of the same. **Any disease, any life problem is a direct out picturing of a misconception, of wrong thinking.**

### Discovery of Freezes

We can, therefore, safely conclude that any area of your life which does not yield happiness above and beyond your wildest expectations is ruled by an freeze. Therefore:

1) **Observe your life from the spiritual, mental, emotional, physical, financial, sexual, etc. angles.** Determine the slightest unhappiness. Do not compromise. Then proceed to ask yourself, "What is it in me that prevents me from conceiving, in this area, happiness beyond my wildest dreams?" You may not see it yourself. However, eventually you will find some sort of wrong association or other (*poor is holy, pleasure is sinful, strength is bad,* etc.).

2) **Observe your body.** Any distortion therein is very simply the result of an freeze. What is this freeze? Where did it come from? Why do you tenaciously hold onto it? How can you give it up?

3) **Discover your blind spot**, which is impossible to do on your own thus making it essential for you to be involved in a community of people who will be willing to reflect—through

confrontation and support—the freezes that you have by now taken so very much for granted. Also, consider your enemies as your best teachers. They will reflect for you exactly what you do not want to see within yourself. Your *bête noires* are your best teachers. Here is the real meaning of Christ's sayings, "Resist not evil" and "Turn the other cheek."

### Requirements for Discovery of Freezes

1) **Faith.** Even if you do not believe it is a good Universe, give it the benefit of the doubt. Even if temporarily, act as if it were good. Think and feel as if it were good. See what happens. You can always go back to your favourite wrong associations of believing that the Universe is bad. Try to see that love is strength; strength is intelligence, and intelligence is love. Again here, we meet the Trinity.

2) **Courage.** Absolute fearlessness is required as you plunge into the labyrinths of your soul looking to slay the monster inside of you as Theseus did, aided by the intelligence of his string and the love of his sweetheart. Slaying the monster involves being open to facing both pains and pleasures which we have blocked in the past.

3) **Honesty.** Have the honesty to admit that you are wrong when it is the case. Have the intelligence and the humility to consider other possibilities than the ones in which you are stuck. Detect the places in you where your mind is closed. No, you do not have an open mind. The last time you had an open mind was the minute you were born. Since then, you have closed your mind with blinding freezes. Finally, have the courage to question your pet beliefs and to risk the disapproval of those with whom you still have unhealthy relationships.

Freedom from freezes will very simply lead you to at-onement with God.

# Chapter 14
# *Creation of Inner Duality;*
# *The Mother/Father Split*

If Parent A is always loving, taken for granted, and depreciated, then anything and everything associated with Parent A will be taken for granted and depreciated. Parent A may be a lover of art or of literature and be very neat and orderly. Art, literature and order will all end up being taken for granted and depreciated. By contrast, Parent B's love of mathematics or engineering and dislike for order and neatness will be idealized, desired, and imitated. A split is thus established as follows:

| *Parent A* | *Parent B* |
|---|---|
| [taken for granted/ depreciated] | [desired] |
| loving | detached |
| commitment | freedom |
| art | messiness |
| order | strength |
| weakness | desirable |
| lack of value | science |
| boredom | engineering |
| value | excitement |

A person with such a pattern will come to associate art with worthlessness and boredom, and with commitment and love. By contrast, science will be seen as the way to freedom and excitement. Art and freedom will be for this person incompatible. So will order and science. This may seem irrational and impossible to someone else whose freeze is different. However, we all have impossible and irrational aspects within ourselves, all very similar to this.

See if you can construct your own split. We call this the Mother/Father Split. See then what is reality for you.

Reality for God is something different; real reality is that all is good. For instance, no art is possible without freedom, no science is possible without order, no love is possible without strength. In the eye of God there is no split, no duality.

The following material was written by me between 1976 and 1980. It has been copyrighted on both dates. It has been given in lecture forms (including the lecture called "The Role of the Unconscious in Career Selection," which was given in 1976 and copyrighted the other material in 1980). It was prepared as a book—the ancestor of this one—with the cooperation of my former wife, Judy Clement Gani.[26] This book preparation was done in 1980. It was submitted to an agent called Jonathan Dolger, who recommended that I rewrite it with the help of a professional writer, which I refused to do.

It will help you identify this fundamental split and freeze, starting with its effects on your life and taking those to their source—your freezes.

### *Conflicts, Dilemmas and Dialectics Ruling Our Lives*
Have any of the following dilemmas ever been a problem for you:
- Either I am a man or I have emotions; it cannot be both.
- Either I am beautiful, desirable, and feminine, or gifted, ugly, and not feminine.

- Either I am a woman, or I am a mother.
- Either I have career and sexual satisfaction, or I have a child, love for my child, but no sexual satisfaction.
- Either I am poor and honest, or rich and dishonest.

Can you think of some more? If you do, write them down at this point, just off-hand. More will occur to you later.

These either/or situations are manifestations of two different currents battling within, creating a constant tug-of-war and an enormous loss of energy.

Most of our energy is spent in this particular way. Most people only operate with what little is left after this enormous battle. Success, effectiveness, happiness, capacity for pleasure are achieved to the extent that these currents have arrived at a peace and an integration. The more that I believe I can be a man and have emotions, the more I will be able to flow and not constantly create situations in which the marriage between the two is an impossibility. As you look at these various splits, see how many barriers you have created to the possibility of bringing the two sides together.

For each human being, these two sides have originated way back in their infancy and, perhaps, before. At one point, we decided that we prefer one over the other, thus repressing one and over-energizing the other, with all of the loss of energy that this entails. It is as if we have squeezed a balloon in the middle and forgotten about the bottom half of it.

Only using the top part has depleted it to the point of exhaustion. In the meantime, never did it occur to us that the bottom part not only exists, not only is not the enemy, but is, indeed, the only answer to our problems, since it contains all of the energy.

The split is created in the very beginning. Out of preference for a parent or an authority figure, we favour an occupation, an attitude, a desire, an expression over another.

In most cases, the split is determined by the personality of the parents, for example, a preference of competitive sports over reading may have its origin in the emulation of father, for a boy, and the rejection of mother.

The result of this in adult life may be an inability to assimilate essential facts, knowledge, etc.—reading, mother—in a competitive situation—father. This can extend to the simplest behavioral patterns, such as the mode of dress. If father was a good dresser, the man in question will dress well in a competitive situation. He will certainly grow up to believe that being well-dressed counts more than being well-informed or well-read.

The reality, of course, is that they are both necessary; being well-dressed—not ostentatiously, which is not in good taste—is important, and being well-read is also important. The degree of emphasis for either one depends on the individual's degree of neglect or over-emphasis in either area.

We cannot emphasize too much that in some cases, the duality is not reflected by mother and father, but in most cases it is. The following exercise will help give you some idea of how far your split goes.

### *Exercise*

Sit down with a friend who knows you well, but not too well, to avoid an emotional involvement and bias. Take a blank piece of paper, divide the page in two by drawing a vertical line down the middle and entitle one column "Mother" and the other column "Father." Relax and be completely open and ask your friend to say the following words to you; as you hear them, write them under "Mother" or "Father." More words may occur to your friend, particularly if you have spoken to them about your career problems, about your aptitudes and abilities. In going through this, be as honest with yourself as possible.

Another way of doing this is to sit down with a friend and have him write down your responses on the divided paper. All you will do, then, will be to respond by saying "Mother" or "Father" to each of these words. Example:

Friend: "Money"
You: "Father"
Friend: "Beauty"
You: "Mother"
Etc.

Again, most importantly, in doing this exercise your responses should come from your spontaneity. Do not try to influence them.

This exercise is similar to the free-association tests usually given in psychology, only you are required to answer specifically by saying "Mother" or "Father" instead of freely associating each with any other word that may occur to you.

**Warning:** Value the first result. If you do this exercise too many times, your unconscious self-defenses will influence your responses and will confuse you. When you do it the first time, please make sure to do it well and to follow the suggestions given to you above.

List of words to be said to you by your friend:

money
beauty
form
success
sex
hate
order
intuition
music

science
brown
accomplishment
red
anxiety
power
love
despicable
divine
desirable

| Mother | Father |
|--------|--------|
|        |        |

These are the results I've gotten from giving this exercise to four persons.

## Robert

| Mother | Father |
|--------|--------|
| money | form |
| feelings | thinking |
| beauty | success |
| intuition | sex |
| music | hate |
| red | order |
| anxiety | science |

| | |
|---|---|
| love | brown |
| divine | accomplishment |
| desirable | power |
| guilt | despicable |
| compassion | math |
| literature | business |
| irrational | God |
| emotional | politics |
| spontaneity | discipline |
| faith | active |
| trust | |
| pleasure | |
| receptive | |

Quite a bit can be explained from the results of this exercise. In the first place, the professional aspect of Robert is tied up with his father. He is successful, he accomplishes, he has power, he has a sense of business in his work. However, the adequacy of his earnings is not nearly commensurate with his immense background, knowledge, and capabilities. One can see, very simply, the reason for that: money is tied up with mother, and therefore, is antithetical to success, accomplishment, and power. On the other hand, despising his colleagues, hating, criticizing, upholding discipline is very much within the habit forms that he has developed in his profession. Notice that God is under "Father" God, the disciplinarian and the law-giver) whereas divine is on the side of "Mother"—beauty, divine intuition, divine faith—the spontaneity and permissive, loving mother who condones the breaking of the rules.

Robert's office is devoid of any pleasurable objects, any plants, paintings, or curtains. He has inherited it from his predecessor, and in the years during which he has been working in this firm, has brought nothing to it to beautify it (beauty equals mother, different from father/profession). He is often commissioned to build churches, but in most cases, gets into personality conflicts with the religious organizations who appoint him to the job. The houses he builds are simple and functional and would not cater to people with an elaborate sense of beauty. All of these difficulties, or course, neutralize his brilliance and impair progress and ability to make money.

His father was a plantation owner, a true patriarch, who had everyone around him treated as servants. The father died, a bitter man who could only express dissatisfaction. Robert grew up to admire him and emulate him. His mother, a compassionate, beautiful woman, came from a very rich background, never had to worry about money, but manifested a totally irrational abandonment to the arts. She would counter her husband's rational discipline with irrational behavior and rambling. Notice sex under "Father." Robert's father had affairs; his mother didn't. Notice pleasure under "Mother." Pleasure is not a masculine experience, as it were, but a feminine, receptive one.

Having literally become his father in his adult years, Robert married a woman who nearly had all of his mother's characteristics. On the healthy level, this marriage is an opportunity for him—and her—to learn the other side of the coin. On the harmful level, it is a quick, but ineffective pseudo-solution since it is an attempt to compensate for the over-development of his "Father" side. In other words, rather than develop his "Mother" side which obviously contains quite a few good aspects that he could use, he married a person who filled the gap. Later in this book, we will see how this is what usually happens when one falls in love. Herein lies the secret of lost interest and how to regain it. If Robert would only trust that love, understanding, colour, and compassion are precisely what are missing in his professional life, he would once again "fall in love" with his profession and infuse it with desire. Chances are that he may have to abandon his profession for a while in order to reintegrate "Mother." The perils of such an undertaking are great, and he knows it. However, as we will see, he has very little choice but to risk this jump into the abyss. In reality, there is no abyss, only, perhaps, temporary loss, if any.

## Susan

| Mother | | | Father |
|---|---|---|---|
| beauty | | | money |
| form | hate | | order |
| success | | | music |
| sex | | | science |
| intuition | | | despicable |
| brown | | | math |
| accomplishment | | | business |
| red | | | guilt |
| anxiety | | | compassion |
| power | | | politics |
| love | God | | discipline |
| divine | | | faith |
| literature | | | thinking |
| irrational | | | weak |
| emotional | | | authority |
| spontaneity | | | |
| dedication | | | |
| will | | | |
| trust | | | |
| feelings | | | |
| pleasure | | | |
| receptive | active | | |
| joy | | | |

      Her father was a Wall Street broker whose power she never saw, since he kept it in the office. What she saw was a person impeccably dressed in unassuming clothes, who didn't talk much, who was highly intelligent, and who, by some magic, managed to bring in all that money. She, as a young child, loved and idealized him. His love of the outdoors was a common ground for the two of them and for Susan's younger brother. Her father was tall and handsome, very attractive to women, very athletic. Another mode of communication with her father was Susan's homework, through which Susan obtained quite a bit of indirect contact with him.

Her mother, a woman of statuesque beauty, would always fill the room with her presence and her extroversion. She was flamboyant in her clothes, always smelled very good, and never stopped talking. She didn't like the outdoors. She preferred the great indoors provided by social life. She would incessantly talk about her talent, painting, and her passion, reading those endless and thick novels scattered all around their house.

As a fashion designer, Susan has obviously recreated to the hilt her mother's personality. Notice the absence of harmful adjectives on "Mother's" side. Although we have emotional and feelings under "Mother," it could obviously follow that hate could also fall under the same category. However, Susan got all confused when hate was mentioned. She could not put it under "Mother," who she idealized, nor could she put it under "Father," who was incapable of emotions, good or harmful. God, a good aspect for her, could not be placed under "Mother" because of the cultural associations of God with the masculine. However, it could not go under "Father" who was weak. Strong mother is receptive, but could not be active, nor could father.

Now, success comes through form, beauty, intuition, and love. So does accomplishment. However, they are incompatible with order, money, and discipline. The good aspect of this is Susan's facility with colour and beauty, her developed feminine touch, a "common touch" which enables her to intuit what women would want to wear this season. For Susan, money is of no importance. Nor is her father. She squanders her money and is unable to find a man for whom she could feel respect. As we said previously, her *bête noire* is the accountant, to whom she is accountable for her budget. The dresses she designs are beautiful, but extravagant. They tend to flow rather than fit. They tend to impress rather than be useful. Susan's office is very bright and overwhelmingly well-supplied with an extraordinary amount of objects to look at or touch. These objects, for the most past, have nothing to do with the business at hand, except to impress or dazzle her customers, buyers, and friends. She spends a great deal of time talking to her peers and her subordinates. She is unable to implement discipline or accuracy with her subordinates, but, on the other hand, is very well-liked by them. Love and charm is ever-present in her environment—disorder, chaos, and unreality, also. She tries to charm her superiors, but, in reality, she dislikes them. She has a pattern of disliking anyone who has been or is her superior. Hierarchy should not exist, for her.

The restoration of the attributes of her father would bring to her professional life an extraordinary sense of peace. She needs to make peace with <u>order</u>, <u>discipline</u>, punctuality, and <u>authority</u>. Her therapist is not helping her, as he is promoting her to the never-ending exploration of feelings and the experiential. Thus, he is leading her—with her devoted consent, of course—to regression and not to progress.

### Ruth

| Mother | Father |
|--------|--------|
| hate | money |
| intuition | beauty |
| music | form |
| red | success |
| anxiety | sex |
| power | order |
| despicable | science |
| divine | brown |
| guilt | accomplishment |
| God | love |
| literature | desirable |
| politics | math |
| irrational | business |
| emotional | compassion |
| spontaneity | discipline |
| faith | trust |
| intellectual | pleasure |
| will | receptive |
| authority | feelings |
| protectiveness | dedication |
| art | joy |
| journalism | weak |
| disorder | photography |
| scattered | ineffective |
| chaos | |

*(center column between Mother and Father: "active thinking")*

Ruth's mother dominated her family by never being able to take care of herself. Constantly sick and bedridden, she nevertheless managed to attract everyone's attention and to dictate her will. She manifested power and will through weakness. Part of her power was also acute perceptiveness. She could figure people our directly. She would then proceed to put them at a disadvantage by shooting out exactly what her perception was. These flashes of perception and utterances would occur quite unexpectedly. Although brilliant and very well-read in literature and politics, although musically talented—she played the piano beautifully—all of this served the purpose of drawing to her people's attention. Her talents were put to the service of self-pity. Her powers of tuning in and knowing, no one quite knew how, characterized the intuitive in her which Ruth later inherited.

Ruth's father, an imposing but soft-spoken man, was also a father to his wife. However, unlike her, he was a dedicated workaholic who enjoyed his business. He could be trusted and he helped anyone in "need." He was Ruth's best friend before puberty. Together, they knew how to deal with mother. Father had a sense of beauty. As an importer, he knew how to select items of quality and how to sell them. Some of these objects, toys, microscopes, binoculars, Christmas decorations found their way into Ruth's home. As a child, she would carefully listen to her father as he explained each item to her. She would ask specific questions as to what they were made of, how much they cost, etc.

Unlike the two previous cases, this one, as well as the next, will seem to be complicated. The difference between the former two and the latter two is as follows: the former two operate under cause and effect. However faulty Robert's reasoning is, he still reasons, "In order to build a house, I must study the terrain," forgetting, of course, the study of the personalities. No matter how irrational Susan seems to be, "The dresses must be short this year, because they were long last year"; there is a linear mode of behavior and reasoning. With Ruth, there isn't. When she takes a picture of a particular situation, she neither knows, nor is she able to explain why her picture is good. It's just that things fell into place. Photography, which is a "Father" aspect, nevertheless, is approached from the "Mother" point of view for her through intuition, anxiety, disorder, and the spontaneity. The good aspect is that she makes room for an extraordinary amount of inspiration. The harmful aspect is that she has incorporated her mother's belief that <u>power</u> can be obtained through <u>chaos</u>, whereas <u>success</u> and <u>discipline</u> are <u>weak</u> and <u>ineffective.</u>

She is what is called an intuitive personality. In that sense, photography gets her to travel towards the sensate, thus healing her split. She took up photography, first, as a hobby, and—typically—things fell into place and it became her profession.

## *Jim*

| Mother | | Father |
|--------|--------|--------|
| success | money | beauty |
| hate | | form |
| intuition | | sex |
| spiritual | music | fear |
| brown | red | indecision |
| accomplishment | | order |
| power | | science |
| love | | anxiety |
| despicable | | joy |
| divine | | light |
| heavy | | guilt |
| desirable | | God |
| literature | | business |
| politics | math | compassion |
| irrational | | trust |
| emotional | | faith |
| discipline | | receptive |
| spontaneity | pleasure | thinking |
| intellectual | | art |
| will | | weak |
| feelings | | photography |
| active | | ineffective |
| authority | dedication | |
| protectiveness | disorder | |

Jim's mother was physically powerful, in addition to which she was an endless source of creativity and inspiration. She wrote a column for a newspaper dealing with feminist issues. She was deeply religious and believed that she had an inspirational channel coming from divine entities. She physically dominated, and she spiritually dominated. Father, a scientist, had very little effect on her or on the family. However, he had his space. He could retire to his den, read his books, look at his paintings, clean his pipes, and touch his miniature cars. He was never successful, however, frequently being fired from his jobs and being unemployed for great lengths of time. During these times, mother provided.

Jim's overwhelmingly powerful mother compelled him, as an adult, to create a personality akin to his father. Had it been the other way around, he would never have felt any sense of individuality or freedom. He would never have been born out of his mother's womb. Thus, in reproducing his father's personality in his career, he remained <u>weak</u> and <u>ineffective</u>. However, the experience of <u>beauty</u>, <u>pleasure</u>, and <u>sex</u> came with it. The sacrifice: <u>success</u> and <u>power</u>, both "Mother" attributes. As a man, he is closer to the figure of a son than to that of a father. Marriage or a permanent relationship are inconceivable to him. The scatteredness and confusion come, in spite of his great efforts to manifest order. Anxiety, for him, is a way of life except in the presence of women with whom he has been very successful on the sexual level. Having manifested his introverted father, he is able to attract and "conquer" woman—usually possessive ones—by manifesting indecision, hesitation, and weakness. Since his mother has all the power, and since she gives all, he sees the companies, organizations, and institutions who commission him as mother figures. By expressing indecision and weakness, he expects a giving and loving response. Much to his disappointment, the response he is getting usually ends up being frustration and rejection. When he is accepted for a job, he has difficulty finishing it and expects considerable amounts of effort and assistance to complete his task. There are always, in the middle of jobs, unexpected difficulties with which or for which he does not use his resourcefulness—<u>intuition</u>, mother. It is as if intuition does not exist. New solutions are terribly difficult. He is over-reliant on what he sees, touches, incessantly measures.

Contrary to Ruth, in his photography he needs to use

intuition and to let go of the sensible world, the sensate. He, typically, is a sensate personality.

+++

I purposely chose two photographers, approaching the same profession from two diametrically opposite points of view. This illustrates that no profession can only rely on a particular set of functions, aspects, or attributes while discarding all others. All functions must harmoniously be present in any profession. The degree to which this harmony does not exist invites failure, unconsciously created harmful situations, boredom, frustration, in short, anything undesirable.

+++

More on what to expect when going through this exercise:

As I said previously, the two columns could be entitled for you Mother/Father on one side, and Profession, Religion, the World, Communism, Fascism, etc on the other side. If this is the case, then just respect it and go through the exercise the parents on one side and whatever best fits you on the other. I have found, for example, that people who have gone through traumatic experiences before puberty tend to have both parents on one side. In Europe, I have taught men and women who have lived through World War II. The majority of them had both parents on one side of the split and Nazi or Fascist or Communist or Bolshevik or Violence on the other side.

Traumatic experiences could also include the extended absence of a parent, extended living in a boarding school, violence on the part of one or both parents, extreme poverty or extreme richness, etc. In no way is this a value judgement, however. No one can say what is normal and what isn't, what is good or what is bad, nor who will be successful or who will fail. We can only look at ourselves and at others with all-inclusive love and understanding to facilitate openness.

+++

This brings me to an essential element. The individual going through this exercise must be willing to cooperate in self-criticism. You must be willing to look with a critical eye at the wrong associations that you have grown up to believe. If you do this exercise with a friend or a teacher, a climate of trust should exist to make room for the confident openness required here.

+++

This is a painful exercise. The mere response of "Father" or "Mother" brings you to the painful awareness of the places where your personality is torn apart and where, therefore, you are at war with yourself. Your war with what you dislike in the world is brought to the war with your mother or father, and therefore, with an aspect of you.

+++

The reality is that all good aspects exist together and are inseparable. Only in our illusion do we separate them. Love and discipline, thinking and feeling, will power and experience, energy and consciousness are inseparable. The goal is to see how they are separated in you, how you perpetuate the separation, and how to bring them together. More on this will be given later in the crucifixion of the ego in the next chapter.

### Application
Let's now see how this specifically applies to your life and your career.

List what you are dissatisfied with in your career and in your life.

From the "Mother" and "Father" lists, determine the side that you favour most. Is it the side of your profession?

Determine precisely where some of those freezes, wrong

associations, destructive equations (work equals no colour, no feelings; or, pleasure equals spending money, etc.) are manifested in your life. We have seen how, for Robert, <u>beauty</u> and <u>love</u> are associated with <u>weakness</u> and dissociated from profession. Specifically, from your own individual list, how is that occurring?

This will take a lot of work. Spend time with it. Improvements will begin to happen. You may feel overwhelmed by the degree to which these things exist. The effort may seem insurmountable. Observe this feeling of despair without identifying with it. Remember, you have functioned with all of this up to now. Awareness will not make it worse. It can, obviously, only make it better.

Mobilize your dream life by sending a thought in before you go to sleep at night requesting a dream that will clarify these problems for you.

If you believe in prayer, pray to find ways to mend this split.

Talking about it with friends will help. Listen to what they have to say.

By now, the more you have cleansed all of this, the more you will find changes in your perception of people and situations around you. Conversely, the progress made unconsciously will be reflected by a change of the way people see you or react to you. It is important to relate these changes as precisely as possible to what you have done through this cleansing. What have you done, specifically, to change this or that? What misconception has begun to dissolve? How can you continue to dissolve it?

On the other hand, if there is no change in some areas, try to relate this to what you may have neglected. A recurring insight which you may have dismissed as unimportant, a persistent criticism which you have decided to ignore may point to more misconceptions which you have omitted from your list. Add it to your list.

Continue to add to this list whenever you can. Every day new things will occur to you to which you will respond, inwardly, "Mother" or "Father." Add them to your list.

## Chapter 15

# *The Crucifixion of the Ego;*
# *Healing the Split*

---

In the Gospel of Thomas (Saying 27, or other depending on the translations used) it says that Jesus, seeing some children being breast fed, told his disciples that those entering the Kingdom of God would be like these breast feeding infants. When asked whether they should become little to enter the Kingdom, Jesus said to the disciples that in order to enter the Kingdom, they must:

- Make the two into one.
- Make the inside be like the outside.
- Make the upper be like the lower.
- The male at-one with the female so that there would be no distinction between the two.
- Make the two eyes become one eye.
- Make one hand out of the two hands and one foot out of both feet.

The little ones who are breast fed are like those who enter the Kingdom. It takes childlike simplicity to enter. You cannot penetrate the Kingdom with your baggage—whether this baggage be material, emotional, or mental. You must let go of all of the misconceptions that you hold onto and advance naked into the Kingdom, naked as the little ones are, innocent.

After which the disciples ask whether they would enter the Kingdom by becoming little.

Here, the Christ shows us how to unify:

1) **Make the two into one,** meaning transcend duality, work on the contradictory parts of yourself as we do on the Path of Purification.[38] We identify those as the Mother/Father Split.

2) **Make the inside be like the outside,** meaning establish causal connections between what is inside of you and what is outside of you. What is inside of you creates what is outside of you; as long as you believe that there is a difference between the two you are deluding yourself, you are living a lie. Untruths themselves are a manifestation of the disconnection between the outside and the inside. The author of a lie believes that what he says on the outside can be different from what he thinks and feels on the inside. All of these disconnections have to be unified, brought together.

3) **Make the upper be like the lower.** Here the Christ is talking about the higher duality, i.e., good versus evil. When the lower duality is worked out—the inside and the outside, then the upper and the lower can become unified. This is the crucifixion of the ego as we understand it.

4) **Make the male at-one with the female, so that there would be no distinction between the two,** i.e., explore the other side of yourself. If you are a man, you must explore the female existing inside yourself; if you are a woman, you must explore the male inside of yourself. By doing so you bring the two sides together. This is the meaning of sexuality, the meaning of relationship and union with another being—union of male and female within one's self. Only when a person is engaged in intimate union with another being on the outer level, **and** intimate union on the inner level with the other side of his/her own being is s/he on the way to becoming at-one

with the Cosmic Life Force, and therefore, able to enter the Kingdom. Here is also proof positive of the Christ's teaching of the sanctity of sexuality and equality of the sexes. Let there be no other interpretation of this in spite of another saying (apparently the last one) in which the Christ seems to condone Simon Peter's saying that women are not worthy of life. It is not true; the Christ always respected women as being equal to men and urged them to enter the Kingdom on the same level as males.

5) **Make the two eyes become one eye, and two hands become one hand, and two feet become one foot.** The existence of two eyes, two hands, and two feet is an out picturing of our duality. The unification of all of these brings unity of sight, one universal vision, one action, one creativity, and one concept of God and of the Kingdom. When this is achieved, when total unity is accomplished, then you can enter the Kingdom of God.

When the two eyes become the same they will merge into one; each eye needs to meet the other by seeing in the other its own likeness, as in two lovers recognizing themselves in the other when they come together. When unified in its purpose, each hand will go with the other towards a single end.

✟✟✟

Here are some more quotes from past sermons which will help you:

"Taking up his cross refers to the crucifixion of the ego. After we have found our Mother/Father Split, the next step is to bring together the good aspects of both sides of our duality and contrast them with our harmful aspects. Then we are to take our harmful aspects and find the good components within them."

"The lower duality means the Mother/Father Split. The Tibetan also talks about a lower and a higher duality. His explanation corresponds to mine. The higher duality appears when the lower duality is on its way to resolution. The higher duality consists of the good vs. the harmful, the good vs. the evil within ourselves. The combination of the lower and the higher duality constitute the crucifixion of the ego and the reaching of the Fourth Initiation."

✦✦✦

"3. <u>The Law of Conflict</u>, the first duality, the lower one. No harmony can be found unless conflict is risked. This reminds us of what we found in the First Ray whereby nothing new could be built unless the old was destroyed. Here then is the connection between the First and the Fourth Rays. The Law of Conflict of the Fourth Ray reminds us of the Law of Destruction and the Law of Repulse of the First Ray. They are connected.

It says in the Mantram of Fire, *Naught in me seeks the way of peace, naught in me yearns for earth.* The seeking of conflict is indeed a commendable search. We must seek the places that are at war. We must seek war in order to experience peace, even if it is merely to consider the conflict between what needs to grow and what resists growth. **The way to find peace is to become at-one with ourselves and decide that we are going to wage war.** This conflict within ourselves is also a conflict outside of ourselves. Thus, we find harmony inside while conflict is undertaken on the outer level. The refusal to fight the battle on the outside internalizes the problem and creates a war inside. Thus is Spiritual Law.

4. <u>The Law of Good versus Evil</u>, the second duality, the higher one. Once the first duality has been conquered, the duality between mother and father in which evil and good have not been quite defined (remember that there are good and harmful aspects associated with both father and mother), one has to undertake this second conflict, the conflict between good and evil. On both the father side and

on the mother side, the good elements are differentiated from the harmful ones. The good aspects are then unified and the harmful aspects are purified. This is called the crucifixion of the ego. One must differentiate between the two dualities as follows: the first duality, the one between mother and father, the duality of the aspirant, he defines with a vertical line dividing a circle."

### *Method of Unification Through the Crucifixion of the Ego*

1) **The Mother/Father Split:** Figure 1 is a picture of a lower duality. The Mother/Father Split, as it first appears, depicts the lower duality. It does not as yet differentiate between right and wrong, good or bad, harmful or harmless.

This exercise must be done first without judgement as to right or wrong. Any such judgement will impair the honesty of the subject who is undergoing the exercise.

The lower split is characterized by the vertical line. The Tibetan shows it like this:

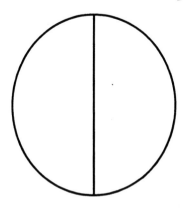

Figure 1:

| Mother | Father |
|---|---|
| success | beauty |
| money | form |
| hate | sex |
| intuition | fear |
| spiritual | indecision |
| music | order |
| brown | science |
| red | anxiety |
| accomplishment | joy |
| power | light |
| love | guilt |
| despicable | God |
| divine | business |
| heavy | compassion |
| desirable | trust |
| literature | faith |
| politics | receptive |
| math | thinking |
| irrational | art |
| emotional | weak |
| discipline | photography |
| spontaneity | ineffective |
| pleasure | |
| intellectual | |
| will | |
| feelings | |
| active | |
| authority | |
| dedication | |
| protectiveness | |
| disorder | |

2) **Differentiating "good from bad" in the Mother/Father Split:** This is clearly done in Figure 2. At this point, having differentiated good from bad, we have identified the higher split characterized by the horizontal line. The Tibetan shows it like this:

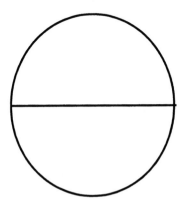

Figure 2:

| Mother | Father |
|---|---|
| *Good:* | *Good:* |
| success | beauty |
| money | form |
| intuition | sex |
| spiritual | order |
| music | science |
| brown | joy |
| red | light |
| accomplishment | God |
| power | business |
| love | compassion |
| divine | trust |
| desirable | faith |
| literature | receptive |
| politics | thinking |
| math | art |
| emotional | photography |
| discipline |  |
| spontaneity |  |
| pleasure |  |
| intellectual |  |
| will |  |
| feelings |  |
| active |  |
| authority |  |
| dedication |  |
| *Bad:* | *Bad:* |
| hate | fear |
| despicable | indecision |
| heavy | anxiety |
| irrational | guilt |
| protectiveness | weak |
| disorder | ineffective |

3) We now have the **Crucifixion of the Ego:**

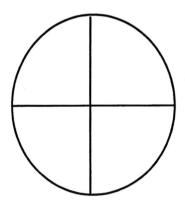

4) Having "nailed it," we can now heal it:

A) First unify each element in Mother with each element in Father, visualizing—conceiving—that it is possible for success and beauty to be one, for faith and thinking to be one, for money and sex, etc. The following chapters on conceiving will help.

B) Second, consider each harmful aspect. Find the good nucleus in it. For instance, hate could be the distortion of righteous anger; indecision the distortion of constructive dialectics, i.e., considering both sides of a question; guilt could be the beginning redemption, etc.

C) Once this is done, do for the transformed badness what you have done for goodness, i.e., bring them together. For instance, healthy anger can help redeem guilt.

D) Every transformed aspect under the horizontal line should be fused with the good aspects about it. For instance, healthy anger, once expressed, transforms into joy and order.

### *Some Observations*

1) This is easier said than done. Painstaking time is needed, as well as the help of a teacher who has gone through it. However, once

done and once your life is penetrated by the renewed soul, it will change for the better. All problems will find their solution in these exercises. All pain will be transformed into pleasure.

2) You will notice how the harmful aspects below the horizontal line are greatly outnumbered by the good aspects above it. This is **not** due to the person being more good than bad. This type of measurement is oxymoronic. Actually, it is due to the fact that most people have not wanted to look at their dark side. Gradually, through these exercises, the aspects below the horizontal line will increase.

3) It is preferable to wait until the dark side is revealed—until more harmful aspects come out—before going to the higher split which differentiates between good and bad. Jumping into the second split too soon will be done from an insincere, idealized self place, not from a Real Self place.

4) Do it right. If you mess with it with your dishonesty and pretense, you will immunize yourself from the benefits of this spiritual exercise.

5) The Crucifixion of the Ego is a first principle. We find it in Plato in the form of a quadrant which we have studied in our sermons this year.

*Section IV*

# The Art of Surrender; Yielding

## Chapter 16
# *Yielding*

---

The formation of human types occurs because we violate nature. If we were at one with nature, we would not form human types that are adversarial to other human types. We would not pit one Ray or a combination of Rays against another or a combination of others. It would not be one aspect in contradistinction to another. Instead, it would be all Ray aspects aiding each other in harmony. It would be balance and equilibrium.

The problem is that we convince ourselves that we have to make choices for the sake of self-protection. Statements such as:

- I will never allow myself to experience this pain.
- I will never allow myself to be rejected.
- I will always appear to be perfect.
- I will always allow my gut feelings to rule me.
- I will always rely on my mind to make decisions.
- I will never repress any sexual feeling.
- I will never allow myself to have any sexual feelings.

These statements are destructive to our nature. Nature never makes contradictory statements like this. Nature suggests, nature invites. It is the insecurity of the ego function that tries to get guarantees of protection and safety which occasion these distortions.

If, as we have seen at the beginning of this book, a child forms a human type for the sake of approval and because he is unable to obtain love, then he must get to the point where he experiences his success in this particular character as a denial of love, as the enemy of love. Therefore, he will consciously or unconsciously want to destroy the type, as well as all of its achievements. If he does not do this, he will never reach a state of balance.

What is your main case against life? How did life mistreat you? See if you can answer these questions as clearly as possible, dwelling on the pain that you have experienced as a result of this prime case against the world. Try to detect how you have constructed your entire life as a guard against this particular pain. Consequently, the formation of the type structure is a guard against the experience of a particular pain which has been deemed to be excruciating, larger than life.

Now ask yourself to what extent is this pain still there? How much do you right now still experience this original pain? How much does the adult in you feel this original pain, to what extent does the child in you experience this original pain?

What you will usually find is that the pain is much less important than you made it, or, amazingly, it is not even there any more. This is a very difficult thing to admit, because that means that now you are reacting to a pain that is greatly diminished or does not even exist. Once you have realized this, you have also learned that you have been reacting for years, even decades, to a phantom. Therefore, in order to save face, you have had to invent pains, create pains, look for pains to justify the lifestyle, the human type that you have built in reaction to the original pain.

Realizing the absurdity of this constitutes a great act of yielding. It is a death; it is the death of what we call the pseudo-life. Basically, the human type is the pseudo-life; it creates great illusions, illusions that are the enemies of illusory fears lurking in the background.

If you resist becoming conscious of the absurdities to which you have devoted most of your life, you will create a crisis. If you yield to your newly found desire to abandon the old ways of life, you will avoid crisis, even though you will have to go through a time of emptiness during which temporary loss must be experienced. This emptiness is necessary. It is necessary to delay the gratification of an addict in order to heal him. Your human type is an addict. As it lets go of its poison, you pass through an excruciatingly painful illusion of emptiness.

The emptiness itself will finally allow new material to emerge to the surface of consciousness. A new identity will come out of this. There is no way to know for sure what that identity is going to be. One can speculate what it might be by studying the inferior functions or by using the Mother/Father Split. However, no theory can describe what will happen when that finally occurs. There is no way anyone can anticipate what one's task is going to be until one is within it. It would have been impossible for Mohammad, while he was going through his drunken crisis, to know that he would be the new Prophet. It is impossible for the larva, as it undergoes the temporary death of confinement in a cocoon, to know that it is going to emerge as a butterfly.

All of this points to one thing: yield. This is very well described in the Tibetan's description of the Initiation of the Renunciation. Only through renunciation can balance be found, can the balance of nature be restored. However, it involves the risk of destroying what we believe to be our most precious possession, our most precious faculty.

### The Fallacy of Goal Setting
It is no use trying to force yourself to liberate what is underneath you. All you will succeed in doing is to create a

cover up, an idealized self which will delay the crisis and make it worse. This was demonstrated, if you will remember, in our example of Richard Nixon, who tried to become a "kinder, gentler" person in the sixties, but who had not actually yielded his tough and aggressive persona.

However, once you have allowed the deeper material to emerge into your consciousness, goal setting will make a great deal of sense, and will be easy to do. You will be able to visualize with elegance, with ease, not with a cover up, not with demand. Whenever it is difficult for you to visualize what you are going to do in the future, it must mean that you are still holding on to something tightly and you are repressing something else—the answer, no doubt. That is why affirmations do not work in most cases.

Affirmations only work when you are ready, when you have already become who you are supposed to be. When the deeper material released by your soul is already there, then you can honestly say that you are strong, that you are loving; then you can inhabit that new position. However, saying that you are strong while you are still weak is dishonest. It will only delay the problem. Saying to yourself that you are rich while you are actually poor is an Alice in Wonderland lie.

So, the method itself as suggested in this book will get you to the point where the new energies will be released and then, and only then, you will know exactly what to do. If you do not know what to do, then you have not done the necessary groundwork in the way it needs to be done, and you need to go back to some of the earlier chapters of this book and start all over again. Do the ground work and allow nature to do the rest.

## Chapter 17
# *The Iron Curtain Revealed;*
# *Surrender to God I*

---

Surrendering to doing your tasks will reveal the true nature of surrender. It means surrendering to the Greater Will, to the fact that we, in essence, are love, and to being and living in the truth.

It means surrendering our little ego. Much on the nature of this little self has been said. But, perhaps not enough. How much do you still hold on to in terms of your:

- **Freezes**: You are still to a great extent holding on to them. See, for instance, how you still react in the same manner; how you still live as if these freezes had not been shown off for their fallacy.
- **Fears**: You still frighten yourself with old hobgoblins which you have already demystified to convince yourself not to give.
- **Despair and cynicism**: Which you mistake for wisdom and which you believe, will protect you from unhappiness.
- **Self-will**: Which among other things tells you that your happiness depends on your outer life responding in predetermined and specific ways; making demands and setting conditions.

As long as this insistence to have it your way still exists, surrender will be seen as a desperate resignation which brings lack of fulfillment and suffering. As long as you are convinced that you can only be happy **your way**, you will continue to hold on to all the construct that constitute your life now. You are condemning yourself to a grey, partial fulfillment which increasingly will diminish until you die.

This "busy-ness," this perpetual "rat race" has no room for the fluid Cosmic Life Force. While holding on to all that stuff, you are caught in a closed energy system that refuses to be penetrated by the infinite goodness of the Universe. You block the light, the ecstasy, the renewal. In fact, you see those as dangerous—and they will eventually appear as such, presenting themselves in your life as cataclysmic, earth shaking events that bring destruction.

In your shortsightedness, you trust what is shaky and temporary while rejecting what is life giving, secure and pleasurable, nay blissful.

By holding on to your old ways you build an iron curtain around yourself. You live under the dictatorship and the tyranny of your old freezes, beliefs, glamours, that all insist to have their way, that, in an attempt at controlling life, stifles it.

Under such a dictatorship, no creativity can occur. Everything produced is pseudo-beautiful, pirated, aped. Eventually you become as poor and pathetic as Cuba under Castro, or as the evil empire, the USSR, or as China.

Within yourself is an ever increasing terror, anxiety, lack of motivation, corruption and stagnation.

Only when the iron curtain is lifted can the free flow of the Cosmic Life Force come in, clean up the old and decrepit—involving, of course, temporary pain—and restore the entity to abundant life.

So, lift up the tightness, the old dictatorship, the self-will, the demands and the insistence. Let in the new, the good and the beautiful, through surrender to freedom and openness, through faith.

✝✝✝

There is a close similarity between the fifties and the nineties, the forties and the eighties, the thirties and twenties and the sixties. The McCarthy anti-communist hearings destroyed the depth of creativity in American cinema. Films degenerated into the innocuous Doris Day types and other musicals. Also, another form of degeneration took the road of violence. It is as if Hollywood's impotency and emasculation gave vent to the violence.

The same phenomenon was happening in the nineties. There no longer was any depth in American cinema. It was emasculated in the nineties by the fundamentalists who, for example, banned Scorsese's *Last Temptation of Christ* from video store shelves. The merchants, of course, knuckled under the pressure of organized so-called Christianity, just as much as the film industry, the schools, etc., were knuckling under the McCarthyist pressure and firing anybody who not only was a Communist, but was also in any way suspected of even befriending suspected communists, or not cooperating with this most unjust oppression.

The consequence of this castration of American cinema has resulted the meaningless films produced today by Hollywood. Compare them to what is being produced in France, or elsewhere in Europe. The depth of creativity and productivity there has far surpassed anything that Hollywood can produce today, not withstanding the hundreds of millions that are being spent there. Hollywood has even managed to eviscerate Nathaniel Hawthorn's *Scarlet Letter*. From a story that carries a profound message of karma and of the powerful effect of the Law of Cause and Effect, they have managed to create a yuppyized version of it, a mere empty shell. The outrageous betrayal of the American film industry is thus perpetrated on classical American writers. The licentious exaggerations of the thirties and seventies are only matched by the restrictive and tyrannical bigotry of the fifties and nineties. One extreme is the cause of the other. At the same time, one extreme abhors the other. They each are each others creator. One is out to annihilate the other. Here can be recognized the mark of evil, the hoof of Satan, clearly showing its ugliness in extreme periods.

Ronald Reagan, who in the fifties was a liberal democrat, but was still an anti-Communist, protested against McCarthyism and the oppressive methods of those hearings. He had the courage to do that then, as well as the courage in the early eighties to reverse the oppressive ultra-liberalism that culminated in the liberal outrages of the late seventies.

Just a reminder of my theories that have been expressed elsewhere and which I have formulated since the seventies when I have become aware of them. The forties were a healthy reaction in the form of action and war against the scourge of Nazism and Communism. This movement became exaggerated and evil in the fifties with the blacklisting of McCarthyism. The sixties brought a healthy destruction of the whole father forties and fifties era, inaugurating the receptive, the mother, the colourful, the rainbow, the all acceptance and the all forgiving aspects of love and of feelings. The seventies were an exaggeration of this and culminated in liberal tyranny and the outrageous ineptness of the Carter administration, facilitating the Soviet Union—the evil empire's finest hour. The eighties were a healthy reaction to the seventies excesses. Refreshingly, Reagan ended the excesses of the left and of the unions with them. He made it possible for the iron curtain to be torn down, along with the Berlin wall. He put an end to the evil empire. The nineties were an exaggeration of this and culminated in the bigotry and fanaticism of those who call themselves Christians.

Today, in the nineties,[27] one can compare merchants displaying the Christian fish symbol in their ads and on their windows to the outrages of blacklisting. One is reminded—in reverse, although the outrage is the same—of the Star of David being painted by the SA and the SS on Jewish store fronts in Germany. Non-Christians as well as genuine Christians should be outraged by this blatant display of open bigotry and exclusivity. It is an open statement that says beyond a shadow of a doubt, "We are better than you because we are Christians and you are not; however, we would love to take your money; so come in and shop anyway." In reality, nothing is more unchristian than the display of a fish on a store front or on the back of a car.

It is not that they have violated any outer level laws. They have violated Spiritual Law. If the problem is not stopped on that level, it will indeed descend on the level of violating human law. You may say that this will never happen in this country. Be reminded by the fact that the entire McCarthy, unAmerican hearings and what followed was in blatant violation of the constitution of this country. It can happen again, this time under a religious banner. Watch out.

There is no way that anyone in his right mind would think of Christ approving such blatant display of conceit, superiority and exclusivity.

Unless there is a fundamental change in the attitude of organized Christianity, it will fall just as surely as did the evil empire, the Soviet Union. Any organization, no matter how powerful, when degenerating into the errors of bigotry, exclusivity, and fanaticism, will be destroyed from within and from without.

✝✝✝

Another oppressive tyranny perpetrated on the American people is done by the medical profession. There is no way in the world that anyone, the average American citizen for instance, can afford the ruinous cost of medical treatment today. Medicine is becoming exponentially expensive. Doctors and the American Medical Association that supports them, are continuously and perpetually acting out their voracious greed by increasing the cost of medicine in an unlimited way. Americans are afraid to go to the doctor because of the prohibitive costs that is involved. It is the same with dentists. Perhaps it is true that the best medical care is found in the United States, but it cannot be found by the average American. The best medical care is reserved for the Arab Sheik who spends his petrol dollars by the millions. It is also reserved for doctors, themselves, who much to my shock, I have found out, give each other discounts and in most cases, don't charge any money to one another.

As the cost of medical care is increasing, the quality of care is decreasing. Indeed, there are frequent reports of mistakes, of the outrageously great percentage of unnecessary surgical interventions, and other astonishing violations. There are figures that show that treated cancer does not prolong the life of the individual any longer than ruinously treated cancer does by doctors and hospitals.

In June, 2001, an article in *People Magazine* reported of the overwhelming percentage of mistakes made in hospitals which endanger people's lives.

All of this is proof positive, an undeniable confirmation that the medical profession is now well under the hoof of Satan. They, too, are in the process of writing their own death sentence. Indeed, about half of Americans are now resorting to alternative medicine whenever they have the opportunity to so. They, too, will fall unless they change their ways in a drastic and fundamental manner.

It is high time that the United States join the other civilized countries in the world and make medical care **free** to its citizens.

✟✟✟

As you can see, the world today is full of very worthy causes to follow. It is only a matter of having the courage to recognize them. The desire not to recognize these causes makes a person as much a coward today as a person who lent a deaf ear to the McCarthy hearings during the fifties. He who has ears, let him hear. He who has eyes, let him see. He who is deaf and blind is a coward and a hypocrite.

### Rebellion Versus Surrender

The little consciousness in you will mistake what I just said with an invitation to rebelliousness. It confuses license with freedom. It forgets that freedom requires responsibility.

Genuine surrender requires the recognition of good authority, within oneself and outside of oneself. Genuine surrender **obeys** genuine authority.

Rebellion and license does not. It establishes another dictatorship, the child tyrant, the terrorist who wants his way or else. So, with rebellion, we regress back to the old iron curtain, to the old stiffness, to demands. We are back into a totalitarian system.

Creativity coming from rebelliousness is either false or short lived.

### Surrender and Love

The need for love in a relationship turns to demand when met with frustration. Then, the individual quickly finds out that the expression of demand for love is met with rejection. This is true. **The more you demand love, the more it eludes you. Demand chases love away.**

The lower self learns this very early. So, it creates a disguise wherein the demand is expressed in more subtle ways. Consider the glamours—all of them, no matter what Ray they distort—as indirect attempts at expressing the demands for love.

Consider victimization, self-pity, power, intelligence as ploys to get others to love you. This is demand, not surrender. It may temporarily fool many. However, in the long run, its effect wanes and the demand is exposed.

Besides, even if love were obtained as a result of the demands subtly expressed through glamours, it couldn't possibly satisfy the craving for it. Indeed, the very fact that it has been obtained through manipulation renders the love invalid. It is the manipulation, the glamour that is being loved, not the individual.

The condition that engenders this subtle demand is the iron curtain that has descended on your faith. It is because you lost faith in love being given to you as a response to your need, to your own love, that you resort to demands.

You decided to barricade yourself behind your iron curtain, where a dictator has decreed never to allow the natural process of longing, of needing, of trusting, of faith. Fundamental mistrust of the Universe is what establishes the condition of demands and despair in a relationship.

**In reality, love favourably responds to natural ways, since it is itself the greatest of all natural forces. Surrender to God and nature is a prerequisite for love.**

✛✛✛

Most people interact on the levels of the glamours, without ever knowing that they do. They end up being very frustrated without knowing why. Their demands for love aren't met. Of course, they deny having such demands even more vehemently than denying their glamours and manipulations.

Then, they enter the Path. They discover that they have to surrender to life, to love, to God. However, they don't know who to trust. If they surrender, they fear that they will lose everything. If they hold on, they must settle for a compromise, for a pseudo-life of relative, conditional and manipulative love.

The only way out of this agony is to work through the areas of glamours, demands and mistrusts.

1) Identify the glamours and how you manipulate others through them. Identify your commitment to them, your passion of and addiction to them. **Humiliating.**

2) Expose the subtle ways of manipulation. Become conscious of their ramifications in all areas of your life. **Humiliating.**

3) Acknowledge the underlying demand to be loved, the pressure, the insistence, the unnatural heaviness. **Painful.**

4) Discover the iron curtain wherein is an ironclad decision never to reveal need of love, softness or vulnerability. This is where you decided that never will you experience pain. **Painful.**

5) Tear down your wall, the iron curtain. Surrender and risk the free and unimpeded expression of your natural needs. This, in and by itself, will be so liberating. Challenge the **terror** of doing so, the desire to revert to the old status quo, the false life.

### *False Life Versus Surrender*
The false life surrenders to the glamours. It accepts compromise. It has sold its soul. It fears the surrender to the real life. It believes in a superficial freedom while harbouring and concealing a dictatorship. It gets heavier and heavier. Through crisis, or through self-search, through giving surrender to nature the benefit of the doubt, the individual gradually discovers that it is a much better course of action

than the old manipulation, demands, despair, glamours and guard.

With your commitment to continuously cleanse it, you get gradually closer to the dissolution of the layers that produce pain and humiliation. With time, you will be able to quickly and clearly see the alternatives and choose the right one.

✛✛✛

"Why would I let go of something that I desperately want? Am I not entitled to a beautiful relationship, to abundance? Why should I surrender those wishes?" Good question. Here is some help.

1) Know that every wish you have has, for destiny, total fulfillment. No one is denying you that.

2) You haven't trusted that fulfillment will come. You haven't trusted in God, in your nature to get you there. You believed that your demands and your forcing would get it for you.

3) This lack of trust cut you off from God, from inner peace and self-confidence. You disconnected from God.

4) Your demands alienated your fulfillment, which can come through surrender to natural need.

5) Your demand fed your lack of trust and your disconnection, which in turn fed your demand.

6) The ruthlessness of the demand created debilitating guilt.

7) So, even if you obtain what you want, it will never satisfy you.

8) In your demand, you have locked yourself into a tight concept of how you should be fulfilled. Those permanently existing wishes to which you are addicted must be abandoned, let go.

9) It is not the wish itself that must be let go, but the manner of fulfillment of that wish. Your wish will be fulfilled,

but not your way. And until you understand that, past your stubbornness, nothing will work.

10) You must understand that the wish itself limits your fulfillment. If it happened the way you want it, you will be disappointed, and unhappy. Think of some of your fantasies. Do you really want them fulfilled. You will find that, for at least some of them, their fulfillment would be disastrous or at least unhappy. Perhaps it is equally true of your other wishes. Why don't you give up, surrender to nature and leave it to God, let God help you.

11) In the present tightness and demand, you can't enjoy anything including what you want the most.

12) In a relaxed state, even not having what you want can be enjoyable. Besides, in that relaxed state, you are much more likely to have it because you make room for it.

Realize all the advantages of letting God conduct your life. Surrender to His will and He will provide you with everything. Surrender to Him and you will naturally have all you want. Let go of your false gods and give yourself to the one God.

## Chapter 18
# *The Iron Curtain Revealed;*
# *Surrender to God II*

Perhaps the greatest advantage to surrendering to God is that, by doing so, you gain the capacity to perceive, and therefore, conceive what is much greater than you.

As long as you keep on merely living your little self, you keep conceiving the same reality for yourself again and again. Surrendering to God means creating the emptiness into which He can fill you with the riches and goodness of the Universe.

Your fear of the emptiness is your fear of death. In that fear, you hold on to what you have. What you hold onto is:

- The old ways of dealing with your life; these ways have become obsolete, yet you don't want to know this out of fear of death; you believe that those old ways are your life. In reality they are gradually becoming your tomb.

- This means that you are accumulating and magnetizing a great deal of falsehoods—freezes. Add to these the original ones, the ones that you haven't as yet resolved.

- The compromises, the status quo, in which you have capitulated your longing for total fulfillment.

- The quick and easy answers, false answers, that have prevented you from the pain of stretching your longing with your integrity to the point of discovering the real answers and resolutions.

So, there is no fresh air entering your system. However, if you were to let go of all of this and let God in, you would de-activate all of your harm. You would stop nourishing them because you would stop believing in them. Look at your present attitude towards them. You are deifying them. They are lesser than you but you act as if they are greater than you. You have sold your soul to them. Giving them infinite powers that can only belong to the only infinite, God. You sacrifice yourself for them. This is your idolatry and, it is evil because it is killing you, stifling you.

✝✝✝

Another reason why you hold on so tightly is because you believe that letting go means never to have what your little ego wants. For instance, you are afraid that if you let go of the way you compromise your integrity in your profession, you will never earn enough money. Your little ego wants guarantees. In its immature consciousness, it doesn't see that it is precisely by letting go that it will obtain what it wants and more. As long as it holds on to the compromises, more and more of your integrity will be sold out. Without integrity, whatever work you put out has no value. And the type of work that used to have value has devalued today.

It is the surrender of the compromise and the commitment to the Absolute, to integrity that will ensure permanency of success.

Surrender means facing and undergoing fear of emptiness. Then, it means experiencing the emptiness with longing, with faith that it will be filled.

This is also true in relationships. The little ego quickly fills itself with already existing, but increasingly stale solutions. This means continuously and perpetually conceiving the same types of partners; continuously believing and magnetizing the same old patterns and fantasies.

Let go if it! With your will and intellect, convince your "feelings" that this is the wrong way. Enter the emptiness. Allow yourself to sustain the hunger. Refuse to fill yourself with false answers, with sickly sweet stuff that can no longer nourish your grownup soul. Let yourself be flooded by All That Can Be, God. **One must let go of what one wants the most in order to get it.**

### *Holding on in Relationships*
**I. The Aggressive[24] Mode.** Observe the intensity with which you dominate others. See how you stifle them with domination emanations. If they are wrong and manifest faults, see how you intensify your pain in order to dominate them through blame.

This is the mode of those who impose their will on others. They are capable—albeit temporarily—of overpowering others and "getting away with murder." Here you find the great magnetic convincers, the forceful sellers. We recognize here the Will Rays. This cruelty is motivated by your fear of letting go. You are empty inside so you try to fill yourself by dominating. You fill yourself with your superiority by blaming, which requires the magnification and the magnetization of your own pain. You believe that this will serve as a substitute for the necessity to surrender to God. You believe that you can escape surrendering, escape your fear of it, by making others surrender to you, afraid of you.

Aside from the intensification of your pain, you will isolate yourself, alienate yourself. You will be very unhappy and disconnected in your superiority.

But, if you let go and face your inner emptiness, you will demagnetize your pain. Other's faults will be accepted with a much greater sense of reality and proportion. You will not have for goal their denigration. You will not have to magnify your pain. This you will experience merely by letting yourself feel your inner emptiness.

And, as this emptiness starts filling up with infinite goodness and possibilities, you will experience that no one can hurt you, not even a little bit. You will truly feel protected and eternal.

With the indwelling goodness allowed within you, you will not have to be right, to forcefully convince or "sell." This you will experience even if you know you are right. In fact, the more you allow God to inhabit you, the less you will have to prove anything.

## II.  The Compliant,[24] Detached.[24]

In the previous, aggressive mode, I feared that if I let go of my little ego stuff, I condemn myself to poverty, misery, slavery, inferiority and humiliation. In fact, in order to sustain my superiority, I must magnify my terror of this collapsed and compliant state. The emptiness that I fear and that I avoid acquires the compliant, collapsed and humiliated hopeless features. It is filled by it.

So, when I decide that the forcing is too much, too tiring, where I can't take the rat race any more, I will collapse into this hopelessness. I will be depressed, poor and humiliated and I will make it a virtue. I will have renounced life. I will have become a "saint," like the swamis.

Have you actually let go of your little ego demands? No. You have merely become more cunning, less honest in your expression of them. You are practicing the oft-mentioned tyranny of compliance. You are actually saying:

- I'll submit and obey so you can owe me.
- I'll lay a guilt trip on you if you don't give it to me; here I gave you my submission and allegiance and you don't give me what I want.
- I have become a saint for your sake, God, by depriving myself of pleasure; now where is the pay-off?

The world is full of examples of false surrenders. Many who renounce life, sex, money, become covertly addicted to those very things. They say they have given up. This is the disguise of the one who has no enemies. He makes nice to everybody. He has no opinions of his own. He never confronts, always compromises. We recognize here the Love Rays.

What is going on here in still the fear and unwillingness to really surrender. The compliant person is filling himself with false expectations. He worships false gods. He makes himself a slave, a groupie, a devotee in order to be a master, to control that to which he submits.

The emptiness and the letting go haven't occurred. God is still shut out. The conception of the infinite goodness is still forbidden behind the iron curtain.

It is now twice difficult to surrender. First, the false surrender, the collapse, has brought about what was feared most. I have surrendered to the worst possible place, perhaps to prove that the part of me that still holds on is right. In spite of that, I am still under the illusion that I **have** surrendered. Second, I still have a demand below the surrender. I still tightly demand instant gratification. The proof is in the despairing collapse. So, I must overcome two defenses against true surrender.

✟✟✟

So, as long as surrender hasn't occurred, the person will be caught between two unattractive choices. He will find himself fluctuating between the two poles of dominance and compliance.

✟✟✟

When one mode is there, the other is there too. The more ensconced you are in manifesting one extreme, the more difficult it will be for you to recognize the other within yourself. Are you blocking the existence of one of these modes? Are you open enough to have it revealed by friends or by your mate? Are you ever aware of doing one of these? In the beginning of your purification, you may not even be aware of your obvious mode of behaviour, let alone what is under it.

✦✦✦

For an extended time, people will get away with acting these modes out. The aggressive will go on for a long time imposing his will, seducing and luring out of fear of collapse and crisis. The compliant will over time seduce through weakness, never confronting or disciplining in order to hide his desire to have his way.

While each obtains what he want through his own mode of behaviour, he will remain limited in his scope, creating and repeating the same scenarios. As long as he doesn't let go, recognize and experience the other side, he will be missing out on life. Maintaining this mode of behaviour gradually increases inner emptiness. It also increases the harmful aspects of the feared opposite.

For instance, the more you are dominant, the more you will have to be compliant when you collapse. The more you are a victim, the more cruelty you will have to live through when you finally rebel.

If you think that your mode of behaviour is bringing you success, you are very much mistaken. You haven't lived yet. What you have now is nothing compared to what you could have if you surrendered and let God unify and enrich you. What you can conceive will dwarf what you so highly keep behind your iron curtain.

So, disengage from the tight routine. Take off the blinders that only allow you to see part of reality. Sacrifice what you hold most tightly. Identify the rigidified ways of life. Observe yourself being tempted to continuously recreate them. Release them. Risk hunger. Create a vacuum and have faith in that it will be filled.

Let your old life die, and, out of the ashes, out of the emptiness, you will be giving birth to a brand new self, a son of God.

## Chapter 19
# *Surrender;*
# *Coercion Versus Love*

---

Suppose you want someone's love. You don't trust that they will give it to you volitionally. So, you force, you control, you seduce, you impose, you manipulate. There are two basic modes.

**1) Aggressive Coercion.** I must have his/her love, so, **I'll control, I'll impose myself on them.** I'll stifle them. They in turn submit, partly because they love you, partly because they unhealthily depend on you. But they resent you and challenge you. This triggers your jealousy and your paranoia. You control some more, in a vicious circle.

**2) Compliant Coercion.** I must have his/her love, but I don't want my desire to control to be obvious. So, I'll exert it through **unhealthy dependency on them, through guilt trips, victimization and self-pity.** They, partly because they love you, partly because they need you in an unhealthy manner, submit, but rebel indirectly or directly, honestly or dishonestly. This makes you weaker, more a victim of a power ploy, etc.

There are other modes of control, such as seduction, manipulation, teasing, sometimes hiding under the guise of being mysterious and interesting, an euphemism for lying.

How does this apply to confrontation, the most difficult,

and therefore, the highest demonstration of love? Remember, **confrontation is surrender to truth, and therefore, love.**

**For the aggressively coercive:** The confrontation will be given with intensity, forcing the other to submit. Actually, it is a false confrontation, since the real issue—weakness, dependency, etc., lies underneath. The forcing is a cover for a collapse, a despair, existing below it. When he receives a confrontation, there will be denial, threats, or a pretense of loss of memory.

**For the compliantly coercive:** He will not confront, or will be reluctant to do so, or find all kinds of justifications to not do it. If the confrontation is given, it is half-hearted, hiding self-created and dishonest fear of reprisals. The fear and the reluctance, of course, hide a demand for approval, which the compliantly coercive person imposes on others by dishonestly refraining from confronting. The rationalization then might be "I don't want to hurt their feelings."

When he receives a confrontation, there will be too easy an acceptance which will feel insincere. Or, the person will react with exhibiting heavy pain, sinking into self-pity and victimization, laying guilt trips on you.

Whichever mode of behaviour is chosen:

A) The common denominator is the forcing of the other to love you.

B) The mode chosen makes you blind to the existence of the opposite mode within you. Indeed, the aggressive controller has, within him a frightened and insecure place for which he compensates. The compliant or victim is blind to the desire to control and dominate, which animates his compliance and victimization.

C) No surrender to God and to truth is to be found.

D) All modes produce guilt.

E) All reinforce lack of trust in life.

F) They temporarily are successful, using talents, assets,

charm, beauty for control.

G) They eventually fail, bringing down with them a whole personality.

✛✛✛

Consider the alternative. Suppose you let go, surrender, refrain from any control. You may lose someone's love. In reality, you have only lost those who respond to your coercion, aggressive or compliant. Those people don't love you. And you don't love them. It is the games and the coercion that they want, not the love. And it is the same with you when you hook in.

Conversely, if, without coercion, they respond to you, there is no question about the fact that they love you. There is no surer way to love them than to let go. It is the safest way. Try it. Surrender.

Trust in the goodness of your simple need to love in truth and to be loved. It is, in and by itself, enough. In its own simplicity it is more magnetic, more attractive then any body or wealth or talent.

Reinvest your power to coerce into surrender and into faith. Put strength in your belief in truth, abundance and bliss, in goodness and love. Conceive of yourself as a trusting, honest, generous, open and rich entity. Practice patience and humility while traveling through the parts of you that still coerce.

✛✛✛

When cleansing your coercion, try to see the opposite side of you and experience it. If you are aggressively coercive, see the compliant side, and vice versa. This will heal and demagnetize you, balance you.

**Say to yourself that demanding love is an oxymoron. Demand cannot exist with love. They are antithetical.**

See if, instead, you can do the following:
- I like you; I would like you to like me. I love you; I would like you to love me.
- I enjoy who you are and I would like to open myself to you and share myself with you.
- You are the type of person with whom I would like to share my life totally.
- If you feel that way, I will expect you to **freely** come to me.
- I will not apply any coercion. I see that obtaining you through coercion is undesirable.
- I surrender in faith that I will get exactly what I deserve.
- If you do not reciprocate, I let you go, in peace, and wait for the person who will respond, and be drawn to me.

This openness allows all energies to flow, back and forth, unimpeded. This is your natural state. Are you capable of sustaining it? For how long?

**Generalization:** This is true of anything you want, in any area of your life, financial, professional, spiritual. By surrendering in this way, you free yourself for receiving infinite energy and consciousness. Whenever you do it, it will be so. Whenever you choose to do it, it will be so.

By surrendering, you will be rich. And the rich will be richer. By tightening and coercing, you will be poor. And the poor will get poorer.

Elevate yourself to the level in which you can sustain abundance. You must qualify by demonstrating inner wealth, which can only be obtained through surrender.

✛✛✛

Behind the iron curtain of demand and coercion, of seduction and dishonesty, of victimization and of self-pity, you are a beggar and you are poor.

He who has surrendered and has made room for inner wealth:

1) Can afford to let go and let the other come to him.

2) He can afford to tell the truth, the simple and unmanipulated truth.

3) He can afford to be rejected.

He who forces is a thief, taking what is not freely given to him. And he cannot get what he seeks, continuously pushing it away by his forcing. So, we have a **poor thieving, lying beggar who lives behind the iron curtain of his demands** and who pushes away fulfillment. That's your fate if you don't surrender. Here, you can see how people will reincarnate behind a political iron curtain, or under a dictatorship. It starts with individual coercion and precipitates—creates—the outer one.

He who has surrendered is willing to sacrifice all illusions, self-idealizations, and glamours on the altar of truth. He knows that they are all lies and he is willing to undergo any pain necessary to give them up. He knows that the pain is a function of his still holding on, in a closed system.

By surrendering you build your wealth, because you accept your emptiness; because you make room for wealth. The wealth is built gradually and, having surrendered, you accept the gradual way, being grateful for what comes every step of the way.

What is preventing you from surrendering? Where? Find the block, the iron curtain and then:

1) Identify the battle between: a) I must have it, and therefore, I must force; b) I sink into despair, collapse, and deprivation if I don't have it.

2) Identify the underlying misconception whereby you cannot have what you want without coercion, and that therefore, you are unworthy, poor, unhappy.

3) Identify why you feel that lack, that insecurity, that

poverty.

- Is it that you haven't wanted to take the trouble of developing this for yourself?
- Is it because you feel guilty for forcing? Or, for you dishonesty?
- Is it because you have expectations that someone else should do it for you, expectations that you have "inherited" or believed?
- How is that connected to the false beliefs associated with your childhood? With accepted societal beliefs? With convenient easy answers that you never bothered to check? In short, our cleansing method.

Surrender will, once again, mean total commitment to fill these gaps.

This should be done in all areas of life, one at a time, determining where you are rich and where you are poor.

When you find areas of lack, of poverty, you must surrender to them, admitting your poverty and fully experiencing it in order to find the strong desire to replenish.

### Giving and Getting

You must expect to get to the measure that you give. You know that. Now how does that become the dishonest bargaining and bartering, the malicious game playing in which you capitulate your integrity and settle for status quo? **Therefore, when you give, you must give your all; that all, then, that capacity of yours will reap what it deserves—and you must accept that.** If you feel shortchanged, you have not surrendered. You are still demanding, still poor. Therefore, you are invited to go through the method explained above.

**Beware of your demand that others take what you give.** They may not want it. Surrender means accepting that, too. Why does it hurt you so? Obviously because you demanded that your giving be accepted, nay lauded. Thus, you gave to get, which doesn't count.

### Self-Love and Surrender

It may seem as if accepting a lack, or an emptiness would destroy self-love, self-appreciation. Wrong. Accepting a lack, an insufficiency is honest. Honesty leads to self-respect, self-love and self-esteem.

Denying an emptiness, a lack, is dishonest. It creates guilt and undermines self-esteem and self-love.

So, surrender to the acceptance and to revelation of your lack is required if you want self-confidence.

This deep sense of satisfaction and reassurance will reduce the need for outer level validation and success. The outer level results will be seen as an added bonus to the already existing at-onement.

✛✛✛

Establish a rich and firm base within yourself. From that base, express a genuine longing, with acceptance of the possibility of lack of fulfillment. With this openness and surrender, you will avail yourself of all the riches of God.

## Section V

# Conceive

## Chapter 20
# *Conceive I*

Having looked at and started liberating our dormant powers, it is now time to learn how to put these powers to good use through conceiving.

Conceiving is creating within oneself the conditions of giving birth. It is becoming pregnant with something, providing inner hospitality for a seed coming from our soul. This seed itself originally came from our spirit and from God.

It is not by chance that the word conceive also means imagining, "giving form to in the mind," as the dictionary says. However, the dictionary gives us more; it says that it also means, "to put into words" (the dictionary in question is the Scribner-Bantam English Dictionary). Thus, putting something into words is the first step to giving birth to it. For instance, when you do Daily Review,[36] you become pregnant with a potentiality which finds its birth in the next day or so.

Thus, words have power of conception. They are the first step to material creation.

Visualization, oft-mentioned in New Age and so-called New Age material, is conception. The blue prints formulated in our minds eventually materialize, creating forms, situations, bodies, harm or good, pleasure or pain, depending on the degree of their alignment to the Cosmic Consciousness and the Cosmic Life Force.

So, creation can only occur if certain conditions are

fulfilled:

1) **The creator must be receptive to becoming pregnant. He must have within himself the active intelligence and adaptability to receive the impetus from higher entities and to become impressed by them.**

As you hear these words, you are becoming pregnant. I am impregnating you with my words.

You are right at this moment pregnant with thoughts, feelings, movies, music to which you have allowed yourself to be exposed during your entire life. Every single idea, note, remembrance, concept, picture, movie, conversation impregnates you. You have already conceived an embryo, the father of which is all of those stimuli.

This is a frightening thought if you focus on it. It instantly makes you question all of the elements to which you are exposing yourself right now. You are immediately wondering "to what will I give birth, what have I conceived as a result of the trash that I have watched last night on TV, of the casual harm that I have left unresolved in my psyche, of the gossip in which I have indulged, of the nonsense which I have read?"

You will start realizing the importance of reexamining all that you have learned. Think, for instance, of what you have allowed yourself to believe, to idealize in your earlier years. To what has that given birth? Has it done so as yet? Obviously, you haven't paid enough attention to it if the thought frightens you. Better late than never. Start now, raising to consciousness what has been assimilated without any consciousness. Reexamine what was taken in with your immature consciousness of the past. Allow now the greater consciousness of the presence to reformulate, reimpregnate, reconceive.

The flip side of this, the good news about it, is that you can now start a brand new conception within yourself. You can choose to expose yourself only to what is good, harmless and conforming to Spiritual Law. You can utter the right words, you can grasp the right plans for your future, you can read, listen to, and watch the right stuff.

The cumulative effect of this will accelerate your capacity for goodness. Soon, instead of harmful occurrence happening to you unexpectedly, good ones will, as if by magic.

2) Your receptivity to my words creates **an active condition in you that will desire a blue print, an application of what I am telling you that has direct impact in your life.** This then is your active participation in this conception. So, as you can see, you must be developed **on the receptive and the active levels.** You cannot afford to favour one over another.

3) **What has been visualized needs to be nurtured, cultivated, protected.** You must not abandon it, abort it, by indulging in other dissipations. You must make yourself a hospitable house for your newly conceived child. What are the impurities within you that could taint its nourishment, its growth?

4) **Finally, creation occurs.** Just as when a child is born, creation is painful. It involves:

A) Sacrifice on the part of the creator.

B) Letting go of his creation.

C) Self-less giving, a true test, and

D) Extensive concern, caring, knowledge, management, order, good will, faith.

Now the birth, the actual creation, will be painful to the extent the creator resists it. If, for instance, the creator a) is not willing to give, b) is too attached to its creation, c) has difficulty conceiving himself or herself as a creator, d) is not used to being a creator, then, the pain of giving birth will be commensurately great.

Think of any innovation brought to your life in this way. You will see the act of conception and the subsequent birth with its pains and its joys. Think of the pain of those who have refused to give birth to what they already conceived.

The story of Jonah is an excellent example of defense against conception and creation. The reluctant creator is brought back to his task through crisis—a shipwreck. He then goes through rebirth—being swallowed by a "giant fish" and beached to accomplish his task.

If you resist your task, if you don't want to be impregnated by your soul, it will happen anyway, in spite of you. The seed is already there. You must do it, no matter how difficult it seems to be, or actually is. If you don't do it, you'll be miserable and attract deadly crisis, only to find yourself back where you started, at the beginning of conception and creation.

Against what are you defending in your life? What is it that you escape from? What do you abhor doing? Here's the neglected embryo of your task. Your soul has already penetrated you, and you don't want its child.

Please know that you have no choice but to nurture and give birth and look after this child. Why **don't** you do it now and thus avoid being another Jonah? So, go directly to all the places you have been avoiding and relegitimize them as your children, your creation, your successors, your contribution to humanity, your task.

5) As we have seen before, **to the extent creation is free of harm, it will have permanency, even eternality.** To the extent it is a product of harm, it will create a crisis for itself and for its creator.

Let's reflect on all of this and see what we can conclude:
- If you let yourself be impregnated by spirituality, **you will become a continuous source of beautiful and permanent creation.** Let's rephrase this: the more you let yourself be impregnated by God's truth, love, personal

responsibility—by Spiritual Law—the more you will create, with increasing facility, happy situations, beauty, pleasure, universes of goodness.
* The idea of immaculate conception finally becomes clear. It is letting yourself being impregnated by God, allowing God's energy and consciousness to impress you, **without darkening it, influencing it by your own distortions. Thus, when creation occurs, it is immaculate, pure, unspoiled.**

The idea of immaculate conception thus acquires new meaning, an actual useful meaning, for all of us. In the act of creation, we are all Marys. On the Path of Purification, we strive for the purity inside which will attract God's power—what we call our inspiration—to impregnate us, impress us. Allowing this power to impregnate us means **conceiving** new possibilities. This method is extended on the various levels of our being as follows:

—**On the mental level**, we conceive through words and frameworks of knowledge.

—**On the emotional level**, we long for the new creation; we visualize it with our feelings, we adorn it with beauty, we nourish it with our love.

—**On the physical level**, we prepare the ground for its arrival. We clear the way by discarding the obsolete, or by liberating our previous creations, which have now a life of their own.

—You can understand now why I put so much importance on keeping these teachings clean. You see now why I resent the darkening of this material through watering it down by those and for those who are too cowardly to accept it in its pure form. It makes the truth into half-truth. And, as we have seen, half-truths are a lot more damaging than lies because they steer you in the wrong direction.

✠✠✠

God creates in His own image. We, His creation, create in our own image. **The creator is superior to the creation,**

1) **Yet, he can let himself be imprisoned in it, if he doesn't let it go and proceed to create another.** This means that he must be a constant channel, continuously receiving, digesting and giving, conceiving.

**You are imprisoned by your own creations.** You have created a degree and a profession to which you are now a slave, expecting it to take care of you. Let's say more accurately, that to the extent you expect it to take care of you, you have become its slave. **To the extent you take care of it, seeing it for what it is—your baby—you are its master, its creator.** You continuously improve it, seeing to it that it grow and that it doesn't stagnate.

If you are its slave, you emasculate it, reduce it. You do not want any changes in it. You see these changes as interference, problems. When your baby acquires a life and a mind of its own, you resent it and you want to stifle it. You want to enslave it, and as a result you become its slave.

2) **Since what is inside creates what is outside, what is inside is superior, more real, more true, more stable. The creator is eternal.** The creation is temporary. The creator is omnipotent. The creation merely borrows for a while the power of the creator. The creator has infinite capacity to conceive. The creation is limited to the way the creator conceived it. Thus, in order to regenerate, rejuvenate, we must transfigure, recreate, ourselves. New forms must be created, new skins are needed for new wines, for a new soul influx.

Thus, your life, your body, your job, all of three-dimensional life is more illusion than the inner life that has created it. We often talk about the inner climate or landscapes, which sometimes clearly appear in our dreams. Well, those are a lot more real than the outer reality they create. They are also more potent, more important.

Here is where we fundamentally differ from psychology. They see it in reverse. It is the outer stimuli that create the inner landscapes.

**The creator is the eternal youth, not his creation which gets old and dies.** To the extent what is created is infused by the creator, it undergoes a continuous rejuvenation. However, this youth essence comes from the creator. It is not an essence of what is created.

3) **Rejuvenation can only be conceived through the shedding of the obsolete and the letting of the new, encouraging it, welcoming it, hosting it, giving it hospitality. The idea of your returning to your youth is therefore impossible, absurd and undesirable.** Think of it, face lifters. Your obsession is in putting youth into what is dying. You are involved in an impossible task which **must become an addiction.**

What must be sought is the creator as the eternal youth. What must be conceived is our own at-onement with Him. This is the only way we will be able to rejuvenate what still has validity and discard what doesn't. **This includes the body at the time of death.** Eventually, clean conception will be so thoroughly developed that physical death will become unnecessary. The physical body will continuously be rejuvenated by the creator who will manifest through it.

**So, conception must be preceded by purification, lest it energizes what must be discarded, what has already served its purpose. If it is not, the regeneration of the obsolete will create perversions and addictions. Addictions and perversions pump new energy in old forms, new wine in old skins, resulting in destruction of form, crisis and death.**

**Investing life in the obsolete creates in it an**

**unquenchable thirst, the thirst of the addict.** He wants, demands to be satisfied the same old way. The little life that is pumped into the old form desperately thirsts for God, fullness, the infinite, yet experiences impending death, collapse, void.

✦✦✦

**If you cannot conceive of—visualize—a new form, it means that you are hooked to the old one.** You are literally hooked, addicted. You are not ready to conceive/visualize. You must do some more cleansing, growing. **You must visualize, conceive the shedding of the old form to which you are addicted.** It would be dangerous for you to now conceive in any different way.

What about those who go ahead and create anyway, without troubling to cleanse? It is irresponsible—nay, criminal—for a drug addict to conceive a child, or, for that matter for any addict to do so. Think of it, those of you who have already conceived a child and raised it. They have inherited **your** addictions. Not that they are your victims, but you bear responsibility in this act of creation and rearing. You knew of your condition, and yet you went ahead and created anyway. Why? What were the motives behind your conceiving? Was your intent[16] the pure providing of hospitality for a soul? Or was it to flatter yourself, your parents, to beat the biological clock, to sink into the glamour of parenthood, to be fed by your creation, now with their unconditional adoration, later when you are old, by their taking good care of you?

What have you done since their birth? How much have you tried to improve as a parent and as a human being? To what extent are you responsible for conceiving their distortions? What can you do to correct this?

Often, after a little more than a decade, it is too late. The task is then to accept the damage in your creation and let it go. It is painful and sad, but it is a fact of life. However, inadequate you were as a conceiver, it is now their responsibility to dissolve their problem. This problem itself, by the way, **they** brought in. It existed before them. They brought it in and chose you as parents to bring it to flowering and fruition, so to speak. You are responsible for not dissolving your problem and for the degree to which that affected them. They are responsible for their problem, their choice of you as a parent, a role model.

✛✛✛

However, you haven't just conceived and given birth to children. Think of how you have conceived of your job and your relationships. To what extent are those conceptions tainted by your distortions and addictions? How have you abandoned your center as the conceiver/creator? How have you then become dependent on your creation? How are you worshiping it, giving it the qualities that only belong to the creator?

You must also realize that you may not retrieve the harm that has already been done. Your creation, as sad as it may seem to you, must go on living its own life now. The only way for you to redeem for the damage is to conceive anew, this time in the right way.

✛✛✛

**If you have disconnected from the creator in you,** you will attribute to your creation the power that only belongs to the creator. If you forget your role as a parent, you will idealize your children who will become tyrants. If you disconnect from your role as creator, you will attach yourself to old and obsolete forms of creativity. You will become addicted to those forms. You will develop insecurity, exclusivity, cruelty, fear. Progress and change will gradually become your enemy. You will, therefore, long for your past youth while at the same time resent and fear all new youth and new change.

✛✛✛

Re-conceive every element of your life. Every moment of your life provides you with fresh Cosmic Life Force with which to reshape everything that exists for you. This reshaping is done by conceiving. Quietly sit down and focus once again on every aspect of your life to reshape it, this time in the right way.

Proceed with order, organizing every single area of your life, preparing it for new conception. Then, reshape it by letting it be impregnated by the fresh incoming soul infusions. Let God be the Father of your creations.

## Chapter 21
# *Conceive II*

We continue with the development of our powers to conceive. Let's consider once again the fact that the creator is greater than his creation. Another implication of this truth is that you can solve all of your problems. Indeed, they are your creation, and, as such, they are lesser than you. You, therefore, can manage and dissolve them. In fact, you are the only one who can since they are your creation.

How does that correspond to the necessary step in addictive behaviour wherein one must admit that the problem is greater than oneself? In the case of the addiction, the person's consciousness has been thoroughly removed from the creator of the problem. The power of conception and creation which engendered the problem has become unconscious. Thus, it appears as if this power is unavailable to the person. It becomes, therefore, necessary for the individual to seek outside help in order to resolve his addiction. It is a little bit the same in everybody. To some extent, we have disconnected from our power of conception and of creation. We have become blind to them. We have to be reminded of them by those around us who can mirror those problems to us. This is why we need the feedback of a teacher of wisdom and the group of friends around us.

✝✝✝

When you have disconnected from your power to conceive and to create a particular problem, this problem is perceived to be immutable. It appears to you as if nothing can be done to change it, that you will always have it, that it is greater than you. Whenever you find yourself in that condition, know that you are not in reality. It is important for you to bring yourself back into this reality, either by yourself through Daily Review, meditation, prayer and application of these divine concepts, or through receiving feedback from your teacher or your friends. You will know that you are back in reality when you will perceive your problems differently, when you will start seeing that your problems can be changed and solved. This is Spiritual Law.

✛✛✛

We are now going to try to turn conception to our advantage. In order to conceive positively, or harmlessly, one has to be impregnated by the right impetus. One has to allow oneself to be fertilized by the right father and be pregnant in good circumstances.

As we grow, we require to conceive in greater and greater states of consciousness. Thus, our inspiration, as well as those who inspire us—help us conceive—must themselves be greater and greater.

One cannot conceive in a vacuum. One has to have and be influenced by a role model. The role model impresses our soul substance, helps us conceive. Using him as an example means allowing him to impress us, to make us pregnant with his creation so to speak. It is impossible to conceive anew without a role model. This is why we have prophets and guides who come and incarnate on our level of existence. They become the examples for us to follow.

The greatest example of all is the example of the Christ. He is the prototype, the blue print, the map which facilitates our own conception.

Perhaps the best word to describe a role model would be prototype. *Proto* means first; *prototype* means the first type, the original, the pure mould. In order to conceive oneself creating what one doesn't have, or reaching a state which has eluded us up to now, one must choose a prototype who has already gotten there, achieved what we want to achieve. Thus, the first step is to choose the right prototype, the right father to our children. Once we have found him, we actively make ourselves available to his influence.

We become susceptible to taking up his habits, his way of life, etc. In a way we allow ourselves to catch his qualities. We let him "infect" us with what he has. We allow ourselves to be "contaminated" with him.

Unfortunately, we are not always wise enough to discriminate between the good and the harmful attitudes of our role models. Thus, when we allow ourselves to take in who they are in order to acquire a particular state of mind, or way of being, we find ourselves also taking in what is harmful about them. We allow ourselves to be permeated on all levels; we take in thoughts, feelings and behaviour.

To what extent have you allowed yourself to be contaminated by your parent's opinions? Examine your political or religious opinions. To what extent are they your father's, or your mother's, or your family's, or your clan's? Through the method that we have so very often studied of looking for people's approval, we allow ourselves to be contaminated by them on all levels.

Needless to say, this method does not only happen on the conscious level. It also happens on the unconscious level. Both conscious, unconscious, subtle, obvious states allow themselves to be impregnated by the person who is admired, held up as a hero.

The more you have purified yourself, the less your

conceiving will be vulnerable to pollution by the harmful aspects of those who are your prototypes. For example, a freeze that you may not have cleaned up will automatically get you to attract corresponding aspects in your prototype. Again, this applies on all levels. A freeze will attract those problems on the mental, emotional, physical, unconscious, conscious levels.

So, the more you are purified, the easier will be the patterning yourself after a role model in a healthy way. In the beginning, you will choose the wrong types. You will not want to choose those types who could really impregnate you in the way you need it. Your line of least resistance will propel you to the wrong examples. The best illustration of this is found during teenage years. During those times of vulnerability, change and crisis, we are prone to emulate the worst possible types, thus opening ourselves to regression.

We have talked in the past about being attracted to your physical parents, i.e., your choice of them. Since, to a considerable extent, you incarnate harmful aspects in order to resolve them, it is inevitable that you will attract as the first role models, people whose features will correspond to the harm with which you are coming in. Of course, this serves the good purpose of repeating problems that you have had in the past in order to resolve them.

So, we travel from incarnation to incarnation, continuously looking for the right role models to follow. Those who are renewers[28] continuously elevate the quality of those role models as they continue their search for God. The freer we are of distortions, the more attracted we will be to the vibrations of great beings, and of course, the more opportunity we will create for ourselves for growth and acquisition of what is missing within us.

One doesn't have to wait for the next incarnation to choose new role models. When enough progress is achieved in a person's life, new role models must be found. This can and should be repeated as many times as needed.

### *Individuality and Role Models*

When we follow a role model, do we lose our individuality? In order to adequately answer that question, we must first bring back a concept that we have encountered in the material about the *I am* consciousness. You will remember that good aspects, or aspects in their positive, infinite, eternal, natural state can be integrated by the *I am* consciousness and can at-one themselves with other good aspects.

In their harmful form, aspects cannot integrate. They remain in an atmosphere of antagonism and separateness.

For instance, good will can be integrated with love and intelligence. Good will is a Universal aspect which is not the possession or the characteristic of any one particular human individual. It is personified by highly developed Masters of Wisdom for us. However, in its purified form, it includes all other aspects with it. In contradistinction to that, a demand cannot be integrated with another aspect. It will not tolerate love, nor will it want to make sense, to be intelligent. Furthermore, it will be engendered, created by its opposite—despair—and, at the same time, will hate it and reject it.

In their separateness, aspects turned harmful, are under the delusion of being special, because they are separate. The infant in order to assert its individuality, says *no* to everything. *No* is the third word learned by the infant after *ma* and *pa*. Thus, it is possible to **pattern** oneself after someone without having to **parrot** him. **Patterning** oneself after the good aspects of the role model, puts us in touch with the Universal quality of those aspects. **Parroting** someone indiscriminately takes on everything about them. **In that mechanism, even what is good in the role model will, through parroting, become**

**harmful.**

So, differentiate between **patterning yourself,** or **modeling yourself,** after someone who is a good example, as opposed to **parroting them.**

This parroting can only occur if the person harbours within himself harmful conditions that would make it possible.

### *Hatred of a Parent Explained From this Point of View*

If our parents were once our role models, why then do we have such antagonism towards one of them or sometimes both? Because, in the very beginning, we parroted them, taking on their harm. Later, when we started becoming conscious of their harm and resenting them, we reacted in a double way, a) against their harm, and b) against the same harm that we parroted earlier, which are now ours and which have now become unconscious. Those harmful traits in the parent, as hated and repressed as they are in childhood, show up in early adulthood in the most unexpected way. The person is stunned when he realizes that he has become exactly the same as the parent that he most hated. That's because he conceived them very early in life, when he parroted the hated parent.

**It is the parroting that creates freezes.** This is true whether a good or a harmful aspect is being parroted. A parrot who says *good morning* to you very nicely, doesn't do so because they are loving and good. They do it because they want a cracker. **The mechanical parroting of traits always harbours a harmful volition behind it.**

**Freezes create their own logic, coming from their own axioms.** Since they are not based on reality, they limit themselves, as well as the scope of their visualization and powers of conception. A parrot that says *good morning* because he wants a cracker has very little power of conception in his psyche. **Not only does he identify with the harmful,**

**but he also negates what is good when he imitates it.**
On the contrary, allowing yourself to be impressed positively by a role model will not lead to freezes. You will be able to freely conceive. Your conception will be resilient and grounded in reality. It will create open energy systems which will allow infinite possibilities for problem solving and change.

## *How to Choose a Role Model*

**You need role models for the development and acquisitions of traits and skills that have heretofore have eluded you.** You may be stuck in "an inability" to develop a particular trait or skill. You may have already identified the freeze which prevents you from doing it. You may even have done a lot of releasing of the harmful volition which keeps this freeze in place and which prevents you from acquiring a particular trait.

Yet, you are still unable to conceive of yourself in the position of having this trait. As a concrete example, suppose you are unable or unwilling to inhabit a position of leadership. You may have identified the freezes of rebellion and the harmful volition behind them that want to uphold them, such as insisting on seeing rebelliousness as the key to power, to success, to happiness. However, you may still be stuck in conceiving of yourself in a position of authority. **You need to find a role model who comfortably inhabits his position of authority. It has to be someone who manifests his power through his authority in a good manner.** Because of your rebelliousness, you may have blinded yourself to the positive, good authorities around you. Thus, you need to open your eyes once again and realistically reassess those authorities so as to find in them the correct role model. Your friends, particularly those who are renewers, or your mate, can be of great help to you as a renewer. They will be able to steer you away from either one of the following pitfalls:

1) Choosing too harsh of an authority which will confirm your freezes of *authority is bad,* and

2) Choosing a too weak and ineffective authority which will also confirm the same freezes, but in another way, namely that *rebelliousness is stronger, and therefore, better than authority.*

The right role model will be an authority figure that can be firm and flexible at the right times. He gives encouragement and confrontation when appropriate. He expresses his feelings honestly and knows how to govern them at the right time.

✛✛✛

Therefore, we arrive at the following rules governing the choice of role models:

1) They must be people who are free of your own particular freezes.

2) They must help you dissolve your human type.

3) They are around you, only you are not seeing them due to your blind spots. You need friends and a teacher to find them.

4) The wrong role model can either:

A) Sink you deeper into your problems, cater to your line of least resistance.

B) Aggravate it by being too much your opposite. Remember, a freeze always engenders an opposite freeze. Example: *If rebellion is good, authority must be bad. If bad authority is strong and cruel, a good authority is weak and loving, etc.*

5) The right role model will have the desired quality well developed. It will be possible for you to conceive of yourself in his shoes, or him in yours.

✛✛✛

When enough cleansing has been done on the freezes and

on the lower self harmful volition, when the individual is clear enough of harm, there will be an organic attraction to the right role model. The person will be drawn to someone who will personify for him the traits that he needs to acquire.

**If enough cleansing is done on the clearing of freezes and of harmful volition, there will be no inner condition in the individual to parrot.** He will just take on what he needs and allow himself to be impressed by it. He will allow himself to be impregnated only by those aspects which are necessary for his growth. It will be clear to him that he needn't be impressed or impregnated by all of the role model's features, but only by those which are in him good and which he needs.

A conscious and deliberate effort is needed to be able to visualize oneself in the act of making the right choice of role model.

✝✝✝

An interesting side effect of choosing a role model is that you are elevating yourself to new heights. From that new position, your vision of your lower self will be much sharper and clearer. Thus, not only is patterning yourself after a role model beneficial from the point of view of the acquisition of the new aspects and attributes, it is also extremely valuable from the point of view of having a new perspective on one's faults and problems. With the new perspective comes a new solution.

From that elevated place, you will be able to observe yourself with new eyes. So, not only is it time to conceive yourself in a new and higher place, but it is also time to revise earlier cleansing that you may have done with yourself concerning areas that are still in their childhood state.

If your role model were in your shoes, what would be their perception of your freezes, your misconceptions, your

Mother/Father Split? From that vantage point, what would they say and how would they handle your life? Pay attention and take copious notes of this new perspective. How much of it can you implement in your life? You will find yourself excited at the prospect of having this new direction.

✛✛✛

Ultimately and eventually, the role models will become higher and higher, reaching the heights of Christ and of God.

## Chapter 22
# *Conceive III*

---

Living within us is the Cosmic Consciousness with its infinite wisdom and the Cosmic Life Force with its infinite love and power. This place of divinity is greater than the little ego. When the little ego is strong enough, it allows itself to be guided by this divine inner place. The ego must make a commitment to surrender to that place. It must reeducate everything that exists within its realm to that surrender.

So, there are many levels of commitment. In the beginning of your self-exploration, you may be under the impression that you have committed yourself to the Will of God, that you are open to all of those divine places within you. However, as long as you haven't gone through the cleansing as it is practiced here, there are places in you that have not surrendered to the Cosmic Life Force and the Cosmic Consciousness. Gradually, as you bring all of this reluctant harm within you to the realization that it is their best interest to surrender to the greater forces within, you are ready to make a total commitment.

When this occurs, when you make that total commitment, your life changes. There is a drastic revolution within you. You become transfigured. The divine within you begins to flow through you and revolutionize your life. In the beginning, this involves pain and destruction. However, this is a necessary step since without destruction there is no construction. You cannot construct anything new as long as the old structures are in the way.

So, what are the places in you that have not as yet made that total commitment and surrender to the Cosmic Force within? Who are those around you who have and how can you pattern yourself after them constructively without parroting?

Do not be fooled by the glamour of believing too quickly that you have committed yourself entirely to the divine within you. Do not commit the same error as do all "positive thinkers," as well as all those who still are trapped in organized religion. It would be a lot better if you said to yourself that there are areas within yourself that are still not quite willing to surrender to the divine. It would put you much closer to God if you admitted that and if you proceeded with the humble task of cleansing them and bringing them about. No matter how intensely you try to delude yourself into believing that you have consciously made a commitment to the Divine Force and that is enough, you will not be able to visualize and create in a good way. There will not be enough energy available to you to conceive and then to create what you want. Furthermore, you will be energizing the parts of you that are going counter your desires, thus creating exactly the opposite of what you want to create.

At some point, you will have reached a total commitment. However, you are not as yet able to sustain it for long. So, you go through a period of fluctuating from total commitment to partial commitment. Still, cleansing needs to be done on exactly the same areas and in exactly the same way of purification to be able to finally surrender to the Greater Will, the inner will.

✝✝✝

What are the features that distinguish a person who has actually made a total commitment to his inner divinity?

Perhaps the following description of his features will help you visualize yourself in that position:

- He is someone who has surrendered **all** of this thoughts, feelings and actions, as well as his possessions, to the Greater Will as it manifests within himself. When a decision has to be made, he knows how to—meaning his ego is strong enough to—let go and allow himself to be guided by his inmost self. All his thoughts, feelings, words, actions and non-actions are guided in that particular manner. His little ego willingly obeys the guidance that is coming from within. This little ego has been witness to too many occasions when his decisions were wrong and the Higher Self's were right.
- He treats all matters with exactly the same degree of importance, meaning 100%. There is no such thing as an unimportant event, thought, feeling, creed, etc.
- Each one of these are seen as opportunities to manifest the Cosmic Consciousness. He cherishes these opportunities, whether they appear to be momentarily good or harmful on the outer level, which means that
- He will transform everything into the good. There will not be for him any harmful occurrence. The most difficult confrontation will become an act of loving and giving.
- He will have developed the tendency to refer to the Greater Self as a habit which becomes more and more natural.
- This habit is so well-developed that there comes a time when, consulting with the Greater Self is done instantly. It is as if he is becoming his Greater Self—and indeed he is.
- There are still areas in him where his purification is still going on. However, the Divine Self is able to come through and talk to him about it, making him aware of a possible danger that may be upcoming, guiding him to doing the right thing. In this case, the ego will recognize

where the right voice is coming from and will follow it.

- The person experiences immense self-love and self-confidence. He is capable of loving and giving boundlessly. He enjoys doing both.

- He experiences the glory of God in creation. He thoroughly enjoys nature, the arts, music, every expression of God.

- He no longer confuses the messages coming from the inner Greater Will as a bad authority. He does not experience it as some superior, paternal figure condescendingly suggesting something beneficial for him. On the contrary, he sees the inner will within him as a blessed teacher, as older brother, the Christ within. Here again is the difference between the Fatherhood of God which is needed in the infancy of humanity and the brotherhood of Christ which is needed at the time humanity reaches adulthood.

- He knows that what is desired by the inner will is what he really wants. He increasingly—through trust at first—realizes how he really wants a lot more what his Higher Self wants. He has developed this capacity by continuously letting go of his utopias and surrendering to the illusory fears of abysses.

- He will receive messages of truth, carrying a wisdom which he never thought existed.

- He will realize, this time with a degree of genuineness heretofore impossible, that all harmful feelings are unnecessary. He will let go of his bitterness; he will stop depreciating himself; he will stop being judgmental and blaming others.

- He will no longer idealize fear, which he will identify as the worst possible aspect of the lower self. Since he has established a close connection between what is within him and what is coming to him from the outside, since he experientially knows that he creates the reality outside of himself, he will not fear it. He will recognize it and welcome it as an opportunity to manifest the Greater Self and to create anew. The at-onement that he experiences with everything in the Universe will entirely preclude fear.

- He will realize that all outer knowledge is changing in accordance with perception. He will reject total reliance on outer knowledge and will rely on knowledge coming from within.

- He will invest all of his powers into genuine enquiry, on the inner and on the outer level. He will recognize this impetus as instinctual. In that sense, he will have recovered the instinctual, insatiable desire for investigation that he once had as an infant.

- He will also realize that all happiness, pleasure and enjoyment that he finds on the outer level is only valid when it is deeply and well connected to inner truth, love and personal responsibility. He will see that without this connection, all of the elements on the outer level that bring pleasure become meaningless and eventually die.

- He will not hold on to any opinion, idea or creed with intensity, allowing himself to continuously be alive and moving, forever looking for new ways of expressing truths in order to keep it clean.

- He will realize that a considerable amount of his past pursuits are totally false. He will give them up. He will be able to watch himself in his disappointment and in his reluctance to give them up, and he will find the resources to clean this up.

- He has given up the apathy of finding quick solutions. He is deeply and earnestly engaged in finding the real ones at any cost, even if he must temporarily accept that he doesn't know what the answers are as yet.

Gradually, as he cultivates these states, he will find himself growing even further as follows:

- He will experience the true meaning of peace and serenity. The security that he has developed through the continuous practice of what we have talked about above, will deeply convince him that there is really no conflict, no struggle. There will be an accelerated increase of this sense within himself. He will find himself in this serene space for greater and greater periods of time, as great as he can sustain them.
- Since he is continuously conceiving and creating, he feels totally satisfied, fulfilled. Imagine how distant the idea of burn-out is from this point!
- Causality for him is a concrete reality. Thus, there is no longer demand and despair.
- Every obstacle becomes a steppingstone, an opportunity to add a dimension to one's life. There are no stumbling blocks; they all have become steppingstones.
- He experiences the world as continuously changing. Nothing is set and immutable, least of all, problems or harm, which are finite. He experiences the finiteness of harm without any doubt.
- Because he is so free and clean, he has an immense capacity for work. He is able to take on a phenomenal amount of work and discharge it with amazing facility.
- Since he is free of guilt, he has an unlimited capacity for pleasure which he does not resist.
- He totally accepts his own anger, and therefore, can breeze through it, putting it to good use. As he grows, it becomes less and less necessary for him to even get angry. He funnels the energy once devoted to anger to conceiving and creating.
- He is capable of a deep and intimate relationship with a mate in which there is total transparency and where there

is a continuous recreation of strength, and therefore, Eros.

- Harmony is to be found in every area of his life, within and without. He enjoys this harmony and glides through it.
- He is enormously resourceful. Since he is not weighed down by freezes, he can freely conceive of any possibility to deal with any situation.
- He shows incredible proficiency and knowledge in an astonishing variety of subjects. Since he is in touch with his Divine Self, he is able to tap into those places without heavily carrying them as baggage.
- He is truly rich. He has so much; he owns the Universe, and yet he doesn't carry it on his shoulders.
- Courtesy and politeness will be emanating from him effortlessly. This will come to him naturally. It is there in this natural state because he no longer desires to appear in a certain way. Having overcome the fear of shame, and shame itself, he allows himself to be giving, to be generous, to give the benefit of the doubt without believing that he will be fooled, or taken. From that distance, he will look at this old self and find how much error there was in him in the past.
- He, in the past, thought that his politeness and chivalry emanated from his idealized self, his glamours. He then when through an antithetical phase in which he purposely was impolite and selfish, believing that was his genuine self. He now realizes that the idealized self, rather than being the author of politeness and good manners, was actually the impediment to them.
- He will have the capacity for being receptive, resisting not evil, allowing himself to experience pain, allowing pain to invade him, knowing that within himself there is an infinite space in which the pain loses itself and must then turn around as Napoleon and Hitler did in Russia.
- He will know how to assert himself, to claim and take

what is his, to take risks, to attack when necessary, even if it is with his physical body. Anger with him can only be healthy. Therefore, there will not be any guilt accumulated, real or false. Thus, when the assertion or even the aggression is expressed, it will be finite, spending itself fully and knowing when to disengage. It will not linger past its useful point. It will not be exaggerated since he will have confidence in the Universe. He will not have the sense of demanding instant results to the expression of his assertion. He will know how to express it and to disengage when the time is right, waiting for the results to come by themselves. The expression of aggression will not be a forced, contrived one, limited to the little ego. It will be a deep one, immensely powerful, but at the same time, relaxed and deliberate.

- Since there are no defenses, he will know exactly what is private and what is secret. There will be no secrecy, only privacy. He will be able to talk about himself with total openness, keeping private at times when it is necessary to do so, when it is not appropriate to open up.
- Thus, he will never feel lonely because he is at-one with himself.
- In addition to which, he will attract people who either are like him, or who, recognizing him for the teacher that he is, will seek his company with respect.
- His ideals will be of the highest nature. He will not be afraid of adopting new and higher ideals if it means changing his mind about something, or if it means that he has been wrong and has done harm in the past by holding lower ones.
- He will be totally devoted to those high ideals, surrendering to them all of his possessions, his body, his mind, his soul, his feelings, his actions and non-actions.
- He will express these ideals freely, lovingly, and with great

enjoyment to whom ever it is who wants to hear them. He will have overcome his shame of these ideals. He will know that the existence of this shame means a desire not to hold them, not to conform to them, but instead, to still want to parrot those who have lesser ones, who are still involved in the false life. He will no longer feel attracted to the false life. Having renounced it, he will also be able to denounce it when ever he sees it, with openness and courage.

- A ceremonial order will permeate everything he does. However, he will practice this with lightness and resiliency, not with forcefulness and heaviness.
- Having transcended duality, he will see no difference between giving and getting, allowing both to flow in an unimpeded manner throughout his life.
- There will be an enjoyment of the act of supporting, of expressing gratitude for every single creation in the Universe, every single entity.
- There will be in this person an inextricable blend of dignity and humility.
- All of this light will have the property of attracting those who can take it and repel those who cannot.
- Gradually, a blissful state of continuous prayer will envelop him and bathe him. All experience, including pain, has become pleasure. All abundance in the Universe is his, offered to him for the taking, yet he is free of it as well since he is willing to share it.

✝✝✝

Take each one of these qualities and ask yourself whether you have it. Ask your guidance, your teacher, your meditation, what it is that still keeps you away from attaining each single one of these qualities and more. Detect the harmful volition within you that wants you not to have one or many of these qualities. Expose its desire. What does it want instead? Why? Then try to convince that part of you that what it seeks cannot be found in the ways of the past. It must change. Show it that its best self-interest is in changing. Present it with role models after which it can pattern itself in its goals.

✛✛✛

In this time of the Winter Solstice,[29] of the birth of the Christ, give yourself the greatest gift you can give yourself. Give others the same gift. You be all you can be and you make it possible for all of those around you to be what they can be. Be in the immense serenity that God visualizes for you. Be peace and God.

*Section VI*

# *Guard Versus Spontaneity*

*Chapter 23*
# *Glamour, Guard,*
# *and More on Spontaneity*

---

The idea of glamour originates in the Tibetan's dictations to Alice A. Bailey in the wonderful book called *Glamour, A World Problem.* I have adapted these to explain my theory of guards and distortions. I have also linked them to the concept of the idealized self in Karen Horney.

Basically, a glamour is an inflation and an idealization of a divine aspect or attribute. It makes the divine and spontaneous into the grandiose and affected.

Let's see how all of this started. At the time of the creation, God distributed great powers to many "angels." These are personifications of the Seven Rays.

The powers given to these entities were immense. They could create at will whatever they could imagine. God's purpose in entrusting His power and authority to these spiritual beings was to penetrate darkness with Light.

Imagine yourself as a child given a great amount of power. How wonderful to be able to do everything you ever wanted to do! Inside each of us there is an aspect that longs for and remembers this state of omnipotence.

However, if we were given unlimited powers, we would not be able to handle them with consciousness. Therefore, we would misuse them, and would develop an exaggerated self-love, an ego aggrandizement. We would fall in love with ourselves. We would make ourselves as gods. We would deny the existence of God. Since there are many of us, all believing that we are gods, we would fight with each other. We would fall. This whole glamour led to the Fall which took millions of years to unfold and which is the origin of evil.

We can see here the formation of the Forces of Light and forces of darkness.

The Forces of Light consist of:

A) The spirits who had not fallen, and

B) The spirits who had fallen and who are consciously struggling to come back to the Light.

The forces of darkness are made up of those entities who consciously deny the Light by perpetrating ego aggrandizement and separating themselves from God, the Source.

Eventually **all** entities will come back to the Light. Some will return as the result of a conscious decision to do so. The conscious decision to return to the Light (cleansing) is an acceleration of salvation. Others will come back to the Light through an unconscious self desire to do so. Their journey will be much longer.

We are all Fallen Angels. Each of us represents a specific quality of Light, a unique combination of Ray colours and tasks. Therefore, each one of us is involved in specific ego aggrandizement.

Take the example of a child with a natural talent. At the onset, the talent manifests for its own sake. The child creates and enjoys creating without thought of reward or approval, he does not require anything in return. However, he soon finds that his friends admire him for his talent, that it makes him appear better than they; what's more, he gets his parents' approval for his creativity and skill.

The child will also be frustrated, feeling he does not get

enough of what he wants from his parents. As a result, his desire for approval will supercede his need for love. After all, approval can be had by the mere manifestation of his talent. Since all children experience frustration by not getting what they want, and since they all come in with a particular talent and quality, we can say that this substitution of approval for love is universal. The talent will be maximized. The child will divert all attention onto it. Therefore, he has glamourized it. And, the more that he identifies with it, the more he idealizes himself through it.

The child will look for a role model to imitate. In most cases, this role model is initially a parent. He will identify with him or her and will emulate their good and bad habits. The talent, along with the idealization of the favourite parent, will be used as a guard against what he considers to be a threat, a weakness. This weakness and threat are usually identified with the other parent. To summarize:

1) A person is born with a specific proficiency or talent, he enjoys it for its own sake and creates from a pure and unimpeded place within himself.

2) He uses it as a substitute for the love he does not receive and, therefore falls in love with the talent.

3) Falling in love with it, he falls in love with himself and the parent that represents that aspect. Here we have the formation of the idealized self image. We also have the definition of glamour. It is the overemphasis of an aspect or an attribute.

4) The glamour is used as a guard against those aspects or attributes that are not as strong or developed. We can see here that the guard (overemphasis of an aspect or attribute) was, at one point in the past, a divine aspect (talent) coming from the Higher Self.

5) Here is the emergence of duality, of the thesis and antithesis situation. Like a magnet, the talent attracts to it a

complex of associations, such as a parent, an attitude, a manner of speech, etc. It also repels, and this is the antithesis, anything that threatens this complex.

We have explained what an aspect or an attribute goes through when it becomes overemphasized and idealized. It rigidifies and gradually excludes other aspects or attributes if they are perceived as threatening.

Let us now study ways in which each Ray of Aspect and Attribute becomes distorted into a glamour.

### *Ray I: Will*

The Ray of Will or Power; the Ray of Leadership; the Ray of Fearlessness; the Ray of Synthesis, the capacity to understand great issues in a large minded way, the Ray of the Law Giver.

Distortion of Ray I produces the following glamours/idealizations:

- The idealization of omnipotence. The belief that I am stronger than anyone else in everything and everywhere. This idealization may also be limited to particular areas which are then exaggerated in their importance. The person tends to maximize the importance of the areas where he believes that he is omnipotent, while minimizing all other areas.
- The idealization of the lone wolf, of detachment. Here, we encounter the idealization of doing everything ourselves, living off of the saddle, as I have often put it. Since the Spiritual Law of Repulse (the law that helps us discriminate between desirable and undesirable) is part of the First Ray, the idealization of it also applies here. It is the state of complaining while secretly enjoying the loneliness at the top; it is the relishing of a detachment and aloneness. Many insecurities inabilities to communicate are rationalized under that banner.

- The idealization of destruction. Destruction, which is divine when eliminating old and obsolete forms, can be carried too far if enjoyed for its own sake. For example, if a complicated piece of machinery requires patient and intricate mending, a person with a lack of patience will destroy it while enjoying its destruction. We can see here that the idealization of emptiness is also the idealization of destruction, and enters into the idealizations of Ray I.
- The idealization of self-centeredness. This is a particularly insidious glamour in our society. It is glorified in people who pursue success, who think of *numero uno* before anything else. As a result of this idealization, the greatest and most brilliant minds are diverted from public service and propelled into the self-endeavor of money making. It is not a surprise then that there is no one in politics who is an inspired leader. The enormous tedium of platitudes spouted in Congress, reflected in untold waste, and per-petuated in mediocrity, are a direct consequence of this idealization.
- The idealization of magnetic personality, being the exaggeration of the ability to attract and lead men.
- The idealization of the self as the saviour in politics. Since Ray I is the Ray of Politics, the idealization of the politician is applicable here. It is best described by the illusion that only through one's own personal ideas can political problems be solved. There are millions of ex-amples here that do not need elaboration.
- The idealization of physical power wherein the person wields his strength at will, settling difficult issues through sheer brawn.

### Ray II: Love and Wisdom
This is the greatest of all Rays since, in our solar system, all the other Rays are its sub-Rays. This is the reason we say

"God is love" and the reason why the Christ, our World Saviour, is the head of the Second Ray. It is known as the Ray of the Glory of God. It is the Conferrer of Names, and here we can recognize our tendency to affectionately give many new names to those we love. It is the Ray of Wisdom, and the Ray of Buddha. This is why love is called pure reason.

One of its names is, also, Cosmic Magnet, alluding to its powerful magnetic attributes. Love is magnetic, is contagious. It is also known as the Master Builder and Great Geometrician, which explains Christ's career as a carpenter, and which establishes a strong link with the Fifth Ray of Concrete Knowledge and Science.

It is the Ray of the Son, Christ being called the Son of God. Thus, it is the product of the bringing together of the Father (Will), and the Mother (Active Intelligence). Here, we have the key to all creation and to all creativity. More words and concepts associated with the Second Ray are: radiance, attraction, expansion, inclusiveness.

The glamours associated with Ray II present a significant challenge. The glamourization of love itself prevents people from identifying the glamour/idealization of love. "How can love be glamourized, be used as an idealized self?," asked an old and very learned friend of mine. With this kind of attitude, great numbers of people have been hurt by love.

Love is not something that takes you out of control. You are not a victim of love. You are a victim of your glamour of love, or of your freezes of love. In those distorted situations, love is not pure.

Pure love is pure reason, and in the last analysis, can only heal. However, in order to find that pure love, one has to diligently identify the ways in which it is used for harmful purposes. For instance, under the banner of love, we can betray, we can justify cowardice in action.

The great distortions of the sixties and seventies, which

were responsible for the denigration of New Age movements, can all be traced to the distortions of love. "Make love, not war" hides cowardice and condones such perpetrators of evil as the former Soviet Union, while simultaneously attacking the democracies that provided the safe and free haven in which the peaceniks lived.

Promiscuous sex, a direct consequence of the glamour of love, gives us AIDS. The "non-conformism" of the sixties and seventies is actually a return of a condition to be found throughout the history of humanity.

One of its notorious precedents was the romanticism of the first half of the 19$^{th}$ Century. Both the movements, romanticism and the sixties and seventies—which I call "radical chic," a term borrowed from Tom Wolfe—can be described as being afflicted with *nostalgie de la boue,* meaning nostalgia of the mud, where tradition is worthless and license worshiped.

Distortion of Ray II produces the following glamours/idealizations:

- The idealization of the religious saviour. A good example of this is the hippies who were so terribly concerned about poverty in India while getting high on expensive marijuana and being unwilling to find a job.
- The idealization of being wise wherein the individual flaunts the fact that he is wise.
- The idealization of being popular. People on the Second Ray pride themselves on having everybody as a friend and having many of them.
- The idealization of duty for my personal satisfaction. Here, similarly to the first idealization considered above, one is enamored by the idea of being responsible; he does not lose himself in his task, or the discharging of his responsibilities.
- The idealization of attracting love. The person caught in

this idealization is not interested in loving for the sake of the beloved, but for the sake of looking at himself in the mirror, so to speak, and being self-satisfied when he sees himself, a loving person, reflected there.

- The idealization of victimization. Those enamored by this idealization are continually complaining and doing their utmost to gain others' pity.

- The idealization of rationalizing out of fear of action, wherein freedom of action is white washed under the banner of understanding. "If I understand, then I do not have to do anything about it, all I have to do is understand, i.e., I do not have to do anything." The Tibetan tells us that the one great fault common to all on the Path is the reluctance to take action. The United States, with its Ray II soul and Ray VI personality, historically shows this slowness of action. World Wars I and II are good examples of crises precipitated by non-action, when a vigorous and focused response was required and would have avoided untold suffering.

- The idealization of fear. This leads to exaggerating every single frustration, making it seem unbearably painful. The opposite of love is not hatred or cruelty, but fear. Since the Ray of Love is the most powerful Ray and most healing Ray, its opposite, fear, is the most insidious of evils. Surprisingly, it seems all right to be afraid; fear is a lot more accepted than hatred. Passivity is a lot more accepted than activity. A bold action, however justified, will come under great scrutiny and criticism. However, a non-action in the face of evil will not, or will be less likely to suffer criticism. Yet, when witnessing an outrage and choosing not to act, one has acted. He is doubly guilty:
  —1) For colluding with the crime, and
  —2) For not using the opportunity that was given to him to do something about it. The perpetrator of the crime is

merely guilty for his crime, one guilt only. This, perhaps, is the most important point to be made to everyone in spiritual development.

* The idealization of self-centered giving. "I serve for appearance sake, I am unselfish only to appear so, and I derive great satisfaction from the appearance and not from the service performed." Many people complain of giving without ever getting anything in return. The very fact that they flaunt their giving will preclude getting anything in return. What is more, if they are indeed giving selflessly, they should not be expecting anything back.

* The idealization of sacrificing one's life for another. A favourite idealization amongst mothers who continuously try to prove how selflessly they lead their lives for our sake. Little do they know that by reminding people of their self-sacrifice, they have stopped being selfless. (Mothers are merely an example here; other very similar manifestations of the idealization can be found elsewhere.)

### *Ray III: Active Intelligence and Adaptability*

It is the Ray of Mother. It is called Holy Ghost by systems of religion that have not wanted to call it Mother, though they have no qualms about calling the Ray of Will, Father, and the Ray of Love, Son. The principle of adaptability is also a receptive principle. Its creativity gave birth to the Son, as well as to the four Rays of Attribute.

Just as the present solar system is ruled by the Second Ray, the Third Ray ruled the previous solar system. The Jews are a group of souls who had not completed their cleansing in the previous solar system. They were reincarnated in the middle Atlantean period (the fourth root race of this solar system), and initiated the emergence of the fifth root race. The fact that they came from the previous solar system and that it was ruled by the Third Ray of Active Intelligence explains the great emphasis Jewish people place on learning, intelligence and knowledge. It also explains the propensity for attracting situations in which they are victimized, a glamour of this Ray.

Distortion of Ray III produces the following glamours/idealizations:

- The idealization of the self as omniscient, all knowing. The person on this Ray is concerned with information, facts. The more he knows, the more he is important; also, the more he is efficient, the more he is important. Therefore, when involved in a task this person would be less concerned with finishing it and more concerned with knowing than being efficient which will, of course, incessantly prolong the task. Here we have people who do not want to complete what they start, who enjoy widening and broadening their endeavors.
- The idealization of being the only one who contributes to the Plan of Salvation. This goes directly opposite to the emerging need for group synthesis and unity of purpose.
- The idealization of having too much work to do. A person caught in this idealization will enjoy being busy to the point of exhaustion: he will be conceited in his busy-ness. In effect, this busy-ness is a form of laziness, a trait of this Ray. This busy-ness will also provide a means of isolation since it is difficult to express emotion and share when one is overoccupied.
- The idealization of giving others work to do.
- The idealization of being an idea person, not an implementation one.
- The idealization of the web. The world wide web, www, is highly suited for Ray III glamours and idealizations. The person addicted to computers—the nerd—can be compared to a spider spinning his web on the www. This is Ray III in action, immobile while spinning and plotting to catch others without their being aware of it. The

widespread deception found in the wide web is appalling in its dishonest intricacies. All of this is stemming from Ray III characteristics.

- The idealization of plots in the mind that are never revealed. Here the person is involved in elaborate thought patterns that no one can understand, finding satisfaction or power in the demonstration of superior intelligence. Needless to say, communication is thus impaired. The idealization of victimization as a ploy to have things done for me. Here the claim artist[SM] concept is most useful (See my book called *Self-Esteem, Not Worldliness*). Ray III is the ultimate claim artist, implying that he is insured by just about everyone for just about everything. This way he can file all of the claims that he wants, catching anyone he wants in his world wide web.
- The idealization of abstract thought which has no practical application. Here we have the glory of art for its own sake, of sophistry, of indulgence in abstract reasoning, of Byzantinism.

### Ray IV: Harmony Through Conflict

Ray IV links the Rays of Aspect and the Rays of Attribute. It is called the Link of the Three and the Three. Aside from being the Ray of Colour, Beauty, Art, it is also the Ray of conflict, of dialectics, of symmetry or asymmetry, and of wide fluctuations.

Distortion of Ray IV produces the following glamours/idealizations:

- The idealization of dialectics, of continuously finding antithesis, of contrariness under the pretense of finding justice and implementing it. This explains the provocative nature of the person on this Ray. They like conflict, they look for it, they create it if it does not exist, they like a good fight.

- The idealization of harmony, as a tool of license and self-indulgence. This is the idealization of the person continually involved in giving pleasure to himself.
- The idealization of the power of clairvoyance. Here is the idealization of divination, negating self-responsibility. For instance, "my guidance says I have to go to Tibet, isn't it beautiful?," as opposed to intuition, which would realize that what needs to he done almost never involves having to escape, to Tibet, or to anywhere else. Here, we also see the warping of the New Age teachings. **Intuition is spontaneous reason. It comes from a well trained unconscious self, or from an area free of freezes, imageless.**[30]
- The idealization of indecision. Here, we have the undecided art student who is in love with his indecision and who glorifies not knowing. Here we also have the glory of feeling, "I don't know; but I feel," making this the Ray of Emotions, par excellence, and giving us the Jungian Emotions Type, and the corresponding Sumo Type.
- The idealization of emotions. "I feel, therefore I am." In this Ray, the individual believes that because he feels something, it must be right. This is the delusion that the irrational is rational, thus catering to self-indulgence which becomes rampant, and which explains the resulting overweight look of this Ray.

### Ray V: Knowledge and Science

This is the Ray of Concrete Thinking in contradistinction to the abstract thinking of Ray III. A person on this Ray is concerned with accuracy on all levels, particularly in the sensible world on which he is focused. It is, therefore, the Ray of the Scientist and Researcher. This person will display great accuracy and attention to detail. He will be concerned with being extremely truthful to the point of pedantism.

Punctual and business like, he dislikes favours and flattery or any type of expression of emotions. He will resent any form of looseness and lack of definition. One can see here how stiff this type of person can be. The rigidity and purism will also create a rigid and perfectionistic body. Fifth and Seventh Ray Types correspond to the Stiff Types and to the Jungian Sensate Type.

Distortion of Ray V produces the following glamours/idealizations:

- The idealization of strict and blind rules. This leads to the idealization of heartless justice, a.k.a., blind justice.
- The idealization of structure engulfing business managers and positive thinkers. This business idealization is now being successfully challenged by Thomas Peters in his books on excellence. His whole concept of MBWA—management by walking around—has finally dealt a mortal blow to old and defunct managerial purism. A good manager, a good leader, does not organize all the time—he feels, he shares, he emotes, he walks around. It is now an accepted fact that there is a lot more effectiveness in doing the latter.
- The idealization of the sensible world. The most spectacular and concrete example of this can be found in the philosophical and scientific movements which developed in the late 19th Century, called positivism. According to its theory, nothing was valid unless you could sensibly prove its existence. This applied to science, as well as to philosophy or psychology. This way of thinking has given us Pavlov and Watson, Wilhelm Reich and Alexander Lowen. The narrow-mindedness of this position is very confining and limiting. The more vehemently they insisted on idealizing their attachment to material reality, the less creative they became, excluding innovations and petrifying

themselves in their positions. You can see here:
- The idealization of reason and
- The idealization of facts and data.
- Also the idealization of security. The idealization of the structural view can be compared to the instinct to be in a herd, to be protected by the masses. If everything is well organized, Ray V gets a sense of safety, having controlled its environment through organization

There is a great insecurity underlying these idealizations. The obsession with the material level is a result of the fear of the inner levels which are less defined qualitatively.

### Ray VI: Idealism and Devotion
This is the Ray of Religious Instinct; the Ray of Absolutes; the Ray of Quality par excellence. The person on this Ray fluctuates between totally adoring a personal God and totally despising Him. It is the Ray of the Saint, as well as the Ray of the Bigot and the Fanatic, the Ray of the Martyr, as well is the Ray of the Inquisitor, of the Crusader, and of the Jihad.
Distortion of Ray VI produces the following glamours/idealizations:
- The idealization of extremism. It is the enjoyment of the extreme response—it is the "holier than thou" attitude.
- The idealization of commitment. There will be undying, unshakable faithfulness to a particular form or a particular person accompanied by oversensitivity and emotional response.
- The idealization of faith. "Look at me, I'm praying," or worse, "Hear me and look at me, I am praying." This idealization is milked to its maximum by the evangelicals, all the Elmer Gantrys of the world. In the Bible, the Christ gives us a good example of this: Matthew 6:5: *And when thou prayest, thou shalt not be as the hypocrites are: for*

*they love to pray standing in the synagogues and in the*
*corners of the streets, that they may be seen of men.*
*Verily I say unto you, They have their reward.* The reward
of course, is the admiration received, not that for which
the prayer was said.

• The idealization of intrusion. Here, we say that the global
idealization of the Sixth Ray has created the Crusades, the
Inquisition, as well as all other religious wars such as
Jihads and pogroms. On the level of personal idealization,
it can be expressed as "I am doing it for your own good."
Since we are at the end of the manifestation of this Ray on
earth, we see its idealizations in ugly extremes, particularly
in the Arab world with the Shiites and Ayatollah
Khomeini. We also see here the imposition of what they
call Christianity on a woman's right to have an abortion.
Indeed, the notion that the embryo is a person is
fallacious. The soul enters the body at the first breath.
Those who call themselves Christians, and who don't
know the true origin of their religion, are attempting to
impose their religious view by legalizing it. This is a gross
interference of church over state. It is a violation of the
Constitution of the United States and of Spiritual Law.

• The idealization which leads to Jesus and Buddha
complexes through identification. Here we see the
excesses of the Baptists, the Catholics, the evangelicals,
the Khomeinis urging people to follow them to the
exclusion of anybody else. We also see here the Buddhists
burning themselves publicly.

### Ray VII: Order and Ceremony
Ray VII is a Ceremonial Ray. The Ray of High Priests and
the Court Chamberlain, and the Ray of the Genius in
Organization, of the Man Who Delights in Ceremonials,
Rituals, and Precedence. Harmfully, it is the Ray of the

Superstitious, and the Ray of Omens and Exaggeration of Diplomacy at the Expense of the Truth.

Distortion of Ray VII produces the following glamours/idealizations:

- The idealization and deification of sexuality. Sexuality is idealized, and its power put above and beyond anything else. The abuse of this sexuality has given us the scourge of AIDS, just as the abuse of sexuality has brought on syphilis and gonorrhea.
- The idealization of the sensible human body which explains why there is such an overemphasis on health in the New Age, the Age of the Seventh Ray. Far from being spiritual, this actually is spiritual materialism. It usually consists in a transposition. Indeed, it is those who feel dirty in their emotions, or in their mental body, due to the warping of their harmful volition, that feel idealized and intensified need for the cleansing of the physical body. They are wasting their time, making the other subtler bodies dirtier and dirtier.
- The idealization of occult wizardry, of knowing what the right word is which will bring on a particular phenomenon. This idealization leads to such New Age fallacies as predictions, misuse of astrology and the Tarot, thus robbing life and individuals of the God-given free will, substituting a sick determinism for it. It creates self-fulfilling prophesies, serving the false prophet a lot more than his followers.
- The idealization of hidden powers which are misused for personal purposes. For instance, the misuse by the psychic, the past-life reader and the astrologer.

### Relationship Between the Guard and Spontaneity

Instinct, spontaneity, can provide us with all the protection we need. Unfortunately, we do not trust spontaneity. We add to it. We cover it up, erroneously believing that by doing so we are providing more protection for ourselves. The mistrust in instincts and in spontaneity, the fear that we will be annihilated by them, propels us into overdoing what we need, thus creating glamours and repressing other aspects that we do not like. Covering up or of augmenting the power or influence of a particular aspect or attribute creates the guard.

The glamour is in itself a guard against spontaneity, separating us farther and farther from spontaneity and from our instincts. It tries to convince us that we do not need our instincts and we do not need our spontaneity. The unnatural, forced evolution of some aspects and the repression of others are at the root of all of our imbalances and all of our problems.

Here we find a progression similar to the one we described above, wherein the talent is not allowed its natural expression and is exaggerated. Similarly, instincts are not allowed to develop harmoniously. The minute we become conscious of the instincts, we exaggerate them. It is as if the emergence of consciousness brings about two equal and opposite responses:

1) An astonishment of how wonderful the instinct is and a desire to use it and abuse it.

2) A mistrust that it will always operate as wonderfully as it did the first time and a subsequent desire to augment the reaction. The exaggeration of the talents is in itself a guard. The talents, if left connected to spontaneity, will grow and deepen on their own accord, without the forcing of exaggeration. This can be seen in art or sports or any human endeavor. The artist who is connected to his inmost self creates an art form that is closest to the truth, that reaches all of us, that triggers in all of us the same spontaneity. In sports, maximum results are obtained through movements that are as natural as possible. Only then can athletes surpass themselves and continuously break records.

So, learning and growth is an elimination of guards. It is

the ability to bring consciousness to spontaneity without letting it go to our head.

### The Effect of the Guard on the Physical Level

All physical stress, diseases are functions of unnecessarily exaggerated guards. If you throw a pillow at someone who does not expect it, his body will quickly respond in an mechanical way to prevent the pillow from hitting him. If you throw a pillow at your friend every time you see him, or if he thinks you will throw a pillow at him, he will develop the tendency to lift up his arm as a guard against the Now whenever he sees you.

There are several other physical mechanisms that accompany this defensive gesture: the blinking of the eyes, clenching of the teeth, tension of the neck and the secretion of adrenalin, to mention a few.

Now suppose this conditioning started at an early age in a situation where this person was subjected to continuous physical attack, punishments by father or mother, rough handling by sister, etc. It is then easy to see that this person walks around being in a continuous state of being on guard. His eyes blink, his neck is tense, his stomach secretes acid. This problem eventually worsens into eye problems, stiff neck or stomach ulcers. It would not surprise me if the propensity for terminal diseases could also be generated by the guards.

### The Effect of the Guard on the Emotional Level

The same principle can apply on the emotional level. If one does not trust, she cannot take in love, nor will she able or willing to give. From the point of view of her personality guards, the world would be divided into two camps: the attackers and those who are attacked. Relationships and personal interactions will be particularly difficult for her. She will even go so far as to glamourize her guards, as well as her desire to attack, seeing both modalities as manifestations of strength and bravery.

### *The Effect of the Guard on the Mental Level*

The same individual will find it very difficult to be permeated by new ideas, to want to learn, to want to think. She will rigidify and oversimplify for the purposes of her guards.

*Section VII*

# *The Many Selves and the Instincts*

## Chapter 24

# The Many Selves

---

## The Higher Self[7]

This is the part of us that is already purified. It is a misconception to believe that the Higher Self is beyond our experience. We think of it as being an exalted state which sometime in the future we may reach. Actually, the Higher Self manifests in many areas of our lives, here and now. These are the areas where we handle our lives with facility, in which things go well and unimpeded, where matters are handled with ease. When in that state, we can make available to ourselves all the necessary knowledge to deal with any situation at hand. The Higher Self also has the capacity to communicate with other Higher Selves  Therefore, it has the capacity to obtain knowledge and information beyond itself.

All instincts emanate[31] from the Higher Self. All thoughts, feelings actions have their origin in these instincts. All instincts are divine in their original state, and long to return to the divine, having gained consciousness, i.e., having attained divine consummation. Let us briefly recapitulate the instincts:

- Survival
- Sex
- Herd
- Self-assertion
- Enquiry

Here is what they become when they self-realize:
- Survival realizes immortality.
- Sexuality realizes religion or faith in God.
- Herd realizes civilization.
- Self-assertion realizes self-actualization.
- Enquiry realizes knowledge and wisdom.

By self-realizing or realizing, I mean reaching its full potential, its divine state.

In the child, these instincts are largely unconscious and only become conscious in adulthood. For example, the sexual urge in a young person is at first experienced in its genital form. Later, the blending of the solar plexus, the heart and the throat chakras create much more integrated, long lasting and pleasurable relationships. Finally, the individual realizes that the search for a mate is also the search for God. The religious longing is finally identified as having its roots in sexuality. Although the young person does not know this at first—it is all unconscious—nevertheless, it exists in the seed plan of the sexual urge.

A great deal of the Higher Self is unconscious. Freud had glimpses of that possibility. Jung was convinced of it although he did not believe in it. It is important to remember that the unconscious self is not all harmful. In our definition, the Higher Self includes the Spirit and the part of the soul that is purified. Other esoteric sources of knowledge, such as Theosophy, the Arcane School, as well as in the Cabala (the Jewish esoteric teachings), have somewhat different definitions of the concepts of spirit, soul, greater ego, Higher Self, glamour, idealized self, etc.

In the Higher Self are to be found all of the Rays. The Trinity corresponds to the three Rays of Aspect:

| Will | Love/Wisdom | Active Intelligence, Adaptability |
|------|-------------|-----------------------------------|
| Father | Son | Mother |

## The Unconscious Self

It has a life of its own. It is composed of freezes (see the chapter on Freezes) which themselves are units of consciousness having lives of their own. It is full of contradictions, hostilities, inner battles, unholy alliances and compromises. As long as it exists, it will create outer situations that reflect its contents.

At the same time, the unconscious self has a divine aspect. All of our instincts, all of those unconscious faculties which we take for granted, that make our bodies, our minds, and our emotions work properly every day, are part of the unconscious self. In fact, the divine aspect of the unconscious self is far more potent than its harmful side. The divine side of the unconscious self is part of the Higher Self, and therefore, is connected to the infinite. The harmful side of the unconscious self is merely the distortion of the divine, and therefore, is finite, being part of the lower self.

## The Lower Self [7]

All instincts come from the Higher Self and are divine. The distortion of these instincts create the lower self. A thought or feeling coming from a person's Higher Self will meet with particular life situations. The more there is lack of development and consciousness in an individual, the more wrong associations (freezes) will be formed. For the sake of the reader's convenience, I repeat here a passage found in the chapter on Freezes:

We form these freezes in a Pavlovian way. We condition ourselves to erroneously associate love with rejection, for example, in the same way as a dog associates the sound of a bell with food, causing him to instantly salivate. For the past 30 years, I have represented these wrong associations as follows:

> Love = Rejection

This is a freeze, a wrong association. These wrong associations slip below the level of consciousness and rule one's life in accordance to the beliefs engendered. The sum total of a person's freezes is his lower self.

### The Shock of Birth[23]

The creation of the lower self is inevitable. As we have seen when we studied freezes, the little baby undergoes excruciating pain when it experiences itself as disconnected. In the state before birth, there was no frustration. It was a state that can be compared to the Biblical paradise—being unconscious. The shock of birth, finding oneself born into a totally powerless state, propels us to create misconceptions for self-protection, i.e., the more helpless I am, the more I will likely get saved. Crying brings me attention, therefore, the more I cry, the more I get attention, etc.

The creation of the lower self is also necessary. Eve eating from the Tree of Knowledge and then getting Adam to do the same depicts an attempt by the individual to acquire consciousness. The attempt itself marks the end of paradise and the beginning of duality. There is now awareness of the difference between man and woman, good and evil, happiness and unhappiness, pain and pleasure.

The individual has passed from paradise, a state of unconscious being, in blissful ignorance, to a state of conscious becoming. In the initial stages of this state of conscious becoming, he hungers for paradise. He wishes he had never tasted the fruit of the Tree of Knowledge. Later, he asks himself whether he really desires to go back to the state of blissful ignorance. Voltaire asked himself the same question and ended up with an emphatic, **"No."** This "no" is actually an acceptance of the state of conscious becoming. It is also the beginning of the realization that there is another state at the other end—a state in which paradise can be recaptured, this time with full consciousness. This state we call conscious being.

### *Non-Being, Being and Becoming*[32]

Therefore, we have three states in the human evolution of its lower self:

1) **Unconscious being:** Blissful paradise, the original state devoid of consciousness. The instinctual pre-human world is still in this state. This is sometimes seen as non-being.

2) **Conscious becoming:** Consciousness emerges, forming an unconscious self. Duality, evil, harmfulness have been created. Everyone inhabiting a body in spite of their will is in this state.

3) **Conscious being:** This is the state attained by masters. Masters, for example Christ, can choose to physically manifest and subsequently end their manifestation at will. In the state of conscious becoming, we aspire to this state. All religions and spiritual paths have for a goal the reaching of the state of conscious being.

✛✛✛

We can, therefore, conclude:

• **Formation of the lower self is necessary for the reacquisition of consciousness.** It would be impossible for a human entity to have reached the state of conscious being without going through forming and resolving the lower self. Atonement with God requires having attained the state of conscious being. The state of conscious becoming is, therefore, the "necessary evil."

- **Evil is finite since it only exists in the temporary state of conscious becoming.** There is no evil in the innocent, instinctual cruelty of the animal state. With the emergence of consciousness, acts of cruelty, which were instinctual and innocent heretofore, have now become evil. The entity must now learn how to overcome this state in order to reach the state of conscious being in which the instinct has been divinely consummated and becomes totally harmless and perpetually creative. Therefore:
- **Good is infinite.** We come in from an infinite state, go through a temporary career in the finite state, and emerge once again into infinity enriched by the experience.

### *The Idealized Self* [33]

The overemphasis of one aspect to cover up the deficiency of another corrupts both. **This emphasis of one over another is a cover up.** The individual tries to disguise his deficiency —lower self—with his proficiency which then becomes an idealized self. This idealized self pretends to be the Higher Self, but actually is not. It is, therefore, a much more harmful and much less spiritual part of ourselves. It is totally unethical and duplicitous by definition. It is a lie.

The idealized self is known by different names:
- The glamours
- The affected conscience
- The superego
- The pretense
- Compensation or overcompensation.

Many idealized selves are to be found in each individual. If I do not want to show my harmful feelings, and I pretend to love, love becomes idealized. I find myself insisting on being loving. In the same way, I can find myself saying, "I must be devoted all the time, intelligent all the time, good-willed all the time," thus transforming devotion, intelligence, or good-will into an idealized self, hiding my lower self.

### *Properties of the Idealized Self*

1) **It is addictive.** My pretense is self-perpetuating, particularly when I forget why I am pretending. "I must be loving all the time, and sometimes I do not know why. I find myself caught up in an addiction of loving. I do not want to even think of the existence of harmful feelings."

Therefore, all idealized selves are addictive and all addictions are products of the idealized self. Substance abuse covers another deeper problem. Those who successfully conquer addiction have just begun the method of cleansing, not ended it as they so very often believe.

2) **It is demanding.** It is in the habit of transforming needs into demands. There is a heaviness in its expression of these demands, an insistence that they be fulfilled, in contrast to the Higher Self whose need is open-ended and tolerant of frustration. The idealized self is rigid, stiff. The Higher Self is malleable.

3) **It is sickly sweet.** There is an emanation that comes out of the idealized self. It feels either too good or too sticky. When we experience this, we almost wish that we could detect the true harmfulness behind it, the genuine bad smell that hides behind the perfume that was poured over it. If we ourselves have a similar idealized self, we will not be aware of this unpleasantness. In fact, we will rather enjoy it and collude with it.

4) **All self-pity and feelings of victimization are products of the idealized self.** They hide an harmful volition of not wanting to do anything about their unhappiness, covering it up by blaming outer level events or other people

for their calamity.

5) **All despair and depression are products of the idealized self.** They are hard to dissolve; they stick to you for extended periods of time. The Higher Self does not experience despair or depression; it experiences sadness which can be gotten into and out of a lot more easily and a lot more elegantly. Behind any despair or depression is to be found a demand. Behind every demand is to be found despair or depression, a feeling of having given up on fulfillment.

6) **Whenever there is an idealized self, there is hidden behind it a lower self aspect supporting it, aiding and abetting it.** This is a Spiritual Law. It is true in every case.

### *The Descent of the Higher Self*

In many teachings, only two selves are presented, as in Higher Self and lower self, or idealized self and real self. This has become too limited. Other selves should be recognized and should be studied in the context of their mutual interactions.

The personality is, in some teachings, combined with the lower self. Here, we intend to clarify all of the selves.

The distortions of the Higher Self descend into the lesser selves, creating different dispositions, depending on the individual. For instance, one individual will have the distortion of the will in his idealized self and of fear in his lower self. Here are the distortions of the Three Rays of Aspect:[34]

- **Will** becomes **willfulness.**
- **Love/Wisdom** becomes **fear.**
- **Active Intelligence/Adaptability** becomes **conceit.**

Let us study each of these distortions:

1) **Willfulness:** This is the distortion of Will (Ray I). It is otherwise called the little will in contradistinction to the greater will, the Will of God, or the will of the Higher Self.

The little will is alienated from reality. It wants what it wants immediately, regardless of the consequences for itself or for others. Here we can find harmful volition, i.e., the use of one energy current to do the work of another, thus corrupting both. Here is where we find the demands, the heavy insistencies that we have studied in the idealized self. The consequences of willfulness are:

A) **Cruelty:** Ruthless demands are implemented through violence in thought, feeling, or action.

B) **Inertia:** This is the reverse of movement, which is a divine attribute of the First Ray of Will. In distortion, exaggerated movement is nothing else but inertia; it is an avoidance of healthy movement in the right place and at the right time. Many people are busy doing nothing. Those who appear to be super busy are usually ineffectual and ineffective.

Do you recognize yourself? Somebody else maybe? Write it down before you continue.

2) **Fear:** This is the distortion of Love/Wisdom (Ray II). Since love is the most powerful force in the Universe, fear is the most destructive one. Hatred is not. Hatred is less damaging than is fear since it is more easily identified. Fear is simply lack of faith. As long as you are afraid, you do not have faith. Fear is based on selfishness. Only out of self-protection and self-interest do you find fear. In the spirit of truly loving and giving, there cannot be fear. Also, it is impossible to love someone when you fear him. It is easier to love someone you hate than to love someone you fear. Love/hate relationships are easily found. What appears to be a love/fear relationship is actually admiration/fear or approval seeking/fear.

A) **Materialism:** Fear, self-protection, self-involvement lead to reliance on material reality for security. Avarice, stinginess, theft, consumerism, all glamours of possession are consequences of fear. Here we find envy and jealousy as well. Living in the glamour of fear is the entire gray world of success/motivation, yuppydom, the glamours of business, the fancy marriages, the respect for parents for the sake of the inheritance, etc.

B) **Bondage:** As a consequence of fear and materialism, the individual finds himself a prisoner, bonded to these attachments, unable to think for himself, create, live. Here there is an obvious connection with the inertia of the First Ray. Obviously, this leads to living death and eventually to actual physical death. It is a definite path of regression.

3) **Conceit:** This is the distortion of Active Intelligence and Adaptability (Ray III). The overemphasize of intelligence will lead us to conceit.

A) **Confusion:** Exaggerated adaptability confuses intelligence. A person with an overgrown intelligence will manipulate through confusion. Here we are in the world of double-speak, of propaganda, of half-truths presented as absolute truths, of quick and easy answers, wrong associations. This is the most subtle of the three levels of evil. Study the relationship between cruelty, materialism and confusion, and you will find in it respectively greater degrees of subtlety.

B) **Blindness:** All of this leads to the shutting off of the mind. The mind's eye is closed. The masses now follow their leader like sheep in the slaughterhouse follow the Judas goat. The 20th Century saw slaughterhouses created by many types of corruption of truth. We saw the Law of Brotherhood —sharing—leading millions of people into the slaughterhouse of communism. We saw the Father/Will Aspect in its distortion lead millions more into the slaughterhouse of Nazism. And we saw the distortion of New Age principles lead Jim Jones and his followers into the slaughterhouse of Guyana. All fanaticism is blindness and leads to slaughterhouses: crusades, pogroms, Bhagwan, Werner Erhart, etc.

This is not merely an exercise in history or sociology. This is to remind you of your own blindness and fanaticism which exist every time you have a set idea that you have not thought through, every time you accept without question something that someone says, or something that someone insists that you must accept. The minute you accept it, you are on your way to the slaughterhouse.

The Three Rays of Aspect are one. So are their distortions. Therefore, in its descent, the Higher Self descends its three aspects, identified above as willfulness, cowardice and conceit.[35]

Where there is one, you are bound to find the other two. Finding one is not enough. Unless and until you have found the other two, you have not actually framed your lower self. When you cannot frame it, you cannot nail it. It will continuously and perpetually elude you.

Persons on each Ray have a particular blind spot. For instance, it is easy for some people to identify their willfulness. It will be difficult for them to be as clearly aware of their fear and/or of their conceit. Let us enumerate the Rays of Aspect:

| *Rays* | *Most Defensive about Admitting* | *Least Defensive about Admitting* | *Love to Admit and Cleanse* |
|---|---|---|---|
| *I* | Fear (Ray II distorted) | Manipulation (Ray III distorted) | Willfulness/ cruelty |
| *II* | Cruelty (Ray I distorted) | Manipulation | Fear |
| *III* | Willfulness | Inertia/Conceit | Conceit/Intellect Inertia |

1) For the Ray I person it would be the worst possible fate to admit to and experience fear. At the same time, if he allows himself to experience it, he will finally open up to love which

will create harmony in his life. He will have less difficulty, however, admitting to manipulation and game playing which are actions. This does not threaten him as much as does fear, which is an emotion.

He will love to admit his cruelty and his willfulness. He takes pride in them; he enjoys being the cruel, willful bad guy. He would not mind acting it out. He would not like to attribute the harmfulness of his life as resulting from distortions of power, of strength, and of will, as are willfulness and cruelty.

2) Ray II, the Ray of Love, has the greatest problem admitting any distortion of the First Ray within himself or herself. In "the glamour of too complete an understanding which negates right action" is a depiction of this guard on the part of the Second Ray of Love. Admitting to cruelty is experienced by Ray II personalities as most humiliating; they abhor it. At the same time, if they were to admit to cruelty, they will open the gate to the possibility of integrating the aspect of movement in their life, and will then find balance.

They will be less defensive when it comes to admitting the distortions of active intelligence and adaptability, i.e., manipulation. Ray II will find it particularly difficult to accept the element of conceit in the way they glamourize their capacity to love. They will be particularly blind to their own self-idealization when they are in the state of loving. A confrontation in which to be shown up as loving for conceited motives will be found to be devastating by them.

By contrast, fear is something they will idealize. In fact, it will be very difficult for the Second Ray Type to see fear as a harmful aspect. "There is nothing wrong with somebody who is afraid," they will say.

3) Ray III differs slightly from Ray II but is very similar. Ray III will guard against admitting willfulness, a forcing current, a tyrannical volition. Here, what we call the

"oppression of compliance" is developed to the hilt under the banner of adaptability. Less difficult to admit will be fear, similarly to Ray II; it is not seen as a necessarily harmful aspect.

However, the easiest to admit for this type is intellectual conceit. They will love to cleanse the "problems" created by their superior intelligence. For example, a mother superior, Virgin Mary, feminist victim type will not want to see any of these characteristics as ploys to obtain control over others. When pointed out to them, they will experience a total destruction of their face—loss of face.

Notice the coalitions of Rays II and III against Ray I. They both are most defensive in admitting that in themselves are characteristics of the will in a distorted state. This represents a powerful coalition against the First Ray. As a result of this, the Devil has always been associated with the First Ray. Power and authority are traditionally seen as harmful, as the bad guys.

Perhaps this is an opportunity to examine some of your misconceptions that still keep you enslaved to these notions.

Notice also, the tendency in Rays II and III to exonerate fear. Remember, there is nothing vainglorious about fear. Fear, as a matter of fact, is the most destructive and insidious distortion of any of the Rays since it is the distortion of the most powerful of all Rays, Ray II. Fear is nothing else but a mistrust in life. It signifies lack of faith. When you are in a state of fear you are petrified, and therefore, you are frozen, i.e., anti-life. All spiritual teachers will attest to the fact that it is impossible to contact someone who is fearful and that fear is the greatest deterrent of spiritual energy. Healers will attest to that, too, asserting that no healing is possible when fear is present.

See if you can find the place in you where you are still worshiping fear and where you are still unwilling to give it up.

## *Relationship Between Cruelty and Fear*

Fear always hides cruelty; cruelty always hides fear. Whenever you find fear in you, you can be sure that there is a cruelty and a demand behind it. Whenever you find cruelty in you, you can be sure you are overcompensating for some place where you feel anxious, insecure and afraid.

All that is being said here about the Three Rays of Aspect is generic in that it can be applied to any and all other Rays. The treatment of fear, cruelty, manipulation, conceit, willfulness and inertia transcends typological lines. For example, a Fifth Ray Type experiences fear (a distortion of the Second Ray). Behind it he will find his cruelty (a distortion of the First Ray). Somewhere in there he will also find his conceit (a distortion of the Third Ray); for example, the conceit found in concrete knowledge.

Do you recognize yourself in any of the above categories? Does this help you detect your lower self in a more complete manner? As you can see, it is easy to identify one aspect of the lower self and even to dwell on it while disregarding one or both of the other two. The one that is more easily identified is usually the closest to your idealized self. It is important to diligently look for the other two as they are alive and well and doing their damage through the lower self.

To review: We have the three Rays of Aspect:

| *Father* | *Son* | *Mother* |
|:---:|:---:|:---:|
| Will | Love/Wisdom | Active Intelligence/ Adaptability |
| *Distorted to* | | |
| Willfulness Cruelty Inertia | Fear Materialism Bondage | Conceit Confusion Blindness |

We have seen the relationship between cruelty, materialism, and confusion. There also is a relationship between inertia, bondage, and blindness. If you do not move, you will become dependent and you will be in unreality. Thus, we have established three types of relationships between these aspects:

* **A linear one within the same Ray:** The relationship between willfulness, cruelty, and inertia in Ray I; fear, materialism, and bondage in Ray II; conceit, confusion and blindness in Ray III.
* **A relationship that goes across the Rays:** The one to be found between willfulness, fear, and conceit; between cruelty, materialism, and confusion; the one between inertia, bondage, and blindness.
* **A relationship that goes across the Rays but not in the same plane:** For instance, willfulness, materialism, conceit; inertia, fear, confusion.

An excellent exercise would be to take each one of these relationships specifically apply them to your life, and meditate on the connections that can be made. Consider, for instance, these relationships, first in the past, then in the present, then in the future. Also consider the causal connection that binds them, once again without ever losing contact with the specific application to your personal issues.

### *Dynamics Between the Lower Self and the Idealized Self*
In a method of cleansing, lower self elements become conscious. The now conscious elements are then raised to the level of the idealized self. For instance, if I have become aware of my anger and I do not push deeper, I will use my anger as an idealized self. (Remember, the idealized self is the overemphasis of one deficiency to cover another.) Now that it is liberated, now that I know how to express it, my anger

will become a tool, serving the yet unexplored areas of my lower self.

In a state of regression, the idealized self level will sink and become parts of the lower self again. By contrast, in a state of dynamic progress, aspects of the lower self are continuously being raised out of the lower self and into the idealized self where they are identified, framed, ridiculed, and finally nailed and dissolved.

What do we mean by framing and nailing an aspect of the lower self?

1) **Framing:** It is the clear cut identification of the harmful aspect in us. Here, we will find ourselves tempted to hedge, rationalize, ill-define the boundaries in order to escape the humiliating reality of the existence of those harmful aspects in us which we find abhorrent, and heretofore, we have so very much attempted to hide.

The clear definition of the lower self, gradually made possible by the continuous practice of Daily Review,[36] meditation, working with others in a class, or individually gets the individual to the point where he can recognize it very clearly. He can see it coming, recognize its features, recognize its methods of making itself known, realize that it wants to take over the entire personality. This is invaluable in that the person will now be in a position to clearly choose between detecting it, and therefore, being able to discriminate himself from it, or *identify yourself with*[37] it as he has been used to doing in his mechanisms. Once the person is in touch with this clear choice he can take action to disengage from it.

2) **Nailing:** The clear definition of the lower self, as in a clearly drawn map, is not enough. It also has to be fixed in terms of time and space. For example, you may have defined very clearly that you have a lot of cruelty in you. You may deny that cruelty is being acted out in a particular situation. Rationalizing the situation as being an exceptional case where

you are not really cruel, but just. Once framed, the "picture"—freeze—must be nailed and fixed so as to become an easier target for cleansing, dissolution and/or disengagement.

How do you craftily guard against framing and nailing? This is a very difficult question to answer yourself. You will need the help of an impartial observer. You could also take into consideration what you create as a direct reflection of your unwillingness to frame and nail your lower self. For example, any harmful occurrence in your life, including inner occurrences such as thoughts and feelings, are a result of your unwillingness to frame and nail harmful aspects of yourself.

The dissolution then occurs when you exercise your choice to disengage from it or to attack/challenge it, dissolve it, break it. Increasingly, you become aware of the fact that going with it will bring you more pain than pleasure, more insecurity than security, in spite of what you have heretofore chosen to think. Your desire to be rid of it, or to relinquish it will grow until you find yourself eager to let it go. This is the point of renunciation which you have now reached. Notice that it is not necessary to dissolve the lower self in order to do right or to act in accordance with the Higher Self. It is merely a question of disengaging from it, choosing not to act or think or feel according to it.

This is different from your usual mode of behaviour which is to:

A) Pretend that this harmful aspect is not there.

B) Supercede an idealized self for it which usually is its equal and opposite. For example, if you are cruel, you may find yourself saying and acting: "No, I'm not cruel at all. In fact, I'm very loving. Look how much I'm giving, doing."

Does the idealized self originate from the lower self?

To answer that question, we must get into:

1) The formation of the lower self.

2) The method of cleansing of the lower self.

3) The progress of regression if cleansing is not pursued.

### Formation of the Lower Self

There are many theories that can be considered here. However, for the purpose of the understanding of the dynamics between the idealized self, let us look at the formation of the lower self through the idealized selves or through the glamours.

There comes a point in the development of an individual when he becomes self-conscious to the point of conceit about one of his attributes or aspects. Let us say that he is conscious of the fact that he is a very loving person and that people admire him for it. The more there is immaturity in the individual, the more there will be a focus on the outer-level results of his capacity to love. For instance, he will be much more interested in the obtaining of approval than in the mere expression of and manifestation of his love and his goodness to others. This shift of focus from the inner to the outer level creates:

A) **Inner deficiency:** Since he no longer is involved in nurturing his inner self, the shift from the inner to the outer creates an inner emptiness.

B) **Overcompensation:** He will accelerate the pretense of being loving, the idea of being loving, the love of being loving, the conceit of being loving. With his willfulness he will push himself to love.

The consequences of the creation of these equal and opposite layers will be a gradual decrease in responses from the outside—the less genuine the love, the less response from others—the less response from others, the more forced will be his current towards loving. And, of course, the more insecure he will feel.

This vicious circle now will reduce the loving current into

a demand, a pressure, a manipulation, a forcing current, therefore, a harmfulness. Since the individual is now aware of the fact that he is being rejected on the outer level because he has that forcing current, he will repress the forcing current itself, which will become the lower self. He will superpose over it a layer that will resemble indifference, or pseudo-lightness, or intelligence, or knowledge, or order, or whatever other aspect he chooses to develop in order to conceal what has become the lower level of his being. He has now formed a lower self in which there is:

A) An insecurity, a despair that he is not going to he loved, a deficiency, and

B) An overcompensation through a demand, a pressure, a forcing current.

All of this constitutes his lower self. His idealized self is whatever he chooses to cover that up with. You can see that this is a distortion of the original impetus to love coming from the Higher Self.

He now enters a Path of Purification.[38] He starts cleansing himself because things are not going well in his life. He talks about and reveals his idealized self of knowledge, or of indifference, or of order. He finally discovers (uncovers) the level of his lower self. The first thing that comes out is the demand for approval, the mechanism whereby he uses his capacity to love in order to extricate other people's approval.

At first, this is very difficult for him to reveal. He feels ashamed of it. Once he takes responsibility for it, he will feel the guilt that comes from it. He will want to redeem himself for it. This method will raise the demand to consciousness. He will become more and more aware of it. That level of demand (in this example, the demand for approval) has become an idealized self.

Beneath this idealized self, still on the level of his lower self, exists the layer of insecurity, lack, insufficiency. As he goes through the method of taking responsibility for insecurity and insufficiency, that too, will become an idealized self. He will see it as an idealized self, a put on, a superposed and affected part of himself. It will be clear to him that it is not as natural as he thought it was. It is second nature, not first nature.

Once all of these layers are out in the open, the emergence of the real self, the Higher Self is possible. Loving is then perceived as a current that is enjoyed for its own sake and is given without expectation of return. There is no pressure for attention or approval, nor is there a sense of lack or deficiency.

Note that I did not say that every layer needs to be resolved for the Higher Self to come through. Nor did I say that each layer has to be resolved in order for you to become aware of the layer below it. In fact, you can bypass all of these layers, become conscious of them, and reduce them to an ineffectual state through your cleansing. You can do this instantly, you can do this now. Of course, it is a matter of being able to sustain this level of consciousness, which is not always possible. Those layers come back when we lower our consciousness, when we go back to inhabit once again the energy forms, the habits, the contacts, the routines that constitute our life.

Suppose now that the individual stops his cleansing. What happens is that the layers will one by one recover their unconscious state. The level of despair and deficiency first will be repressed and will become again the lower self. Then the layer of demand and the manipulation of his love feelings will again sink into his lower self. At that point, the idealized self will then be reestablished as the original cover of thinking, or indifference or knowledge. If the regression goes on, it will be covered by yet another layer of idealized self which eventually become the lower self, and so forth.

**Which creates which, the idealized self or the lower self? It is a classic chicken/egg question.** For instance, in overemphasizing one aspect at the expense of another, we can see the creation of both at the same time. Let's take the example of the overemphasized love. "I want to love so as to make sure that you will love me back. I am willing to falsify myself in order to ensure that you love me." Or, "I'll submit to you through my love in order for you to love me in return."

In both cases we have two things happening at the same time:

1) The revving up, the falsification, the making heavy of love. This is the idealized self.

2) The intent for doing this, which is the insuring of the other person's response under false pretenses. It is a form of tyranny. It is a demand for a desired response from the other. This is the lower self.

The lower self will be less apparent as time progresses. The volition will be repressed while the individual will only be aware of the overemphasis of an aspect or an attribute. The individual will be aware of what flatters him, what, in his view, is an asset. He will hide the obvious harmful volition constituting the lower self.

Phenomenologically, one will reinforce the other. The idealized self of love will pay diminishing results. This, in turn, will exacerbate the lower self volition, making it want to tyrannize and manipulate that much more. This exacerbation will energize the idealized self of love which will become more intense and more heavy. bringing less and less results, etc.

The whole thing hinges on one misconception in the case mentioned here. The misconception is that the natural, organic expression of love will not be satisfactory, will not be enough, leaving the individual vulnerable, or open to rejection. It is the insurance against rejection that propels the individual into wanting to manipulate the environment by falsifying himself.

I guess one can say, generally speaking, that the formation of the lower self thus precedes the formation of the idealized self. The misconception is formed in the lower self. The lower self is closer to the Higher Self, and therefore, closer to creation. However, as time progresses both idealized self and lower self get involved in a mutual cause and effect relationship of reinforcement, as well as antagonism. That is why, for the purpose of renewal, it is important for the individual to accept himself wherever he is. If he is more in touch with his idealized self than his lower self which is usually the case—then he should proceed from the idealized self, looking for the lower self underneath and becoming aware of how his idealized self is indeed reinforcing his lower self. (See **center of gravity** below.)

### *Insanity—Psychosis*

Since addictions, pretenses, demands, despairing are part of the idealized self, insanity and psychoses are products of the idealized self, not the lower self. Neuroses are a product of the lower self. The neurotic person tries to escape from the lower self into the idealized self and cannot. Therefore, the neurotic person is disconnected from his Higher Self. However, the psychotic person finds it difficult to get out of the idealized self. He fluctuates from one idealized self to the next. He is disconnected from his lower self and, of course, from his Higher Self.

Here is another demonstration of why it is preferable to be in touch with and experiencing the lower self, instead of hiding it, pretending it does not exist. The pretense that it does not exist leads to insanity, to the huge ego trip of positive thinking, to the illusion of having already become God.

This is where we find that there is a lot of truth in the conventional Judeo-Christian belief that positive thinking—belief that you can create your own reality—can indeed lead to insanity, and therefore, is evil. However, it is true that you create your own reality when you dissolve your lower self, when you focus on it rather than denying its existence. The evil comes when the illusion of the nonexistence of the lower self is cultivated. Then the idealized self is propped up and insanity sets in.

### How to Cleanse the Lower Self and the Idealized Self

1) **What is rational and what is irrational?** The concept of rational versus irrational was developed by Aristotle. For him actuality is reality. For us, too. Later, Hegel develops the concept of "the rational is the real."

The definition of the rational and the irrational within us defines Higher Self, the rational, from lower self, the irrational, and idealized self, the pseudo-rational, i.e., the doubly irrational.

Just as with Aristotle, the Higher Self cannot be defined without defining God and His Laws.

In order to facilitate the detection of the lower self and the idealized self, one has to take into consideration the Higher Self. Only when one trusts in the existence of the Higher Self can one launch into the exploration of the idealized self and of the lower self. If the Higher Self is not accepted as a reality, there is no trust in the Universe. The person then feels extremely insecure, unwilling to reveal harmfulness emanating from him because he is afraid that there is nothing else to him, that he is fundamentally harmful and unacceptable, that he is fundamentally a bad person. This is the reason spirituality must exist if change is to be permanent.

Therefore, we need to differentiate between what comes from the Higher Self, the rational, and what comes from the lower self and the idealized self, the irrational. However trite and tedious this seems to be, it is an essential exercise. Do not under estimate your own confusion as to what is rational and what is irrational.

Also, detect your tendency to confuse the two, to want to believe that what you feel or want is actually rational when it actually is not.

The reverse is also to be detected. It is impossible to do this by yourself. You must have help. You are fighting your own shadow.

2) **Don't condemn, nor condone.**[39] When you have discovered a part of your lower self, you will be tempted to condemn it and yourself. Shame is a type of self-condemnation. Self-punishment, obviously, comes from self-condemnation. The more this condemnation exists, the more the real dissolution cannot occur. You must remember that you cannot cut out your lower self. You can only reeducate it. You can only help it find its way back, show it new and healthier ways of fulfillment.

You may also be tempted to condone it and yourself, finding excuses, rationalizations, back doors. The more this tendency exists, the more it will be impossible for you to dissolve it; you are perpetuating it. The practice of healthy detachment is needed here. The razor's edge, the narrow path in between the two must be found. This is sometimes called positive neutrality or proactive neutrality.

3) **Owning up**[40] **to it without acting it out.**[41] When a new aspect of the lower self is discovered we find ourselves afraid that, if we admit to it, we be more likely to act it out. We think that greater awareness of it will lead us to be more likely to perform it. In reality, the greater the awareness, the more there is consciousness of the harm that can occur if it is acted out. The less the desire to act it out. As long as we do not admit to it, we will act it out, consciously or unconsciously, while owning up to it will dissolve it.

4) **Determine your center of gravity.** This is a concept which I have developed through the years. Indeed, in order to

be effective in cleansing and renewal, one does not necessarily have to go deeper. Instead, one has to deal with where his center of gravity is in the present.

For example, if the idealized self is more damaging in its manifestation, going deeper into the lower self would be escaping the problem. Also, we may speak here in terms of layers. If a more superficial layer is doing the damage, it must be concentrated on, rather than dig deeper and escape.

The mistake of going deeper is more widespread than it appears. Take for instance sexual issues which may be seen as the deepest and the darkest. There may be a lot less reluctance to talk about them than to talk about issues of financial dishonesty which appear to be more mundane. Yet, it is those superficial issues which are the culprits.

A surprising number of misguided so-called New Age "guides" are guilty of this fallacy. This doesn't mean that other mundane psycho-logists, iatrists, therapists do not commit the same mistake. The mistake is committed by a combination of glamours coming from guide and guided and being in cahoots with one another.

Where is your center of gravity? Sit on it, no matter how unpleasant—the more unpleasant, the surer you are that you are hitting it—until you establish a valid connection between it and what makes you unhappy.

### Crisis

When the idealized selves are not faced and dissolved voluntarily, the individual will attract life situations, both inner and outer, that will attack and eventually destroy his idealized self. The destruction of an idealized self constitutes a crisis. During the crisis, the hidden material of the lower self is finally revealed in all of its harmful splendor.

There always are many warnings presaging a crisis. Elsewhere, I have explained that crisis is preceded by, first, opportunities, which then become challenges, and then explode into crisis.

If the opportunities or the challenges are heeded, the crisis is averted. However, unless one is involved in cleansing, the portents are not recognized and the crisis comes to pass.

✛✛✛

Hopefully this material has enabled you to realize the importance of detecting and dealing with the many parts of you. It is an unending, perpetual exercise. Dissolving the lower self and the idealized self is the primary task of the individual. It will take a long time, perhaps many lifetimes. Believe it or not, it becomes enjoyable. What once was unpleasant and against which you defended gets to the point where it is longed for. The exercise of detecting and dissolving harmfulness becomes a continuous prayer. Eventually, your entire life will he nothing but this prayer.

You will know that you are nearing the end of it when it becomes ferocious, when the three aspects come together in what is called "The Dweller on the Threshold." The dying lower self now presents its last battle, using everything it possibly can to pull you back into the old ways. If you pass this final test, you cross the threshold of initiation. You find the Angel of the Presence.

## Chapter 25

# *Plotinus and the Graphic Representations of the Self*

---

Plotinus' system helps us conceptualize in form the many selves:

1) At the center, **the One,** from which everything emanates. This may be considered the center of the Higher Self.

2) Out of the One, **the Nous, i.e., the intelligence,** corresponding to Plato's perfect forms. For instance, mathematical forms originate from the Nous. But this extends to the perfect table, the perfect dog, the perfect human. Thus, the perfect model for anything in our material world exists in the Nous. Conversely, anything in the material world is merely an imperfect image of what exists in the Nous. When in the Bible it says God created us in His own image, this is what is meant.

**1) and 2) constitute the Higher Self.**

3) **The soul.** In it is potentiality, that which needs to be developed in space and time. **This corresponds to the lower self.**

4) **The face,** turned outward or inward, for right and wrong reasons. This is the non-self, the seat of evil and of falsehood.

The above, therefore, can be represented in concentric

circles, as suggested by Plotinus and as demonstrated by Dr. Phillip Cary, Head of the Philosophy Program of Eastern College in St. Davids, Pennsylvania.

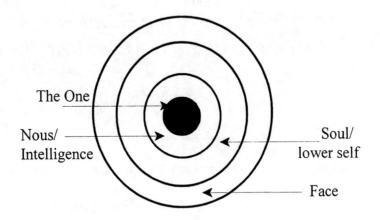

Some ignorant and misguided people believe that they have invented this representation. They should educate themselves before arrogating what is not theirs.

### New Representation of Plotinus' Concentric Circles

I prefer to see the Higher Self as infinite, not limited by any circles. Thus, the Higher Self is everywhere, all over. The one is in all.

The intelligible Nous, emanating from the Higher Self, which is everywhere, is already a descent from the One.

From it, the soul is created with its potentialities, its unresolved problems, offering a task to the individual who brings it in. We represent this as a defined circle, inside the Nous/intelligence.

The descent from that gives you the not self, the idealized self, or the grandiose self, the most confined place in us, the most isolated, the smallest, giving you the following representation:

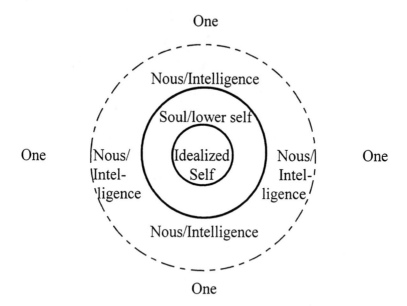

This makes a lot more sense. The idealized self no longer appears to be greater and more encompassing. Yet, in order for it to reach the Higher Self, it must go through, dissolve, integrate or assimilate the lower self/soul.

## Chapter 26
# *Instincts and the Distortion of Instinctual Needs*

---

Within each human being's soul is contained his task. If he remains unified with his instinctual needs without distorting them, his life task will be accomplished. If he distorts his instincts by overemphasizing one and minimizing or diminishing another, he will lose touch with himself, and his task will either be hidden from him or will manifest in a lopsided form.

And so it is with the other kingdoms of nature. If an animal or plant lives in its usual environment without interference, it will go through its normal and necessary life cycles. However, if it is in anyway hampered, its development and essence will be lopsided. The expression of its life will be distorted. Its task will not be accomplished.

An individual who allows his instincts to live through himself will discover and accomplish his task. Permitting these instincts expression is not in opposition to the development of consciousness, it encourages it. In a like manner, the development of consciousness will facilitate and promote the expression of the instincts, thereby giving the individual the protection and help it must have to take the necessary risks for growth.

There are five basic instincts. Of these, the first two

underlie all the others:
1) The Survival Instinct
2) The Instinct of Sexuality
3) The Instinct of the Herd
4) The Instinct of Self-Assertion
5) The Instinct of Enquiry

## The Survival Instinct

From the harmful point of view, fear activates this instinct. From the divine point of view, the search for immortality activates it. This is true on all levels of being: physical, emotional, mental, and spiritual.

From the physical point of view, we can very well understand how the Survival Instinct operates by itself without us having to interfere, encourage, or embellish it. However, if we now consider that it operates in the same way on the emotional level—protecting us from emotional pain—we can see that there is a vast difference between what constitutes emotional pain for the child within us (the lower self), and for the adult within us (the real self or the Higher Self). From the point of view of the child, it is necessary to make any and every rejection, frustration, defeat into a mortal emotional danger in the belief that having triggered the all powerful Survival Instinct, he will be rescued from experiencing the harmful occurrences. The result is overprotection, over concern with safety, inability to reach out and love, inability to allow pleasure.

After a cycle of self-protection, the person decides (albeit it unconsciously) not to operate under fear all of the time. It is, after all, very fearful to be there continuously. He becomes aggressive to compensate for the fear. By making others afraid of him, he creates in them the condition that heretofore existed in himself.

Therefore, we can talk about the following phases of a

person's life:

1) A formative period of life in which the sense of safety and security is lacking. Physically or emotionally violent or brutal parents are the usual cause here. However, the effect of a cataclysm or crisis (war, famine, disease, etc.) while still young can produce the same results. So, we have identified two states: the victim who is incurring the threat and who feels afraid, and the victimizer/aggressor who inflicts the state of fear and anxiety in others. Neither of these positions permits love or pleasure. Love and pleasure are considered a threat or a necessary evil by both the victim and the perpetrator.

2) Consequently, fear engenders self-protectiveness, overprotectiveness through the oft triggered Survival Instinct. The person lives under a cloud of fear and creates a protected cocoon for himself, shaping his life accordingly. In Hegelean Dialectics terms, this is the "slave."

3) Tiring of being the slave, or gradually having acquired power over the master, this person at some point or other switches and becomes the master, developing an aggressive persona, an idealized self that is steeped in omnipotence and invulnerability. This person lives according to certain codes of conduct, rules. Here, we have the rules of machismo, of being the greatest, of being invincible, the rules of dominance, aggression, etc. This person expects to be loved for all of these characteristics. His loving of others is seen as out of the question, as a dangerous, vulnerable position that can only be taken by others towards him. Extreme cases here are people who do not want to be touched in the act of love, or who will not open up to others while being "good listeners" to another's revelations and problems. This person is unable to take defeat, and although he boasts courage and honesty, he possesses neither. In his obsession always to win, he will have no courage to risk. In his obsession to never admit any defeat,

he will conceal any frustration, any rejection, and any set-back, thus being dishonest. He will be much more willing to commit suicide or hara-kiri than to admit his defeat.

Typologically, we have here the Will Type and the Stiff Types. Nevertheless, let's be flexible and admit the possibility of this happening with any of the other types. Indeed, we can imagine that even love can be used as a powerful, controlling weapon to justify one's omnipotence.

Here we see that the creation of this aggressive personality is a direct result of the over emphasis of the Survival Instinct. Therefore, the Survival Instinct is the creator of this personality type. That explains why it is difficult to:

A) Dissolve the personality type, which is the key to personal growth.

B) Take confrontation from someone who deflates this personality type, challenges it, or denounces it for its cowardly and devious ways. Since the Survival Instinct is the author of this personality type, it will equate confrontation or opposition with death, and therefore, will defend as if it were a matter of life and death. Here, one can see the reason for a great deal of defensiveness found in the dominant type.

The master-slave switch usually occurs during the crisis of puberty. However, it can occur in other life crises, such as a divorce, or a change of life conditions. A crisis is the shattering of the formation of a human type. It propels the person into the experience of its opposite.

One can also see that the underlying fear experienced as the slave and the aggressive boastfulness of the master are mutually antagonistic. The aggressiveness is in reaction, contradistinction, compensation, and negation of the fear experienced by the slave/victim.

At the same time, fear is the author of the over aggressiveness of the master/perpetrator. If it were not for the fear of the victim, the aggressiveness of the perpetrator would have no reason for existing. Therefore, the aggressiveness of the master will see to it that there will always be frightful and threatening issues in life to justify the aggressive overreaction.

Conversely, from the fear point of view, the fear will see to it that there exists an aggressive and irrational "hammer" outside of it so that it can justify its position as the anvil, continuously hardening itself in protection (Survival).

Throughout the cycle thus described one thing is missing: the Instinct of Sexuality/Pleasure. This person has missed out in a very important area of his life: love, pleasure, beauty, perhaps even faith. There are big gaps in his experience and great needs in a state of infancy that remain not fulfilled.

Here, one can see that the swinging of the pendulum does not necessarily guarantee unification and healing. One can swing with the pendulum and still, to a great extent, never allow oneself to experience "the other side," which in this case, happens to be sex, love, beauty, faith and pleasure supreme. The other side is then experienced as a necessary and temporary evil, endured while waiting to go back to the "good" or "right" side. Or, after a crisis, the other side is experienced as an ever present inferno in which the individual is stuck.

### The Instinct of Sexuality, Pleasure Supreme

Nothing is ever created without the experience of pleasure. The accomplishment of one's task is always a result of pleasure, of longing, of loving, and of the deep resulting satisfaction and bliss. Plato calls this longing Eros.

Therefore, in reality, the Instinct of Sexuality is much broader and deeper in scope than is traditionally believed. It is not merely two pelvises coming together and creating the shell that holds the human spirit. Sexuality goes way beyond that, representing equal and opposite forces coming together, longing for each other, and in the satisfaction and the consummation of their longing for one another, they create.

Any act of creation can be an opportunity to verify the truth of this. It holds true whether you consider the creation of an idea, of a feeling, of a work of art, of a baby, of a building, or of a movement. Every person at birth expects a total, unconditional and infinite climate of love, beauty, pleasure, bliss. Once again, Plato knows this as he describes Eros in his *Symposium.*

Here, we must each consider our own inner split; the mature part versus the immature part. The mature part of us realizes that in this, the sensible world, life is a matter of accepting imperfection and striving for the perfect state of bliss.

This striving for perfection is a human condition that is well described by Aristotle. The relative longs for the Absolute. The sensible longs for the intelligible. Why does philosophy see a contradiction between Plato and Aristotle? Can we just simply realize that Plato focused on the Absolute, the intelligible, while Aristotle focused on the relative and the sensible, trying to reach the Absolute and the intelligible? Why is it so difficult to realize that the two beautifully blend, fuse, and complement one another, separated only by the limits of terminology in human language?

This dualistic view in philosophers reveals their unwillingness to resolve their Mother/Father Split. Generically, but not necessarily personally, Aristotle represents the principle of Mother/Matter, while Plato represents Father/Mind. Unless you resolve your Mother/Father Split—albeit to some extent—you will neither be able to see, nor want to see the reconciliation of the two trains of thought. The irreconcilable split is in the eye of the beholder, who would rather revel in it, glorify and intellectualize it rather than resolve it.

It is our task—is it not?—to blend all goodness, to include, not exclude, to resolve, not create problems.

The life task of accepting imperfection while striving for perfection, although seemingly contradictory, is the only thing we have to do. What else is there to do?

This requires maturity, wisdom, and an expanded consciousness. Our immature parts (those areas where consciousness is not as developed) demand to be satisfied now, to have unconditional love from everyone now. For example, there will be a demand that mother and father (or mother and father substitutes) unconditionally, totally, and exclusively love them. However, there is also going to be a demand that they love each other in the same manner, which is an impossibility.

All of this is not reality and creates frustration. With the frustration, there will be an overemphasis of the search for pleasure supreme, and thus an abuse of the Instinct of Sexuality. Here we have the following sequence:

1) The individual needs love, pleasure, bliss and beauty.

2) Lack of fulfillment of this need creates frustration which is regarded as defeat, rejection.

3) The feeling of defeat engenders an aggressive, hedonistic demand for satisfaction at all costs. Inordinate risks are taken for the sake of pleasure and love. This manifests in the drunken sailor, in epicurism, in hedonism.

4) At some point, it becomes clear that the demands one made in number 3) above will not be satisfied unless he complies to certain rules of conduct in order to be lovable. Here, the key word is **comply**:

- The person capitulates to what is expected of him.
- He becomes a martyr for the sake of love.
- He espouses the theory of "in order to be loved, one has to be weak."
- He sees principles as being the enemy of love.

- He also sees self-assertion as the enemy of love.
- His compliance for the sake of love and for the sake of pleasure has become the enemy of the demand that lies underneath.
- At the same time, the demand underneath, irrational as it is, justifies the compliance on top. If the demand underneath were not irrational there would be no reason to comply.
- Thus, the demand underneath has to be kept irrational, violent, and childish in order to justify the overcompensation for the glorious compliance and victimization.
- He is in quite a dilemma.

Once again the switch between the demand for satisfaction, and the submission in order to get satisfaction occurs at a time of crisis, usually at puberty. The pampered little girl becomes the dutiful wife. Before puberty she had all her whims fulfilled by her parents. After marriage she has to comply to her husband in order for him to provide what her parents did.

Here again, there is a great gap in one's life: there is no room left for contribution to society or humanity. The joy of order, concrete knowledge and good will is completely lacking. These aspects are seen as enemies, not as friends. And therefore, will tend to be totally disregarded in the person's life. These "will" aspects and attributes, these "hard" matters are seen as a necessary evil to put up with, while the demand and the search for childish pleasure supreme goes on.

Quite a bit can be explained by this sequence:

- The business man, the engineer, the person who has developed the "hard" part of life considers this love stuff as a necessary and messy inconvenience which must be put up with or purchased. He uses the Survival Instinct, with

which he is familiar, to obtain for himself the satisfaction
of the Sexuality Instinct, where he is still an infant.
- Conversely, the painter, the artist, the psychotherapist, or
  the priest considers money, concrete science and order as
  necessary evils to be endured. They become terrible record
  keepers. They do not want to do their paper work, nor do
  they want to deal with financial matters.

Here is a chart in which this can be easily followed:

| I | II | III | IV |
|---|---|---|---|
| Instinct | Triggering Condition | First Level Distortion | Second Level Distortion |
| Survival | Danger | Fear; self-protection | Power hunger, omnipotence; overt tyranny; dominance lovelessness |
| Sexuality | Deprivation of pleasure | Demand; abject need | Love hunger; compliance; covert oppression; powerlessness |

The first and second level distortions are blocks to a
person's task. They are false answers. They do not work. In
spite of the fact that they do not work, the person will
stubbornly maintain them and insist on acting in accordance to
their rules over and over again.

In fact, the less they work, the more the individual will feel
compelled to reinforce them until a crisis comes and
completely destroys them. The destruction of distortion is
indeed the first task. No task can be discovered unless it is

uncovered. The more one's distortions are dissolved, the more the real task of the individual will be liberated, and therefore, revealed.

What do you believe is your task? How have you glamourized yourself in your particular pseudo-solution? What are your pet peeves? What are your pet demands? What do you believe must be over anything else? What are some of the conclusions that you refuse to let go of? What are some of the "truths" that you refuse to give up? What are the deepest of your secrets? You do not have to tell them to anybody else but yourself. However, at least have the honesty of being forthright with yourself. List your secrets and see if you can make a connection between them and those other parts that you are so proud of, What do you see?

### *Risk*

In order to study our attitudes concerning risk, let's go through the distortion of the Survival Instinct again, perhaps a little differently this time, going deeper.

1) The main focus in this individual's life is on safety and security with great dread of the unknown and untried. Natural lightness, ease and balance are lacking, so the Survival Instinct is distorted.

2) Consequently, the legitimate need for love and pleasure is repressed, feared, denigrated.

3) As the need for love and pleasure is repressed and denied it gets more and more intense and rebellious.

4) The individual is now torn between need for safety (the superior function), and need for pleasure and love (the inferior function), both of which are legitimate.

5) He thinks that to obtain pleasure he must risk, he must be adventurous, must be brave.

6) However, this negates the main focus of his Survival Instinct which demands safety at all costs.

7) He is now demanding both safety and pleasure without risking, which is impossible.

8) He sinks into harmfulness, depression, victimization, self-destructiveness, followed by addictions.

If you take this in reverse and apply it to your life by asking yourself "why am I depressed," or "why am I addicted," and follow it through, you will find at its source the frustration of your instincts. It is impossible to get out of depression by negating the fact that you must be unfulfilled somewhere. You can and will rise from depression by accepting that you are unfulfilled somewhere. Anything short of pleasure supreme constitutes lack of fulfillment. Anything less than the total sense of safety and security is also lack of fulfillment.

You cannot obtain anything without risking and without commitment. Half of a commitment is no commitment. A task done badly is a task not done. You cannot cheat life by making deals and expect to be fulfilled; there are no deals.

Check out your:

- Desire to compromise, not to risk, yet demanding to be fulfilled.
- Unwillingness to admit that you are unfulfilled in particular areas of your life from fear that you will then have to take risks or commit yourself.
- Complaints that, having not committed yourself totally and having consequently failed, your failure (rejection, set back, confrontation, criticism) is so unbearable that:

   1) You will push your aggression even further than before, or

   2) You will sink into a false renunciation—serenity, a euphemism for detachment.

All of this is sure to do one thing: totally negate the

possibility of love and pleasure supreme.

Consequently:

- All the Love Rays are negated. There will be no beauty, no faith, no love, no wisdom, no patience, no pleasure, no bliss, no sweetness, no fragrance, no music, no tasting, etc. Your soul will be parched and dry.
- You will miss out on essential life experiences constituting your seed plan.

It is like removing the flowers from a tree because they smell good, give pleasure and produce wasteful fruit. The damage is considerable. Your Higher Self will not put up with this. Its disagreement, and the action it will take against you, is very serious. It has all kinds of options. Rest assured that they will be exercised, one way or another.

### *Distortion of the Sex Instinct*

Let's also dig deeper into distortion of the Sexuality Instinct.

1) The main focus in this individual's life is on pleasure, with a great fear of lack. Therefore, the natural Sex/Love Instinct is overdone and distorted.

2) Consequently, the Survival Instinct—need for safety—is repressed. Foolish risks are taken for the sake of pleasure and love.

3) The suppressed Survival Instinct seeks safety by complying. This way, by becoming a slave, by being taken care of, it is hoped that both pleasure and safety are to be found.

4) Safety is sought **because** I am weak, compliant and helpless. "You will protect me because I am weak; so I'll compromise."

5) The glorious risk of sacrifice is glamourized.

6) Masochism, inability to assert, is born.

The consequences are:

- True danger sets in. The soul atrophies and is unable to be creative, to take initiative.
- Perpetual anxiety and depression.

When distortion of one instinct exists it engenders the others. Therefore, we all must have all of these. And discovering one is a good start.

However, you have to discover the others if you are to know yourself.

Experience is the next step, followed by a deep need for fulfillment, for abandonment of those false answers.

You may experience the coexistence of both distortions, tearing you into two equal and opposite vicious circles.

Don't escape. Stay with it and take it to the source. Only then can you resolve the problem.

If one distortion is not obvious or appears to be weak, it does not mean that it is weak or absent. It may mean quite the opposite—that, being hidden, it is stronger.

Since the creation of one engenders the other, the healing of one may instantly remove the other. It will certainly do that in the long run.

However, attacking **both** at the same time will yield the best results. They really are one and the same problem.

# Section VIII

# Inferior Functions

## Chapter 27

# *Inferior Functions*[42]

It is essential that we realize the difficulty in predicting an inferior function. Indeed, any Ray can constitute the inferior function of another Ray, because on the soul level can be found all other Rays. The most accurate conclusions, of course, will result from the study of a specific individual and the particular split pertinent to him or her. Generally speaking, this split is between mother and father, but it can be found in other fundamental conflicts in a person's life, as in parents versus society, and so forth. Nevertheless, as a general rule we can find antithesis to each personality type. This is what we shall attempt to do below.

## *Fundamental Split*

One can say generally that there is a fundamental split between the Will Rays (I, III, V and VII) and the Love Rays (II, IV and VI). Our society has erroneously identified the Will Rays with the masculine and the Love Rays with the feminine. This is not at all reality, since the self-actualized person has all of the Rays harmoniously developed. In western societies, the Will Rays and the Love Rays alternate as a dominant function: as the one becomes the dominant function, the other (being its opposite) becomes the inferior function.

It would be a very useful exercise for the reader to investigate to what extent does he adhere to these collective freezes/images about love and will, or to what extent has he rebelled against them, creating their opposites within himself? What then have been the consequences of these distortions?

### Inferior Functions
### *Inferior Function of Ray I: Will*

Generally speaking, the Will Type hides a deep disconnection. The upper part of the body is disconnected from the lower. This fundamental split creates deep propensities that are very reminiscent of Ray VI, the Intuitive. As a rule, one can say that the gate to the inferior function of the Will Type is the disconnection of the Intuitive, Sixth Ray Type. Once the bullish onslaught of the will has been exhausted the Will Type disintegrates, collapses and even becomes compliant in his despair. He will then exhibit characteristics of Ray VI. If you look up the description of the harmful aspects of the Sixth Ray in this book you will have a very good picture of what the Will Type becomes in times of crisis or in times of switching from one function to the next.

Once this phase of disconnection has been worked through, the true inferior function of the Will Type is revealed —Ray II, Love and Wisdom. Look at this sequence in operation: Ray I's connection to the Love Rays is made through Ray VI. Ray I is connected to Ray VI much more strongly that to Ray IV or to Ray II. Through the gate of Ray VI, Ray I finally allows in his system the energies of the Love Rays (IV and then II). Can you see the connection between the Will of the First Ray and the devotion of the Sixth Ray? Can you see the connection between the devotion of the Sixth Ray and the Love of the Second Ray? This is then the route that the First Ray takes when in reintegration.

### *Inferior Function of Ray II: Love/Wisdom*
When all of the glamourized and overemphasized

goodness of the Love Type is spent, what usually emerges is a ferocious onslaught of will. This can be clearly seen in Love Type wives who heretofore had exhibited compliant tendencies but who through divorce develop militancy, control, aggression leading to hostility, and a tremendous drive.

Another possibility, less likely than the one we have just considered, is that the Second Ray Type will reveal a Stiff structure (Rays V and VII). The over flexibility and malleability (and occasionally disconnection, since the Second Ray is so very much associated with the Sixth) heretofore exhibited by a Second Ray person, is replaced by a tremendous attention to detail, by a sense of blind justice leading to cruelty, by a meticulous sense of impeccable order. Notice, however, that in either case the Second Ray inferior function will be represented by a Will Ray, usually a First Ray reaction, but it could also be another of the "Will Rays" as in V or VII.

Another reaction of the Second Ray in its inferior function is to adopt the characteristics of the Third Ray. To best illustrate this example, let's consider a marriage of long standing. A Ray I man marries a Ray II woman. In the beginning of the marriage she is self-effacing and compliant, demonstrating economy of effort and movement. As the marriage progresses, and particularly if the marriage goes beyond menopause, she will start exhibiting the control mechanisms to be found in the androgynous mother of the Third Ray, even developing the inflated bottom features that are characteristic of it. The switch—in a sense rebellion—is not allowed to go above the waist. She now controls the situation with her pelvis.

Of course, he also switches, and as we have seen, acquires features of disconnection. However, in a long standing marriage there is a mutual pact which maintains the illusion that change has not actually occurred. The result is that the male still believes that he is in control but actually is not; the female is in control. You will often find in these households a terrifying, though toothless, bark coming from the husband. The woman will even actually say that in so many words: "Let him rant and rave; he will calm down in a little while and then we can do whatever we want." We have here the consequence of a deep change that has not been acknowledged and accepted on the surface.

## *Inferior Function of Ray III:*
### *Active Intelligence and Adaptability*

Amazingly enough, we find that the inferior function of both men and women of this Type is a return to the unbridled experience of two basic instincts—Survival and Sex. Heretofore, they had concentrated on the development of the mind at the expense of these instincts. Their adaptability was focused on subjugating themselves to what was "needed" in their lives or in society. Now, in their inferior function, the "oughts" are abandoned and instincts so long repressed can emerge—and wreck havoc in their lives. The Professor in "Blue Angel" is an excellent example of this.

The Professor was a man who had completely given himself to the mental world of teaching, of reason, of thinking, thus denying his sexuality. All of a sudden he finds himself hopelessly in love with a floozy and behaving like a lovesick, horny, petulant teenager. The explosion of his basic instincts when the inferior function is finally released is an attempt at reconnection with nature. However, since nature had been so long repressed, it has very little consciousness.

This is explains why these people are capable of totally uncharacteristic acts of childishness and acting out merely for the sake of pleasure or for personal possession when the inferior function manifests. Have you ever asked yourself

"Whatever happened to my old teachers or professors in my university?" You will find an amazing percentage of them trying to recapture their adolescence by taking up with a graduate student. We find here the emergence of Rays IV, V and VII characterizing the inferior function of Ray III.

The heavy emphasis on adaptability found in the Catholic Church has the same results. At some point, the priest or nun who has been subjected to such incredible tour de forces, trying to adapt (Ray III), finally rebels and we have the plethora of cases of child molestation and sexual acting out that we have seen in recent years.

There is also the great number of clergy leaving the celibate church and getting married and raising a family. This is a much more honest and direct way of dealing with the emergence of the inferior function. Those clerics who choose to stay in the church continue their fruitless battle against nature. However, that energy must eventually be expressed. When it is, their religious vows are broken either in pederasty, whoring, homosexual promiscuity, or in the formation of committed "arrangements."

The Catholic Church, in response to this problem, is now requiring applicants to priesthood to undergo extensive psychological tests in an attempt to find out which are the ones who will more likely develop the "undesirable" traits of sexuality. Actually, this cannot and will not work because the mere forcing of instincts into a celibate regimen will eventually create distortions.

### Inferior Function of Ray IV:
### Harmony Through Conflict

The Ray IV holding pattern and the tendency to be explosive will have the following inferior function. Ray IV will all of a sudden become obsessed with economy of effort and energy (Ray II). The generous, expansive quality of Ray IV will be totally reversed into self-protective, almost avaricious behaviour.

A good example of this is to be found in the dichotomy between bulimia and anorexia nervosa. The overemphasis on eating and exuberant expression to be found in bulimia gives way to the deficiency and the incapacity to take in food in anorexia nervosa. In many cases both coexist, creating what psychologists nowadays call manic depressive. It would be very helpful if they would begin thinking of this method as an attempt by nature to reestablish its balance in the individual expression.

### *Inferior Function of Rays V and VII: Concrete Knowledge and Science; Order, Ceremony, Good Habits and Magic*

These rays are both representatives of a Stiff function. The common denominator between all of the subtypes in this category is a focus on the sensible world. Consequently, the inferior function will be represented by the Sixth Ray, the Ray that disconnects from the sensible world and focuses on inner levels. The Stiff Types (Rays V and VII) who go through a crisis will collapse into a "Ray VI break." This means that their Sixth Ray will come through very powerfully. Their lives will be disrupted. All of the safety heretofore found in material success or in sexual attractiveness will vanish and the person will suffer an extraordinary crisis of identity. In short the worst aspects of the Sixth Ray will manifest in a crisis undergone by the Fifth and the Seventh Rays.

It is no surprise that the worst aspects of the inferior function show up first; it is a general rule. Indeed, whenever the expression of faculties has been impeded, harmfulness accumulates at the obstruction similarly to a dammed up river. When the dam is finally broken it is the impurities that first violently invade the established order of things and disrupt it or destroy it. Eventually, equilibrium is reached and the limpid flow of the river is reestablished.

As this applies specifically to Rays V and VII, it means that they will have to start taking into consideration matters that pertain to the inner levels such as faith, trust, a philosophy of life, or a religion.

We can find many examples of this in the collapse of people who are outwardly successful and who, through a crisis, find religion. The initial success of the outer level is usually accompanied by a sense of ruthlessness and a lack of principles. The crisis reveals the inner life and after a time of suffering and of loss of identity, the person in question "sees the light," i.e., becomes very much aware of the importance of ethics, of religion, of the existence of God. The former addiction to outer level values diminishes and/or disappears.

The result of this is a peculiar inability of people in this category to recover their initial success in the outer world. If one goes to an AA meeting one will hear this story repeated many times: the drive for success drove them to drink. During those increasingly besotted years they were Stiffs, being very much aware of outer level realities and creating for themselves a yuppy life. The crisis came, destroying everything. They stopped drinking, collapsed into a loss of identity and material possessions. They managed to have a subsistence level of living, but never quite recovered the success they had in the outer world. They have a new found faith in a Higher Power.

An excellent example of this is the Prophet Mohammad. Before Mohammad's contact with the Archangel Gabriel he was a successful businessman who managed a camel trade with his wife, Khadija. In fact, there is every reason to believe that he married her for her money and position. We have here the life of a yuppy, concerned primarily with his outer level success. All of a sudden, Mohammad began to rapidly sink into heavy drinking and irrational behaviour. He lost his reputation very quickly. One day, as he was taking refuge in a cave he heard the voice of the Archangel Gabriel who ordered him to write. What he wrote was the Koran.

It was impossible for Mohammad to recover his reputation in his hometown. He left with his wife and his best friend, Abu Bakr, and fled to the city of Mecca. The year 622, called the Year of the Flight, marks the first year in the Moslem calendar. Mohammad brought about a religious movement which served the purpose of destroying the old and obsolete forms of two empires, the Byzantine and the Persian. His success in propagating the Moslem religion in Mecca and his ability to bring together all of the Arab tribes under one leadership, thus launching the Arab conquest, is proof positive that his newly found idealism and devotion, Ray VI, through his crisis, actually enhanced his outer level skills (Rays V and VII) which he had developed previously as a businessman and a trader.

If a person is on a program of cleansing and renewal, there is no reason why the emergence of his inferior function will not actually enhance—not destroy—the assets of his dominant function. Also, the person on such a program can avoid or minimize the crisis, although examples of this are very few and far between. Sometimes, cleansing merely accelerates the emergence of the crisis. Granted, it is a lot more easily handled when one is on a program of cleansing and renewal, still the crisis must represent a temporary loss and must take the person through the type of pain in which he will lose his identity. In fact, the loss of identity constitutes a very necessary death without which there is no rebirth.

There are some cases of people who get religion through crisis only quickly to forget about it and go back to their merry old ways. However, a closer study of these people reveals that they never are the same again. The "return" to the old ways is really a holding onto a shattered image. The holding onto it makes them more fanatical, more rigid, less effective, more self-protected, and eventually more paranoid. It is only a matter of time for a full blown crisis to come in and deal the final blow to the guards.

One of the most revelatory signs of an impending crisis is the fanatical holding onto a particular trait or to a particular way of life. The more tightly one holds onto something, the closer one is to its death. A good example of this is Richard Nixon.

Richard Nixon in his early political career developed the tough-minded ethical aggressive image. It was valid in the beginning. A lot was accomplished through this as demonstrated in his book "Six Crises." However, by the end of the fifties this had become much too tight and too fanatical. If one remembers, for example, his kitchen debate with Khrushchev, one will see how rigid he was and how his attitude was producing diminishing results. By 1960, when he ran against Kennedy, his tightness, heaviness and over confidence lost him the election, even though he himself was convinced that he was going to win. In 1962 he lost the California election for governor which precipitated a personal crisis. He was very antagonistic to the press, completely alienating just about everybody in political life, and disappeared from the political scene, i.e., lost his identity.

My hunch is that he then went through some kind of cleansing. The new Nixon that emerged from this in the late sixties was much more flexible, much more adaptable, and much less adversarial. This new Nixon won him the 1968 election and the 1972 election.

However, the old form was not completely destroyed. It was still there very powerfully, except that it had gone under ground, it had hidden.

Whatever cleansing Nixon underwent was not thorough enough, not deep enough. It merely created an additional facade, put on the previous one.

It is the old facade reemerged that created Watergate. The old stiffness and heaviness came galloping back. The Watergate scandal is the result of Nixon's repressed fanaticism and heaviness. He **had** to win, and so he had to illegally break into the headquarters of the Democrats to see what they were doing in order to insure victory.

The irony of the situation is that his victory was cinched before the Watergate break in. Yet he had to make doubly, absolutely, completely sure. This type of insistence, this type of tightness, this type of demand is usually the indication of the breakdown of a form of life or a dominant function and the emergence of a new one. Nixon was never able to completely integrate his new function. To a large extent he was a Stiff, he was a V and VII with a lot of I. And he could not integrate the incoming Ray VI and Ray II energies. Finally, in his old age, was he able to do this. For those of us who saw him on television mourning his wife Pat with his uncontrollable sobbing, it was clear that the old tough inquisitor was finally dead. In the waning of his life, the full blown loving and giving person had emerged.

### Inferior Function of Ray VI: Idealism and Devotion

The renewal of a hippy into a yuppy epitomizes the emergence of Rays V and VII into the consciousness of Ray VI. The Ray VI hippy who in the late sixties and seventies worshiped poverty, rebellion, nature and abhorred earning money and conforming to conventions, undergoes a powerful switch in the eighties. All of a sudden he wants to be successful, he wants to make money, he wants to have a family, he wants to have a house and wants to be concerned with all of the values that he had heretofore denigrated. In essence, we have witnessed an entire generation undergoing that switch when passing from the seventies into the eighties.

A perfect example of this is a very well known leader of the sixties who participated in a top leadership position to the 1968 Chicago events. This man appeared in my office in 1980 saying "I want to make money. I want to work hard. I want to get married. I want to have kids, and I want to own a house. I know that I am nearly 45, yet I would like to do all of this, and I would like your help. I have heard that you epitomize the blending of the sensible world with New Age philosophy in terms of career success. That's why I am seeking your help." He also told me his name. Although I knew who this person was, he was so different from what I imagined him to be that I could not make the connection. Only when he left my office and was sighted by a colleague of mine did his identity sink in. My colleague said "That was ____."

However, my new student could not sustain the rigor required in this turn around period. He felt that his era had come to an end and that he had to change, but he did not want to put in the work required to do it. After a few lessons he disappeared and I never saw him again.

Another example of a switch of this sort is the passage from teenage years to maturity. Teenagers, since they are in a period of transition from childhood to adulthood, have the tendency to lose their identity, thereby exhibiting a lot of Ray VI characteristics. They do not know what they want to do, they do not connect with their new bodies. They also have a great deal of psychic and esoteric experiences. A lot of us have had those experiences, which are a characteristic of the destruction of the old type form.

The passage into teenage years and on into adulthood requires an apprehension of the sensible world, as in getting a job, dealing with sexuality, handling responsibility on the outer level. Adult responsibilities tend to develop Ray V and VII characteristics in everyone. So, for the teenager, or for the hippy (who after all worships the teenager and tries to be like him), Ray VI is a dominant function, and Rays V and VII are the inferior functions, powerfully trying to emerge into that person's consciousness. Reaching adulthood brings about conditions that are reminiscent of Rays V and VII in somewhat of a universal fashion.

A famous example of this is obviously that of Rimbaud, whom we discuss in the chapter on "The Switch at Puberty and Menopause." His abandonment of Ray VI poetry and his embracing of business at age 19 constitute the emergence of Rays V and VII and the destruction of Ray VI and perhaps Ray II that were his dominant functions in childhood.

Generally speaking, if you want to know what your inferior function is, consult these chapters, consider the Rays that we have indicated to be your possible inferior function, and then consult the descriptions of these Rays. This will give you an accurate picture of what you will look like when you go through a crisis. During the crisis you will have the harmful traits of the Rays. Hopefully, past the crisis, you will integrate the divine traits of the Rays with the divine traits of the Rays that you already have. However, this requires cleansing, cleansing that you cannot do on your own, cleansing for which you need a good mirror and a lot of help.

## Chapter 28
# The Switch at Puberty
# and Menopause[43]

In 1975, I gave an assignment to members of a career class that I led. I asked them to define the area of their strongest interest from birth to age 10, and then to write about the influence of this subject on their lives. Likewise, if they liked something that was not taught at school, that subject was to be the focus of their essay. I had them take their lives in five year blocks of time, 0 to 5, 6 to 10, 11 to 15, etc., writing a few paragraphs about each time span. They were not to change subjects, even though their interest in the original subject may have faded, but to trace the evolution of their strongest interest in their lives at age 0-10.

When the essays were read and compared, sixteen of the eighteen participants showed a distinct switch of interests at the time of puberty. It was as if at puberty the forces of sexuality and adulthood came in, energized new and unexpected interests, and toppled the old and overemphasized ones. This was reminiscent to me of Jung's similar switch at "menopause," or around 45 to 55.

I was, of course, fascinated by this discovery and started to study it in individuals to whom I was a teacher, as well as in historical celebrities. First of all, I wrote my own autobiography in the same vein, focusing on my favourite childhood subject: mathematics, carrying it through the age of thirty-five.

### *My Own Personal Example*

**From 0 to 5:** I was good in math. I remember learning to count at a very early age. I would number the tiles in the kitchen and be complimented by my grandmother on how smart I was. With my facility with numbers, I used to impress my little girlfriend who lived downstairs. I felt a sense of superiority over other kids because I was able to do this, and I would think and sometimes say, "I can't understand why he's so dumb."

My ability was immediately recognized by my teachers, from whom I received immense amounts of praise and privileges. I remember the feel of arithmetic class as being far more glowing than any other class. As a result, I began to neglect other subjects; a certain amount of contempt existed for what did not have the exactness of numbers. Huge conceit and self-worth were attached to this subject and I was, without trying very hard, the best arithmetic student in my class.

**At age 10:** I was asked by the teacher of a higher class to demonstrate to older students how simple and easy it was to understand mathematics.

Since math was so easy for me, I decided about age 10 that I did not have to concentrate on it. Without studying, I was able to wing it and pass with brilliant marks. It was accepted by everyone, including myself, that I would be an excellent mathematician and that I would have a career as an engineer. I had already resolved to be a buildings engineer. I knew which college I would attend and what my life was going to be like.

**Around age 14 or 15:** Even my interest in girls was influenced by my mathematical proficiency. I believed that it was easier to be liked by girls **because** I was excellent in mathematics. Much to my surprise, not to mention my shame, my marks at the end of this period were no longer at the uppermost. Rather than being the undisputed number one, I began to be one of the best. Some of my friends, who were originally considered dumb, but, who unlike me, had spent many hours poring over the math books, were catching up with me.

**From 16 to 20:** My grades and my interest dwindled. However, I had to continue pretending to be interested, since everyone expected a great mathematical career from me. As I progressed through adolescence I was drawn more and more to the humanities. My pull towards sex and romantic involvements grew in inverse proportion to my pull towards math. I finally received an early degree in math, after which I experienced a great feeling of relief—relief from not having to do math or exact sciences any more. I felt that now I had graduated I had proved to the world that I had "made it" in mathematics, and, having made it, I no longer had to stay in the field of exact sciences.

**From 21 to 25:** Good-bye math, and hello to a brand new area where human relations were a lot more important and where my languages could be used—business. I entered the business world, not having prepared for it or studied it, but through the back door, as it were. Consequently, my first years in the field were difficult and very tedious. Mathematics was of almost no use to me then. The very limited way in which I could use numbers did not hold a candle to the extraordinary amount of "numbers" knowledge I had amassed in the previous period in my life. I could not accept this, and I insisted on looking at business transactions from the point of view of exactness and calculation.

**From 26 to 30:** I began to realize that I was uselessly trying to live up to others' expectations of me, expectations that I had heartily and completely accepted. I finally understood that I much preferred human relations to science. Consequently, success in business immediately ensued and at the end of that period, I enjoyed my work and had a responsible and challenging business position.

**From 31 to 35:** I begin to experience sort of a boredom in my business. I had proved that I could meet the challenges, that I could be successful. However, "Now what?" and "So what?" is how I began to feel.

As you can see from my own case history, there are two functions at play here. Let's call them **Function A** and **Function B**. If we call Function A what manifests pre-puberty, and Function B what manifests post-puberty, the following diagram describes the general evolution of a human being's professional interests.

| *Birth* | *Puberty* | *Menopause* |
|---------|-----------|-------------|
| Function A | | Function A |
| ――――――――――→ | Function B | ――――――――――→ |
| | ―――――――――→ | |
| 0 | 12-18 | 45-55 |

Therefore, the pre-pubescent tendency is reversed to its opposite at puberty. At menopause, the pre-pubescent tendency returns. Many expressions illustrate this, such as in the comparison of older people to children, the second youth, coming of age, etc.

To be more specific, this reversal is an attempt at integration. What gets toppled are the aspects that have been overemphasized, that have been used and abused for motives such as pleasing authorities, self-aggrandizement, greed, etc. These attitudes and belief systems take the person **away** from the interest itself. Thus, the interest in the subject and the developed skill are doomed to fail. Pleasure, which used to be associated with the subject itself, dissociates from it and becomes attached to the distorted motive.

Now that you have read this far, write your own autobiography, focusing solely on your favourite interest or subject as a child before age ten, and describe your attitude toward it until the present time. Then complete the following two steps.

1) Detect the wrong motives experienced before puberty. Your focus on this favourite subject was for approval seeking, or for love, or for the sake of getting something in some other area; thus, you lost your center as described earlier. (Of course, this is all unconscious.) In order to cleanse the nature of your interest you must clearly define the wrong motives you have attached to it. Through the cleansing you are doing here they will be gradually discovered. In the beginning you may not even be aware of any wrong motives and you may find yourself strongly guarding against the mere suggestion that there might be such things attached to this passionate interest you had; yet you find yourself unable to explain its disappearance. Keep an open mind to the fact that nothing ever disappears unless it is repressed by us and nothing is repressed by us unless it is associated with something harmful, or something erroneous.

2) The second step is to legitimize these interests. They lost their legitimacy through association with the harmful or with what was erroneous. You may experience this as a peculiar sense of shame associated with some of these prepubescent interests; you may not even want to talk about them. Look for the shame and beneath it the guilt, both of which prevent you from allowing these natural interests to burst out into your life and enrich it. Come to the point where you can naturally claim the legitimacy of these interests.

Notice the emphasis on the words "naturally claim" as opposed to "unnaturally claim". We are not here advocating

the unnatural cover ups of affirmation, or of those phony
practices that are called "assertiveness training" which are
nothing else but the unnatural forcing of one's dishonesty on
the Universe. Keep it natural, keep it simple; if you are not
ready, do not do it yet, wait until you have cleared enough
brush for the sun to shine upon your repressed childhood
interests and allow them to grow once again.

### *Examples of the Switch at Puberty and Menopause*

#### *Grandma Moses*

Grandma Moses is a great American painter of the
twentieth century. You may have heard that she started
painting at the age of 70, became very famous, and died at the
age of 101. Actually, she started painting at age 57. Her early
attempts are dated 1918 and 1920, and she describes one of
them which is called, *The Fireboard*:

> One time I was papering the parlor, and I ran short of
> paper for the fireboard. So I took a piece of paper and
> pasted it over the board, and I painted it a solid color
> first, then I painted two large trees on each side of it,
> like butternut trees. And back in it I did a little scene
> of a lake and painted it a yellow color, really bright, as
> though you were looking off into the sun light. In the
> front, to fill in that space, I brought in big bushes. I
> daubed it all on with the brush I painted the floor with.
> It run on three or four years, and we re-papered the
> parlor and papered over the picture. When we
> re-papered the room again a few years ago, we took
> the paper off the fireboard, but the colors had faded

somewhat. That was my first large picture.[1]

Notice the almost spontaneity way in which she creates her first work of art. It is as if an inexplicable force came in through her and used whatever material was at hand—"the brush I painted the floor with" and "the paper over the fireboard." Clearly the talent was latent and was suddenly energized. It was "born" at age 57, not at age 70. However, being aware of the equally important switch at puberty, I researched what she did when she was a little girl, and we find that:

> . . . my father would get me and my brothers white paper by the sheet, it was used for newspapers. He liked to see us draw pictures, it was a penny a sheet and it lasted longer than candy. My oldest brother loved to draw steam engines, the next brother went in for animals, but as for myself I had to have pictures and the gayer the better. I would draw the picture, then color it with grape juice or berries, anything that was red and pretty in my way of thinking.[2]

See here the unmistakable sensate tendencies, berries, grape juice, a sheet that lasted longer than candy. Unlike her brothers, who drew only steam engines or animals, she drew "pictures," not individual, exclusive representations of one thing or one being, but all-inclusive representations of her reality.

She describes her life to age 10 as follows:

---

[1] Otto Kallir, *Grandma Moses,* Harry N. Abrams, Inc., 1973. Distributed by New American Library. Grandma Moses words, 18.

[2] Ibid., 16.

I Anna Mary Robertson, was born back in the green meadows and wild woods, on a farm in Washington Co. In the year of 1860, Sept 7, of Scotch Irish paternal ancestry.

Here I spent the first ten years of my life with Mother Father and Sisters and Brothers, those were my happy days, free from care or worry, helping mother, rocking sisters creadle taking sewing lessons from mother sporting with my brothers, making rafts to float over the mill pond, roam the wild woods gathering flowers and building air castles.[3]

Then, there is a distinct break of this joyous sensate period:

1870, now came the hard years, schooling was in those days in the country three months in summer, three in winter, little girls did not go to school much in winter, owing to the cold, and not warm enough clothing, there for my school days were limited, altho I was kept busy helping at home, and the neighbors, when twelve years of age, I left home to earn my own living as then was called a hired girl.[4]

A hard-working life, full of misery, poverty, child bearing and infant mortality occupied her adult years. It is only at the end of that period that the resurgence of her talent occurs (1918); she was 57. In 1927, her husband died and the youngest son and his wife took over the farm.

Leaving me unoccupied, I had to do something,

---

[3] Ibid., 11.

[4] Ibid., 12.

so took up painting pictures in worsted, then in oil.[5]

Notice that the early attempts at serious painting preceded the death of her husband. Thus, the return of her talents cannot be attributed to that loss and to her youngest son and his wife taking over the farm. **The resurgence of the talent occurred in spite of the life conditions.** It was reinforced by her life circumstances then. It is as if the existing trend created the events to make room for its emergence. It is not the other way around as we are very tempted to believe. Events are not causes of emerging trends—events aid the flowering of them. Events come in to reenforce an existing direction. This is a very important concept. Grandma Moses' talent did not occur because she had time to spare. **The time to spare occurred because the talent was emerging.**

One more word about Grandma Moses. There is a distinct link between her paintings from age 57 to age101 and her childhood. She writes, in 1947:

> How do I paint? Well first I get a frame, then I saw my masonite board to fit the frame. Then I go over the board with oil. Then give the board three coats of flat white paint. Now it is ready for the scene, what ever the mind may produce. A landscape picture, an old bridge, a dream, or a summer or winter scene, childhoods memory, what ever one fancys. But always somthings pleasing and cheerful and I like bright colors and activity.[6]

---

[5] Ibid., 15.

[6] Ibid., 145.

These are childhood memories, pleasing and cheerful with bright colours. Thus, she reproduces the magic days of pre-puberty.

### *Domenico Scarlatti*

Domenico Scarlatti was a brilliant harpsichordist who was brought from Italy to the Court of Philip V, King of Spain, as were many other talents at the time. For 25 years he performed on the harpsichord, then, at age 53, he started composing hundreds of sonatas. However, unlike his contemporaries of the 18th Century, these sonatas were inspired by the fiery, sexual rhythms of Spanish flamenco. The intricacy of 18th Century counterpoint was enhanced by the rhythm, colour, and potency of Spanish dance. At the time of his death at age 72, he had composed more than 550 sonatas.

An amazing fact about Scarlatti is that nearly all of his "sonatas" and "essercisi", as the early works are called, were written during the last few years of the composer's life. There would be nothing peculiar about this if he had only lived to be 24 or so, but since he was about 72 when he died, one must wonder what sort of phenomenal crystallization of his musical language must suddenly have possessed him.[7]

And, again, Fernando Valenti says:

For all practical purposes, Scarlatti's career began with the "essercisi" of 1738, published in London in early 1739 and dedicated to Joao of Portugal. Before

---

[7] Fernando Valenti, *Domenico Scarlatti: Sonatas for Harpsichord,* Vol. 4, Collectors Series, Westminster W9317 (18831).

the appearance of this collection, nothing Scarlatti composed seems to have been particularly distinguished, nor have any of his works before 1738 noticeably affected posterity. The "essercisi," as Scarlatti called them, are the earliest known expressions of a composer who, at the age of fifty-three, with the aid of the musical influences of a foreign country, had at last forged his own medium of musical invention. From 1738 onward until his death, however, Scarlatti maintained a rate of musical growth and development that more than compensated for the relative musical unimportance of the first half century of his life.[8]

Thus, we have another Grandma Moses here, with an incomprehensible upsurge of creativity past age 45 or 50.

### *Arthur Rimbaud*
If creativity blossoms past "menopause," does it also blossom pre-puberty? A good example of pre-pubescent creativity and brilliance which was interrupted at adolescence is illustrated by the life of Arthur Rimbaud, born in Charleville (Ardennes) in northeastern France near the Belgian border in 1854.

His father was an officer in the French army who abandoned his family after seven years of marriage and five children. Arthur was then six years old. Life was difficult for Madame Rimbaud and she was a difficult woman.

Statements from contemporaries are unanimous. Mme. Rimbaud was haughty, inflexible, severe. This authoritarian

---

[8] Ibid., Vol. 1, (XWN 18328).

woman believed firmly in "work, money, [and] religion." [9]

Rimbaud was an excellent student, showing brilliance in the town's college and doing remarkable work in Latin verse.

Distinguishing himself in Latin shows Rimbaud's early adherence to his mother. As adolescence approaches, his new function (rebel/soldier/father) comes in ("he would scrawl 'Shit on God' on the park benches of his home town" [10]), and blends with the previous function (brilliant Latin student/mother) creating his extraordinary poetry. The new function conflicts with the old one and finally takes it over.

Rimbaud stopped writing poetry at age 19, at the end of his tempestuous affair with Verlaine, who shot him in the wrist. By then Rimbaud was totally immersed in his father function. In 1876, he joined the Dutch colonial army (age 22), a year later, he wrote "to the American consul in Bremen to inquire about enlisting in the U.S. Navy, but he apparently forgot to include a return address"[11]. In 1887, at 33, he tries "to make a fortune by selling guns to King Menyelek II of Shoa"[12] in Ethiopia.

Rimbaud's life as a colonial reflects the unconscious development of his father side. He backed into it, the way so many aspiring artists today back into business, out of unfortunate necessity. It is not "unfortunate necessity," it is the irresistible pull of the other side of the personality, trying to establish a balance in spite of the person's conscious will.

---

[9] Peschel, Enid Rhodes, *Four French Symbolist Poets: Baudelaire, Rimbaud, Verlaine, Mallarmé,* Ohio University Press, Athens, 1981.

[10] Ibid., 21.

[11] Ibid., 28.

[12] Ibid., 28.

The unconscious will, the will of the inferior function, energized by the nascent forces of puberty, establishes itself. In Rimbaud's life, one senses the cynicism and mercenary attitude he seemed to attach to his post-pubescent function.

Rimbaud returned to France in May 1891 and died in Marseilles on November 10. He never knew that in Paris the "symbolists" were reading his works.[13]

Rimbaud died completely immersed in his father function, the function of the businessman. He was oblivious, cut-off, from the poet. He did not want to be aware of the poet. It was too painful for him. However, at 37 years old, he was close to facing a switch, the switch of menopause, which would have brought him back to the rebellious agony of his adolescence. One is almost tempted to think that Rimbaud died to escape it. Rimbaud's innovations in poetry, the free-verse, the search for the new, the search for illumination, reflect the infusion of the rebel/soldier/father into the brilliant Latin student/mother.

### *Theodore Roosevelt*

Theodore Roosevelt, known as the rough-and-tumble adventurer, explorer, man of action, and President of the United States, describes his childhood as follows:

> I was a sickly, delicate boy, suffered much from asthma, and frequently had to be taken away on trips to find a place where I could breathe. One of my memories is of my father walking up and down the room with me in his arms at night when I was a very small person, and of sitting up in bed gasping, with my father and mother trying to help me. I went very little to school. I never went to the public schools, as my

---

[13] Ibid., 28.

own children later did... my aunt taught me when I was small. At one time we had a French governess, a loved and valued "mam'selle," in the household... I had been a clumsy and awkward little boy, and while much of my clumsiness and awkwardness was doubtless due to general characteristics, a good deal of it was due to the fact that I could not see and yet was wholly ignorant that I was not seeing.[14]

Here we see the sheltered and frail little boy, taught by his aunt and raised by a French governess. He describes his aunt as follows:

My aunt Anna, my mother's sister, lived with us. She was as devoted to us children as was my mother herself, and we were equally devoted to her in return. She taught us our lessons while we were little. She and my mother used to entertain us by the hour with tales of life on the Georgia plantations.[15]

And his mother:

My mother, Martha Bulloch, was a sweet, gracious, beautiful Southern woman, a delightful companion and beloved by everybody. She was entirely "unreconstructed" to the day of her death. Her mother, my grandmother, one of the dearest of old ladies, lived with us, and was distinctly over indulgent

---

[14] Theodore Roosevelt, *The Autobiography of Theodore Roosevelt*, New York, 1958, 11, 12, 14.

[15] Ibid., 11.

to us children, being quite unable to harden her heart toward us even when the occasion demanded it.[16]

A lot of women surrounded this frail child. This is the opposite picture of the Teddy we know.

The switch at puberty is illustrated by the difference in his reaction to his first trip to Europe at age 10, and to Europe and the Middle East at age 14.

> When I was ten years old I made my first journey to Europe. My birthday was spent in Cologne, and in order to give me a thoroughly "party" feeling I remember that my mother put on full dress for my birthday dinner. I do not think I gained anything from this particular trip abroad. I cordially hated it, as did my younger brother and sister. Practically all the enjoyment we had was in exploring any ruins or mountains when we could get away from our elders, and in playing in different hotels. Our one desire was to get back to America, and we regarded Europe with the most ignorant chauvinism and contempt.[17]

It is the opposite of the great traveler, isn't it? The second trip:

> Four years later, however, I made another journey to Europe, and was old enough to enjoy it throughly and profit by it.... When I was fourteen years old, in the winter of '72 and '73, I visited Europe for the

---

[16] Ibid., 10.

[17] Ibid., 12.

second time, and this trip formed a really useful part of my education. We went to Egypt, journeyed up the Nile, traveled through the Holy Land and part of Syria, visited Greece and Constantinople; and then we children spent the summer in a German family in Dresden. My first real collecting as a student of natural history was done in Egypt during this journey. By this time I had a good working knowledge of American bird-life from the superficially scientific standpoint. I had no knowledge of the ornithology of Egypt, and I picked up in Cairo a book by an English clergyman, whose name I have forgotten, who described a trip up the Nile, and in an appendix to his volume gave an account of his bird collection.[18]

Here is the birth of the man of action and the infusion of vigorous curiosity into zoology, ornithology, natural history, whose interests were, at an early age, on the level of story telling and fairy tales.

At about 13, "I got my first gun.... My gun was a breech-loading, pin-fire double-barrel, of French manufacture."[19] The hunter is born.

The grown-up Teddy, the strong man with discipline, dedication, and high moral standards is more like his father:

My father, Theodore Roosevelt, was the best man I ever knew. He combined strength and courage with gentleness, tenderness, and great unselfishness. He would not tolerate in us children selfishness or cruelty,

---

[18] Ibid., 12, 15.

[19] Ibid., 14, 15.

idleness, cowardice, or untruthfulness. As we grew older he made us understand that the same standard of clean living was demanded for the boys as for the girls; that what was wrong in a woman could not be right in a man. With great love and patience, and the most understanding sympathy and consideration, he combined insistence on discipline. He never physically punished me but once, but he was the only man of whom I was ever really afraid. I do not mean that it was a wrong fear, for he was entirely just, and we children adored him.[20]

Ultimate justice, strength, active caring, use of power, and (sometimes physical) threats to support what is believed to be right: it was the father function in him that intervened in Cuba because "conditions in the island had become so dreadful as to be a standing disgrace to us for permitting them to exist."[21]

To recapitulate, before puberty, Theodore Roosevelt was frail and sickly; surrounded by women, he identified with them while seeing his father as an unattainable ideal. The identification with the women and the frailness is demonstrated by his dislike of his first trip overseas. At puberty, 14, a drastic change occurs that brings him enjoyment of a trip abroad and that evokes the active, aggressive man of action portrayed in his childhood by his father.

### *Wolfgang Amadeus Mozart*
How about those people who have always had the same interests, such as child prodigies? They do not seem to switch

---

[20] Ibid., 7.

[21] Ibid., 119.

at puberty. What we need to remember here is that the switch at puberty occurs in areas that:

A) Have been overemphasized before puberty.

B) And/or need development and were neglected.

Let's consider Mozart's life, for example. Mozart was born with a violin in his hand, practically.

> The boy's compositions were so remarkable that skeptics accused his father of having written them. [22] His loving but ambitious father raised him on the principle that he was a performing bear: from his sixth year he was dragged over the map of Europe, and exhibited as a marvel—which, indeed, he was.[23]

Then things began to change. As he grew up, he could no longer be exhibited as a child prodigy.

> [People] had found it easy to believe that such a delightful little creature was a genius; at nineteen they found him less convincing.[24]

Mozart reacted to this change and "to compensate for his insignificant appearance, he began to affect embroidered coats and an excessive amount of jewelry, and took special pains with his hair, of which he was very vain."[25] He began to

---

[22] Wallace Brockway and Herbert Weinstock, _Men of Music,_ Simon and Schuster, New York, 1962, 125.

[23] Ibid., 124.

[24] Ibid., 133.

[25] Ibid.

develop a taste for "boon companions, billiards, dancing, and good wine."[26] He developed an excessive sexual urge, but he was under the domination of his ambitious father and until his twenty-fifth year it never entered his head to question, much less disobey, Leopold Mozart's fiats on every subject under the sun, and he never tired of saying that he considered his father "next to God." Unfortunately, this touching attitude was partly an excuse for his own unwillingness and inability to make decisions for himself. It had served a certain purpose in the past, but was no weapon for the struggles of the future.[27]

The rebellion against father finally manifested through keeping company with people of ill repute and marrying a person who was considered homely, dull, and unattractive. He joined Freemasonry, which at the time was considered iconoclastic. Thus, Mozart's switch went from the exquisite rococo six year old man with powdered wig and miniature sword, promising to be perfect in his social bearing and his looks, to a rebellious, iconoclastic young man, enjoying boon companions, sex, and joining a socially questionable spiritual institution. It is, therefore, in his personal life that Mozart switched. In music, however, the rebellion had beneficial effects. It is during adolescence that Mozart's compositions began to be permeated by his own genius and strength. His musical channel was open enough to successfully integrate the force of creativity/sexuality, while his personal and social life were not; they had to be toppled by puberty.

✝✝✝

There are other examples of integration of this fantastic

---

[26] Ibid.

[27] Ibid., 133f.

force that comes with the emergence of Function B. Johann Sebastian Bach is certainly one of them. Integration permeates his sexual life—he was the father of six children with his first wife and 14 with his second, and his music, in which romanticism, faith, exquisite intelligence, and power are to be found. It is this type of integration which produces extraordinary changes in fields of human interests. It took a 100 years for us to begin to recognize that Bach had done just that for music.

Meanwhile, Mozart, Beethoven, and many others drew enormous amounts of inspiration from him, while his sons considered him old-fashioned and out-dated. Bach never had great monetary success, nor was he a royal court musician; nevertheless, he seems to have lived a financially comfortable life. The fact that his wife died in poverty is much more attributable to his son's oblivious or harsh attitude toward her than to his lack of financial success.

# *Betrayal of Love;*
# *Formation of Personality*
# *Through Violation of Divine Law*

## Chapter 29
# *Betrayal of Love Forms Human Types I*

---

Love is the most powerful force in the Universe. It makes us, creates us. We live, move and have our being in it. It is God for us, and the other two aspects of the Trinity are, for us, sub-aspects of it.

Yielding to love is the most ecstatic experience ever. However, the more we are limited in our consciousness, the more this yielding will be painful. So, we guard against it. We even antagonize it, vilify it and betray it. This betrayal aspect is what we focus on today.

Significantly, Judas' betrayal of the Christ very much comes to mind. Also, appropriately, the issue of betrayal is very pertinent when considering all of the transferential problems that we encounter here.

Indeed, we have seen that the loving nature of this cleansing and renewal is wrongly interpreted by the lower self as being license to dump. We say, here, that all of yourself is acceptable. The lower self itself is the gate to the Higher Self, to any success and improvement. So, the lower self prides itself of that and takes this method for granted. All of the outrageous behaviour that was not allowed with parents, and, by extension, all of the outrageous behaviour that is not allowed today in your life, all get dumped here, since, a) it is allowed, and b) the lower self is full of conceit about being the gate to the Higher Self, about holding the key to progress.

So, the love of this place is more easily betrayed and demeaned than any other aspect or institution or person out there. It is allowed here, according to the lower self, to have the audacity to break commitments, on any level, including on the business level. Anywhere else, you would be sued for this type of behaviour. Here, not only do you betray, but you dare show your face and pretend that nothing happened.

Actually, what is expected of you is the reverse of this: a) You are expected to take responsibility on the level of thoughts and feelings. b) You are supposed to have gone **beyond** the mundane outer level responsibility which is expected of those who are not even on a cleansing and renewal program such as this one. c) What's more, you are supposed to serve this faith. Yet, you act as if it is supposed to serve you, change your diapers and cover for your childish outrages.

Here are some of the consequences of this behaviour:

1) If it is OK to dump on what has the most value in your life, this faith, then gradually you'll do the same on the rest of your life, you will not only regress, but sink lower than you were **before** you entered this faith. That's why it is better if you leave this faith when you find yourself acting in an outrageous manner towards it without taking responsibility for it.

2) Even if you don't act this out, as long as you haven't resolved this problem of denigration of love, you will demean this faith and this cleansing and renewal. Thus, you will demean yourself, never realizing the great strides you have taken here. You will not be able to recognize yourself as the leader you have become. You will feel isolated in your life, in despair.

That's betrayal of love and its consequences.

The betrayal of the love force is at the root of all of our problems. Thus it is what crystallizes, decelerates and materializes, forming the personality and shaping the body.

Let us begin by studying once again the familiar method of formation of duality which we have encountered in the Chapter 13 on Freezes (page 119):

A child is just born and has two parents: Parent A and Parent B. Parent A is perceived as always there caring, loving, giving, feeding. The child does not long for that parent's love or care—he has it, and therefore, he takes it for granted.

Parent B, however, is perceived as not always there, as less giving than Parent A, as detached. Therefore, Parent B becomes the object of curiosity, in other words, desirable. Since the child desires Parent B, and since Parent B is detached, detachment becomes desirable. Detached equals desirable is a freeze that this child will carry with him. "In order to be desirable, I have to be detached, or simply absent." I, therefore, grow up always wanting to leave, thinking that I am desirable this way, or I play hard to get, or I tease, etc. Detachment, non-loving, is absurdly seen as desirable, which of course will result in great pain and suffering later in this person's life.

Detachment, or absence, is the opposite of love. In no way is it magnetic. It may work for a while with some people, but its life is finite. Eventually, detachment will meet equal detachment and will result in loneliness, frustration, and pain.

Meanwhile, since Parent A was loving and present but not desirable, another set of equal and opposite wrong associations is formed. Love and/or commitment and/or presence and/or service and/or selfless giving equal worthlessness, not being desirable, being taken for granted. This same person will find himself disappointed or put off or turned off by someone who loves him. Only when a person is detached, will he become desirable. The minute a desired, detached person turns around and loves them, they will lose interest and leave.

Perhaps you can take a moment to look at the patterns of your life. Does the above remind you of anything? Have you in your life taken love for granted, destroying very valid relationships only to regret what you have done once the person has finally decided that he has given you enough and it is time to withdraw?

✜✜✜

By opting for the rejector, the child betrays love. The taking for granted of love is also a betrayal. Look back in your childhood. You have betrayed love in a certain way. Whose love was it? You have, in one way or another chosen to emulate one parent or aspect while denigrating another one and, with that, rejected and betrayed love in a particular fashion.

Desiring the rejector, admiring and emulating him, leads to severe distortions, as we have seen. For example, if I desire to become as my rejecting parent, if I admire him, and if I perceive him, at the same time, as having rejected loving and generous giving of feelings, then this loving and this expression of feelings become shameful, contemptible. I must, therefore, repress them, alienate myself from them.

The betrayal of the aspect of love results in the formation of typology. We adopt a lifestyle that betrays love. As we will see, this also applies to the formation of Love Ray Types. They too have betrayed love, as expressed perhaps by a Will Ray type parent. The betrayal may also appear as a falsification or an exaggeration of love, an affectation of it, a manipulation of feelings, arriving at their distortions: emotions.

Let us now see what happened to each individual Ray type, as he betrays love and forms his type. As we do this, let us remember that the parental figures may not necessarily be the parents themselves. The betrayed love aspect may be represented by someone else. So is the emulated aspect with whom we side.

## Formation of the Ray I Type

**Loving Parent A:** is receptive, adaptable, compliant, humiliated, weak, feeling, loving, but a victim of Parent B. He/she may not be a victim when expressing love to his/her child, but he/she is a victim when he/she interacts with Parent B. He/she is probably a Ray III type, compliant, adaptability distorted. This parent can also be Ray II, the Son/Love. A combination of the two is usually the case. Therefore, although this parent could be male or female, the aspects represented here are Mother and Son.

**Rejector Parent B:** is aggressive, hostile, unfeeling, willful, arbitrary, irrational, violent. But he/she is perceived as strong, effective, an "achiever." Although this parent could be male or female, the aspect represented by it is Father. **The child opts for Parent B, represses his love for Parent A, as well as Parent A's love for him.** Early in life, before puberty, he identifies with Parent A. He may even hate Parent B. However, out of fear/cowardice, he will side with Parent B and betray Parent A.

Therefore, the child's achievements—even in adulthood—however good they may be, are a betrayer of love, which he denigrates. Strength for him is conquest, domination, promiscuity. He has contempt for adaptability, seeing only its harmful aspect, lack of integrity and spinelessness. However, he reserves the right to be dishonest and deceptive, to lack integrity when it comes to achieving, conquering, i.e., when it comes to Parent B's values.

He mistrusts Parent A and any love that comes to him, seeing this force as manipulation, fearing to be engulfed and enslaved by anyone whom he would love or who loves him. He develops an abhorrence at being touched. He wants to touch, but he doesn't want to be touched. When he touches, he is in control, he can manipulate, he can have his way. When he is touched or given to, the discomfort that he experiences comes from his demand to always be in control and from his fear of any force outside of himself that he cannot control.

Thus, achievement, conquest, skill, talent are all developed in contradistinction to love and adaptability. They are the enemies of love, thus they automatically manufacture guilt by merely existing. Obviously and ultimately, self-destruction must occur.

Sometimes, both parents are seen as being totally irrational and out of control. So, he has to take care of them both. Sometimes, as loving as Parent A may be, he/she turns on the child, displacing onto him all of the outraged feelings of anger and rage that are accumulated during his/her interactions with Parent B. So the child experiences violence from both. No love seems to come from either parent. The love that he then experiences is identified with someone outside of the immediate family.

### *Formation of Ray II Type*

**Loving Parent A:** for him is **actively** loving and giving with abundance (combinations of Love with **Will** or even Emotions, Ray IV). The child is blind to the active aspect of loving which threatens him. He sees this as too blatant an expression, too much out in the open, to easily identified. Therefore, for all of his/her strength, Parent A seems vulnerable since exposed.

**Rejector Parent B:** is withholding, and therefore, in control, to be admired, non-committal, therefore, **sitting on the fence,** having the "power" to go either way. The balance and tension are used for the purposes of playing hard to get.

This balance is false. However, it is reminiscent of the point of tension which is love. The false balance is the opposite of love. It is fear of commitment and it is a teasing power trip.

- **So he opts for Parent B.**
- He betrays love by betraying **active** (Ray I) abundance (Ray IV), committed giving.
- He betrays the law of abundance by adopting poverty consciousness.
- He betrays the law of attraction by attempting to attract through withholding.
- He loves and admires and emulates the withholding parent, be it mother or father.

### *Formation of Ray III Type*

**Loving Parent A:** actively loving, **but not there!** He/she is also seductive and attractive and **dominant.** Yet, he/she can be easily seduced by the child. The child feels enormous power over Parent A. Because the existence of this condition the child experiences contempt for him/her as well, a sense of ownership and superiority. Although the role of Parent A could be male or female, we are here talking about the Father principle, combined with the Son principle.

**Withholding Parent B:** is compliant and unattractive but holy and safe—**asexual**—victim. Pseudo-love. Yet, this parent seems to have captured Parent A's sexuality and attention. This parent also expresses contempt for Parent A, who is seen as easily manipulated and is portrayed that way. Although the role of Parent B could be male or female, it represents the Mother principle.

**So, the child betrays Parent A by opting to become Parent B**, having contempt for A, putting him/her down, yet being conceited about A's attraction to him/her at an early age, and concluding that "all men/women are the same; all they 'want' is sex." "They all want sex," i.e., **the child has**

**great sexual power. This power, however, is motionless, immobile. It is intelligent and knowing, but it doesn't have to do anything. It is convinced of its own magnetism.**

In this type, one can also replace the word *sex* with the word *intelligence* or *mind*. For example, the child has seductive mind powers which loving Parent A finds as irresistibly attractive as would be sexuality or being cute. Thus the child venerates and idealizes his own mind. Once again, there is nothing to be done. No movement is necessary. The child feels desirable as is. In fact, movement is gradually seen as endangering desirability. All movement is relegated to Parent A who desires, who is attracted and who has been seduced by the child.

- Actually, **the child** wants sex. Early **stimulation** through the seduction of Parent A creates the big pelvis and the exaggerated sexual desires. This is denied. The child may not be aware of the seductive aspect as being such. He will perceive Parent A as a mean seducer who victimizes him, while secretly enjoying the "sexual victimization." Then guilt and shame for this enjoyment will set in. The whole thing will be turned around and constructed as a case against Parent A. Thus Parent A secretly becomes responsible for providing sexual stimulation and enjoyment, but gets blamed for it at the same time. The shame, guilt and denial that set in around sexuality create the over development of the pelvis in a holding pattern, i.e., holding, exaggerated sexuality, along with guilt, shame and emasculating hostility.

- In case the child is feminine, she will display an overt abhorrence for male sexuality. She will reject males who are attracted to her while colluding with her offsprings. We have here a desire to become a mother **before** making love, i.e., before being penetrated, impregnated by a man. (Artificial insemination.). **We have here the genesis of** the virgin birth, what we at the Church of the Path call the **"emasculate conception**," since it denies the existence of the role of the male. Let us remember, however, that since there is sexual overstimulation, there is great sexual desire. Thus the violent contempt and rejection of the Father on the outer level is, in effect, a seductive ploy! What a set up for unhappiness!

- She pseudo-loves, as does her Mother. She loves as a compliant victim, who is trying to convince you that loving has been so humiliating for her.
- Her goal is to exclude Father. **She will become both parents, thus accomplishing her lower self goal of becoming androgynous.** This androgyny has been reached through the denial of her gender, not through the full acceptance of it and through the living of it. That is why it is a distortion and not the blessing that she claims it to be. The idealization of this regression leads to the abstinence and the celibacy that is ruining so many religions and their practitioners. It leads to the worshiping of the Virgin Mary, Isis, etc.
- The Ray III male also **betrays the Father aspect.** He is not always there; however, he has structure and principles; he is a lot more straightforward than the Mother aspect, thus his love is a lot more genuine and direct.    The Ray III male opts for the **compliant and victimized, thus unloving Mother aspect**. He colludes with this aspect—Mother, whether male or female parent—who is always there to "hatch," brood over, and mollycoddle him. Both form a cocoon that excludes the Father aspect. It is the betrayal of the Father aspect's straightforwardness and direct honesty that creates the Ray III male typology. Both male and female types will tend to have over developed pelvis. We are reminded here of Toynbee's *Chrysallis*.

## The Mass Freeze of "Free Spirituality"

You are all familiar with the misconception that says that spiritual help should be free. Here you have a double standard. Indeed, if you consider it fair that you should pay the price for other goods and services, and if you consider it fair that you should be paid for what you produce, then why should spiritual help be free?

It too involves vigorous training, the same as any other, perhaps, even more so. It too is given responsibly, even more so than in other professions. So, why should you feel that it owes you? Why do you have double standards towards it, thus demeaning it and taking it for granted? Because you still consider it as a source of love, which it is. As such, you reject it as you rejected your loving parent. The same contempt, devaluation, taking for granted that you experienced then, is experienced now. You demand unconditional, free giving, as well as the simultaneous right to demean it and betray it. "If it is all loving, it is all forgiving and I don't have to be afraid of it. So, I can dump on it. At the same time, the devil, harmfulness, meanness is unforgiving. So, I'll respect it and pay homage to it. Furthermore, any harmful feelings I have for the harmful, I will transpose onto the divine."

It is safer that way. "It is easier and safer to be angry at the all loving, Almighty than to be angry at the devil." The consequences of this are:

1) Any goodness in **you** will receive the same treatment, the same devaluation. Consequently, any happiness, success, achievement in your life—always a consequence of goodness—will instead wrongly be attributed to the evil in you. Since you have now convinced yourself that happiness and success are achieved by meanness, withholding and greed, you will cultivate those and reap unhappiness and failure. These will in turn be attributed to the goodness in you which is seen as naive, unknowing, innocent, childish. You will,

therefore, proceed in cutting out more of this niceness in you. "No more Mr. Nice Guy!" This will bring you more failure and unhappiness, etc.

2) Not wanting to pay the price for spirituality, you will not value it, thus thwarting your progress. You will also find spiritual teachers who, because they are cheap, devalue their own work. Because they do, they themselves become lazy and don't give their best. Because of that, they lack, which feeds their greed. Thus they are unable to teach you anything, from fear that they will rub you the wrong way, and lose a client. They are more concerned with what their livelihood is than with the quality of their work. Yet, they daren't charge because they themselves devalue spirituality, love.

At the other end of the spectrum, you find doctors and lawyers. They do not deal with love and they know it. So, they grossly overcharge to assuage their guilt for lovelessness.

### The Way Out

The early childhood betrayal is being perpetrated all over the place in adult life. The way out of this pattern is to experience the original betrayal, to feel the pain of it. You erroneously believe that if this pain is felt, you will hang yourself as Judas did. That's how much this early pain is feared.

In reality, and as continuously demonstrated, pain, when faced:

A) Appears to be considerably less intolerable than once thought.

B) Gradually diminishes and then stops when fully accepted and fully experienced.

C) Yields healing and transforms your life, always for better.

Judas committed suicide because he wanted to **escape** the pain of betraying the Christ, the embodiment of love. Suicide is **escape from pain**, not experience of pain. It inflicts on the self the ultimate pain of death because it believes that it is preferable to the experience of the pain of the guilt. Why?

Because the pain of the guilt of this betrayal of love involves the dissolution of the personality. Type formation, having been done in opposition to love, has for foundation, guilt, which it is continuing to manufacture. The facing of this guilt endangers the entire structural error on which the personality is founded—a crack in the foundation of a house, which puts in question the entire value of that house. The more the person is identified with the house, the more he will believe that, facing the crack endangers, not only his safety, but, worse, his identity. "Better to end this life than to face total loss of identity," he erroneously concludes.

Of course, if he allows himself to feel the crack, feel the pain of the guilt of betrayal, he may destroy his present identity. However, he will also discover that identity was not only false, but was preventing him from finding his real one, from actualizing, realizing who he really is. The pain of having betrayed love must be faced and overcome. Without that, it will be impossible to liberate the total capacity for love.

At the same time, when that guilt and pain are faced, the flood of love will dwarf all of life's problems, all the conflicts, all the other pains. They may not be all resolved right away, but the way to recovery is certain, clear. So:

1) Experience the love of the parent you betrayed and rejected.

2) Allow yourself to desire to redeem yourself for your betrayal.

3) Experience the guilt/remorse and the pain of it.

4) Allow these feelings to put in question your entire approach to life. This is going to be the most threatening of all. It means the death of the old ways. But, haven't you wanted renewal? Haven't you been wanting, at last, a creative

solution to your old and insoluble problems? Well, here it is! Of course, it is going to put in question the old stuff. And why not? After all the old stuff didn't work, did it? It failed miserably. You failed through the personality that you constructed.

5) Allow, at least, the consideration of the new ways. As you finally experience the love of the betrayed parent, do you see a new approach to life? Do you see a new vigour? As you dissolve the betrayal, love floods you and reshapes you. You find yourself naturally doing what was heretofore impossible, excruciatingly difficult, seen as risky and humiliating.

6) The love that will flood you will shape you, will make you, will motivate you, will propel you, will reveal to you your own task and will finally make it possible for you to live as a soul, not a personality.

The faith has finally been embraced. Spirituality is respected and valued, when received and when given. Self-love and self-respect are restored. The dignity that is thus found reveals the ever presence of the love of God.

## Chapter 30
# *Betrayal of Love Forms Human Types II*

---

We continue our study of type formation from the point of view of betrayal. As so very often mentioned, we have within us all types. As we go through this study, see if you can find, within or outside of yourself, the types, their descriptions, their betrayals, their pains, their problems. If you find yourself being sarcastic, know that you must have judgments in that particular area, and that therefore, you haven't resolved problems within yourself related to that particular type. See if you can differentiate between humour and sarcasm. In humour, there is compassion; in sarcasm, there isn't any. Humour tolerates sadness; sarcasm doesn't. Humour passes over you like a breath of fresh air, i.e., you are not involved; sarcasm stays with you as an unpleasant emanation, yours.

The Rays of Attribute are more involved in matter and crystallization than are the Rays of Aspect. That's why what creates a human type in the Rays of Attribute is a double betrayal, in contradistinction to the single betrayal found in the Rays of Aspect. Although the personalities formed through the Rays of Attribute are further removed from the Higher Self, they appear to be "coping" better than the ones formed by the Rays of Aspect. This adjustment is false. It seems to be desirable because it is supported by so much collusive falsehood around it. "When in Rome, do as the Romans do." It is strange, indeed, that the rigidity of the Roman Empire lasted for as long as it did. Its collapse is reminiscent of the collapse that comes when a Stiff experiences a crisis. The whole thing crumbles and the person is lost for a long time. The West was lost for a thousand years after having, for so many centuries, sold out to the rigidity and the conformity of the Roman Empire.

When you adjust at the expense of goodness, rightness, good will and harmlessness, you create a false equilibrium. The price you pay for this is much greater than the price paid by the one who seems to be somewhat maladjusted.

## Ray IV Conflict
### Indulgence Versus Restraint

Here, **Parent A** could be a withholder, Ray II or one of the Stiff Rays V or VII. The aspect of love here is expressed through reason, good sense, thinking, order or science. The child doesn't see the love coming through any of this. He only sees restriction, withholding, coupled with interference in what the child is doing. There is too much attention placed on the child in every possible respect, particularly food and excretion.

**Parent B** is self-indulgent. He doesn't care much for the child. He cares for himself, indulging himself. The child opts for Parent B because he likes this way of life. Everything is allowed, permitted. That's the way to live.

Also, the self-indulgence in this parent creates secrecy and guilt. As a result, the child trains himself to hold, hold secrets, feelings, or food as a protection against feeling the pain of the guilt that would emerge if and when all of this holding is released.

Parent A may even be sexual, developed, mature. However, sexuality is not particularly cherished by the child whose self-indulgence is created by displacing sexuality onto food or on to other controllable substances. If he indulges in sex, it is always through control. The sexual partner is objectified.

The opting for Parent B creates a condition of hostility for Parent A and all that he represents.

**Double Betrayal:** Thus continuous conflict arises between insatiable self-indulgence and restrictiveness. The child, and later, the adult will spend a lot of energy provoking any restrictiveness. The child will also fluctuate between bouts of indulgence and bouts of restrictiveness. In extreme cases, particularly when the Will is associated with this type, there will be sociopathic behaviour.

By restricting himself, he betrays the indulgent parent. By indulging himself, he betrays the healthy limits of the disciplinarian. In either case, he betrays someone and creates guilt. The intensity that characterizes the holding pattern in this type will make the restrictiveness as well as the indulgence go to extremes. Thus, he will continuously punish and reward himself by going one way or another at different times of his life. The same lack of balance will be found in just about everything he does, including over-working.

Of course, the intensity itself must be given up if this person is to solve this problem. He must face the betrayal, and most importantly for him, forgive himself and forgive others. The return of loving will restore the balance.

✝✝✝

We now enter into the world of stiffness. This is the world of adaptation and coping *par excellence*. Thus it is also the world of double betrayal "perfected." Since the Stiffs represent the societal norms and expectations, we will all to some extent, identify with them, since we all tried to emulate them one way or the other.

## *Ray V*

**A) Apollo:** It is a stiff, unbending, blind justice, militaristic type. For us it is the male aspect of Ray V. In a way, we have here a similar condition to the betrayal found in the formation of Ray I.

The **Loving Parent A** is mother. She is all giving, she is adaptable which is perceived as compliant. She may be intelligent, but she nevertheless is seen as dumb. She loves the child, who identifies with her in his early years before puberty. Yet, he has betrayed her even then, by siding with and idealizing his father.

Mother also praised him for his handsomeness and his intelligence. He knew this all too well, gradually but surely developing an idealized self of the most handsome, the most intelligent, etc. Deep down, he grows up to believe this.

At puberty, the betrayal of mother is complete. The identification with father is now total, at least consciously.

**Rejector Parent B**, father, is stiff, willful, unfeeling, unloving, proud, way past conceit. He treats his wife as an inferior, a servant. He takes every opportunity to demonstrate his superiority to her. The child opts for Parent B, denigrating his mother, his feelings, his women, his spontaneity—by the way, making it very difficult to have an orgasm. He denigrates happiness and joy, favouring the somber, introspective, Wagnerian moods. In Mythology, this ominous quality, coupled with cruelty, is revealed in the following story, one of my favourites for Apollo:

Marsyas, who had accidentally found Athena's double flute, challenged Apollo to a music contest. The crowd was to judge who the winner was, and the winner could then do whatever he liked to the loser. After some preliminaries in which both contestants delighted their audience, Marsyas played a very joyous tune, the most joyous and merry anyone ever heard. How could Apollo top that? Apollo then played a sad and somber tune, the saddest that anyone had ever heard. Everybody was in tears. When voting, the crowd, in true betrayal fashion, voted for Apollo, opting for the tears and taking laughter and merriment for granted. Apollo, the winner, had Marsyas killed in a horrible fashion for daring to challenge him. Here is Apollo's cruelty. He doesn't forgive, nor does he forget. He will punish to the full letter of the law. He will demolish anyone who opposes him, anytime he can.

Apollo, the Obsessive Penetrator doesn't like to be challenged. Particularly not by a woman, or by a feminine aspect. And anything that is not stiff and somber, is feminine. Remember, it is Athena's flute with which Marsyas threatened Apollo. A woman was behind it, of course.

**Double Betrayal:** While Apollo, the Obsessive Penetrator denigrates and betrays his mother, he also venerates and idealizes his father. At puberty, he starts **selling out to his father**. Now he is to his father what his mother is, compliant. Both Apollo, the Obsessive Penetrator and his father are masters to mother. However, between father and son, father takes on the role of master and son the role of slave, and therefore, of woman. He submits. He doesn't like it. But behind the submission is a hidden agenda against father. When strong enough, he will "kill" and replace father.

Thus, **inside, he betrays father as well.** This betrayal of father consists of a double game: total compliance to father on one hand, total devotion, reminiscent of the oath to Hitler by the Munich Youth, energized by an enormous demand to be taken care of, led, fed on all levels, and hiding a volition for total rebellion and destruction, a biting of the very hand that feeds him.

This is the jock, proficient in sports, totally self-controlled. He has contempt for disease and for anyone who is sick. He has particular contempt for "weak men." In this definition are the men who display anything reminiscent of the feminine, such as art or even indecision. Of course, we are talking here of the Ray VII, Femininized Male.

There is here a demand for total supremacy and superiority, which one day will pit him against his father. As we have seen above, there is a hidden agenda. One day, it becomes a revolutionary reality.

David Koresh, the cult leader in Waco, was such a stiff type, pushing his rigidity to the point of fanaticism. The cruel revenge displayed in Oklahoma City in the past few days by one of his followers is a typical Apollo, the Obsessive Penetrator reaction. In fact, the man arrested on Friday looks like an Apollo himself, with his crew cut and his wiry but rigid body.

At some point or another in Apollo's life, the feminine side will catch up with him. Although he will desperately try to hold on to his Spartan old ways, he will unconsciously hate them, longing for the softness, the beauty and the love of mother who he also betrayed through seduction. He will react to that by further betraying his wife in a midlife affair—or more than one—with a younger and more hard bodied woman or women, in order to assert his phallic superiority.

The double betrayal here makes the following statement: I love no one. I am committed to no one except myself. I use and abuse whoever and whatever I please to aggrandize myself. Of course, this can only work for awhile, sometimes even brilliantly. However, having betrayed love on both sides, it is bound to collapse.

✚✚✚

**B) Venus:** Here, we have Cinderella, the sexy woman *par excellence*, the paragon of beauty.

**Parent A for her:** The loving parent is Mother. She is always there, loving her, giving, caring and educating her. There is lots of education in being a woman, in arts, in crafts, in knitting, in music. Nevertheless, little Cinderella only sees how inferior she is to mother. She sees herself in the ashes, while her mother is invited to the ball. When Prince Charming lifts her out of the ashes, she won against mother.

**Parent B, father:** Is not always there. She doesn't identify with him, nor with males. However, by submitting to them and by being helpless and seemingly dumb, she betrays her femininity, the fullness of womanhood, adult womanhood.

**Double Betrayal:** In another sense, of course, father is betrayed, too. He is disregarded, or taken for granted. He is supposed to support her in the grand style.

Later, with Prince Charming, after she lands him, of course, there will be the same demands as with father. Only they will also be accompanied by the unfulfilled demands for mother. Thus the Prince Charming husband will have to fulfill both roles. There will be no gratitude for father, even less for Prince Charming who will never be able to fill the shoes of father, let alone of father and mother combined. In spite of her compliance, in spite of believing that she is irresistible, she will not obtain the satisfaction that she seeks.

No distortion can bring happiness. So she will, either gradually or suddenly change, from the little doll Cinderella to an unkempt and matronly bitter person. The change will happen either in a midlife crisis—age 42 to mid-fifties— or it will be precipitated earlier by a form shattering event. This could be an affair on her part or on husband's, a death in the family, a collapse in her financial situation, or a windfall of money, through inheritance or through winning the lottery. Nothing like an infusion of money—energy—to precipitate a crisis!

Meanwhile, the guard against crisis will create a great conflict in the person's life, particularly, or shall we say in most cases, around ages 28 or 32. She will find herself desperately holding onto her girlish figure. She will dread and resent pregnancy and motherhood, both of which threaten to propel her into the unpleasantness of matronliness.

She will compete with and "castrate" her female offsprings, feeling devastated if they surpass her. She will feel particularly devastated if her daughter shows that she can be attractive **and** professionally promising. This would be a deep threat to her entire philosophy of life. It would invalidate her entire *raison d'être*. Meanwhile, while her daughter, or daughters, are in childhood, she will collude with them—as mother did—against Prince Charming become King Grouch. Her princess world, in her beautiful—sometimes opulent—home, with her daughters, studying the true arts of ballet and music, wearing dainty clothes and going to Tuesday Tennis League at the country club, will sharply contrast with the unattractive, bland, sometimes downright dirty place of work of the husband/father. He, along with other men, will be perceived as grouchy, uncultured, dirty, unkempt, i.e., to be tolerated at the dinner table and seduced for the money to pay for all that business. Shame for father will set in.

It reminds me of two points:

- My mother used to sing an old French song that goes:
    *L'habit qui ne va pas, c'est pour mon papa.*
    *Les plus beaux vetements sont pour ma maman.*
  Translation:
    *The clothes that won't do (or don't fit, or both), that's for my daddy.*
    *The most beautiful clothes, that's for my mommy.*
  The song is all about how dainty and attractive is mother and how ridiculous and contemptible is father.
- When I visited clients across the US, back in the early seventies in my business days, I was always astonished at the incredible difference between their offices and their homes. The offices were shabby old places, with gory stuffed animal heads staring at you from the walls. They

were dusty, dirty, disorderly. By contrast, the homes were immaculate, sometimes stylish, sometimes ornate. The wives were always either explicitly or implicitly hostile to their husbands and to their guests. It felt as if we, in business, were intruding on their immaculate, pristine paradise of female nobility. When, however, under other circum-stances, I would visit the same type homes—say that we met after a cultural event, outside of the business context—then women's attitudes towards me would completely reverse itself. As long as I was associated with the fine arts or with the country club, I was charmed. If I was associated with business—the unfortunate, but tolerated source of their money, father—I was treated with covert, and sometimes, overt contempt.

The destruction of this outrage must happen at some point or other. The soul does not tolerate for long the extent of this distortion. Cinderella must find a job.

✛✛✛

The two Ray VII types, as well as Ray VI, will be studied in the next chapter.

**So:**

1) Experience the love of the parents you betrayed and rejected. How did your father love you? How did your mother? How fully did you experience this?

2) Allow yourself to desire to redeem yourself for your betrayal.

3) Experience the guilt/remorse and the pain of it.

4) Allow those feelings to put in question your entire approach to life. This is going to be the most threatening of all. It means the death of the old ways. But, haven't you wanted renewal? Haven't you been wanting, at last, a creative solution to your old and insoluble problems? Well, here it is!

Of course, it is going to put in question the old stuff. And why not? After all, the old stuff didn't work, did it? It failed miserably. You failed through the personality that you constructed. Now try through your soul!

5) Allow, at least, the consideration of the new ways. As you finally experience the love of the betrayed parent, do you see a new approach to life? Do you see a new vigour? As you dissolve the betrayal, love floods you and reshapes you. You find yourself naturally doing what was heretofore impossible, excruciatingly difficult, seen as risky and humiliating.

6) The love that will flood you will shape you, will make you, will motivate you, will propel you, will reveal to you your own task and will finally make it possible for you to live as a soul, not a personality.

Live, love and be loved totally.

## Chapter 31
# *Betrayal of Love Forms Human Types III*

---

We continue our study on the formation of typology from the point of view of the betrayal of the love force. Our method takes us on ever deeper spirals of study. The same issues recur offering us more profound insights.

We have previously examined betrayal as it applies to Ray V Stiff Types. We focused on the conventional types of our culture—Cinderella and Prince Charming. We now focus on the popular types of the counterculture, Ray VII, the romantics and the revolutionaries. Here, they are looked at again in context of the betrayal of parents.

### *Ray VII, Counterculture*
**A) Dionysus:** The Feminized Male. In mythology, he appears as an effeminate god, having been raised by the nymphs. His father is Zeus, who endows him with all kinds of masculine powers and with potency. However, he betrays his father's love and giving by opting for women and staying/dwelling, being controlled by them.

So, **Parent A, the Loving Parent** is mother, androgynous mother, since father is never there. Since mother represents both parents, she is controlling, aggressive—probably Ray VII herself, if not Ray III or Ray I. She pampers him, adores him and sexually charges him. He is attracted to her on many levels including the sexual. He is usually surrounded by women, her coterie of friends or sisters or nieces or maids. He is mother's buddy, friend. He would have preferred being a woman. His tastes go thoroughly towards the feminine. There is collusion with mother against father and against men in general.

**Parent B, the Rejector Father:** is not always there. He may be strong, a hero who is very difficult to match, let alone surpass. Even if he isn't, he will appear to be. So, the child will long for him, but will repress this longing. Later in adolescence, he will search for him and try to emulate him, in the hope of being liberated from the controls of the androgynous, Amazonian mother. Mythology bears this out. Past puberty, when Dionysus discovers that his father is Zeus, he pursues the Amazons who take refuge in the temple of Artemis (Diana)—where else?!

Another beautiful expression of this is to be found in Ulysses's son Telemachus. As a very young man right out of adolescence, he leaves his native Ithaca and his mother Penelope, in search for his father who is trying to return home from the Trojan war. Here is the post-adolescent search for father, and therefore, for male identity. It is also interesting to note how this myth was used in history, albeit unconsciously. Fenelon was the tutor to the Dauphin, Louis XIV's son. In order to teach the story of Ulysses to the Dauphin—who was no doubt emasculated by the coterie of women surrounding him, as well as despairing about ever reaching his father's achievements—he wrote a novel about Telemachus's search for father. It became very popular in its original French and its translations.

Fenelon no doubt was unconsciously helping his pupil to become a man. Here is true love set in motion. It connects with the infinite, achieving unconscious self goals of goodness and love. It also creates, never for a moment knowing that the novel would become as popular and as wide spread as it did. The novel was written for the education of only one pupil.

The physical structure of this type reflects his conflicts. He has a strong pelvis and strong legs. However, his chest is sunken. He usually has a protruding jaw which seems to compensate for the hollowness in the chest. Believe it or not, he is a sexual symbol—the shuffling adolescent so very much adored by androgynous and controlling women during the cycles of "romanticism," i.e., in the sixties and seventies, the twenties and thirties, as well as the first half of the 19th Century.

The strong pelvis in this type is the result of early sexual stimulation by the women who raised him as their little darling. The sunken chest is the result of shutting off of the heart, and sometimes of the Will (back). The protruding jaw is the stubbornness and hostility, homologous to the pelvic strength and aggression. So, we have seeming compliance, with stubbornness and resentment, on top, with the sexual seduction and aggression below.

**Double Betrayal**: This type, in a way, is an exaggeration of the Ray III type. However, unlike Ray III, there is here betrayal of both parent's love.

His desire for mother and his collusion with her constitute an obvious betrayal of father. This is what creates the charged and strong pelvis.

The sunken chest is a betrayal of mother. Basically, it says "I will never love you; after all I am a man and both of us know that eventually you will reject me. I will never love you, nor will I ever love any woman. I will seduce and reject them and I will get them to take care of me by stifling my manhood. Then when the time is right, I will long for, look for father."

Although he identifies with her and betrays his father and his nature, he also betrays her by rebelling against her, acting irrationally towards her, while still expecting her to take care of him. His weapon of betrayal is through indecision, and through seduction of mother. By seducing mother, he betrays both parents.

**B) Diana:** I call her Masculinized Woman. I gave her this name because the goddess Diana, the huntress, was very close to an Amazon. Indeed, she did not like men very much, controlling them. However, she desired them. Endymion,[44] a young shepherd, was asleep when she saw him, was attracted by his youth and seduced him. Here is Diana's obsession with the Dionysus type.

I could very well have also named her Athene. Indeed, her father, Zeus, gave her birth through his skull. He had an enormous headache which was relieved by having Vulcan or Prometheus make a breech in Zeus's skull to allow Athene to be born, fully armed, screaming a victorious shout. Where are the women? Only men are present, even at her birth. What happened to her mother? Her mother Metis was a Titaness who would transform herself into many shapes to escape Zeus—typical Ray III adaptability in its distortion and its duplicity; typical also in her size. The child, who was supposed to be born from Zeus's union with Metis, was to be male and was to depose Zeus as Zeus deposed Cronus and Cronus deposed Uranus. So, she was to be the heir apparent. Well, father Zeus was not going to put up with that. While Metis was asleep, he swallowed Athene in embryo form out of her mother's womb. Athene was hatched in his skull.

We learn a lot from all of this:
- The tomboyish quality of this type of female. She would rather be male.
- She is surrounded by males and denies/betrays her femininity.
- The big head and big pelvis reflect her having been energized mentally and sexually by her father. The sunken

chest represents her despair when it comes to love. Indeed, she knows that she is not a man, and that one day she will be seen as inferior compared to them. So she hates them and eventually, after puberty, discards them from her life and becomes her own soldier—as androgynous as her sister Diana.

So, **Parent A, the Loving Parent** is father. Mother is not always there. Father pampers her, adores her, sexually charges her. She is father's little buddy. Her tastes go towards the masculine. She mistrusts women, preferring the company of men who she trusts and with whom she identifies.

**Parent B** is mother, who is not there for her. Later in life she will look for mother and try to identify with her. In that attempt, she will embrace women's issues in a militant—masculine—manner.

No matter what mother's typology is, this type will project on her aspects of victimization and compliance in order to justify her own aggressiveness and vengeance to which she is blind. By portraying women—and therefore herself—as weak victims, she can remain blind to her own hostility expressed through aggressiveness towards men. Men, particularly the strong ones, will continuously be seen as the perpetrators of all evil. Thus she will continuously be attracted to the weak, indecisive and compliant ones—Dionysus.

**Double Betrayal:** Again here we see an exaggeration of the Ray III type with the exception of having here a double betrayal instead of a single one.

- The early alliance, identification, emulation and glamourization of father is a betrayal of femininity and of receptivity—a betrayal of self for that matter since she is really a woman.
- The later rejection, control and castration of men, becoming androgynous, constitutes a betrayal of father/men. Since she confines herself to being attracted to

the weaker men who deny their masculinity, and since she herself compensates by providing the missing masculine aspect in them, her relationships will be deeply dissatisfying. Her only chance is in restoring her receptivity and femininity and trusting that a man's love will not hurt her.

- Just as with Dionysus, we have a sunken chest, a strong pelvis and legs and a big head with a protruding jaw. Believe it or not, again, we are talking about a person who is considered a sex symbol during the same periods of prevailing romanticism.

### *Consequences and Connections*

Looking at the typological structures from the point of view of betrayal, reveals quite a few startling realizations:

1) The four Stiff sub-types to be found in Rays V and VII, all have betrayed both parents. Ray V, Cinderella, betrays mother's full womanhood. Mother tries to teach her culture, womanhood, the finer things in life. However, Cinderella still sees herself as inferior, convincing herself that she will never be able to achieve or surpass what her mother is trying to do for her. This is rejection of mother's love. She expects Prince Charming to rescue her from the ashes just the way she is. When she achieves that goal through using her weakness—in essence, her lowliness, her inefficiency, her inabilities—she proves to mother that she can get all of this without self-development.

At the same time, she takes Prince Charming for granted. She takes also her father for granted, who albeit absent, is supposed to provide for her and for her mother. The providing aspect is totally taken for granted, and therefore, betrayed. Little princesses are not supposed to be concerned with the Survival Instinct, or with making one's own living, etc.

Apollo, the Obsessive Penetrator male, betrays the love of

mother by colluding with father and maintaining mother in a compliant, subservient, and inferior position. At the same time, he betrays father by viciously competing with him, wanting to kill and replace him. This is reminiscent of the Will type, only with a double betrayal.

With Diana, she sides with father early in life, becoming a tomboy, and betraying her mother's love and femininity, which she discards. However, she also betrays father by taking him away from mother and by seducing him without giving him her heart. This she does later, with her mates as well.

The male Ray VII type, Dionysus, seduces mother and identifies with her. Thus he betrays father by becoming sexually charged with mother. Later he betrays mother, too, by pursuing her, rebelling against her, chasing her and expecting her to take care of him, i.e., not loving her.

2) The double betrayal of the Stiffs is what creates the pseudo-balance in them. Having betrayed both parents, they have reached a false equilibrium, the equilibrium of evil, the one that is capable of seducing and betraying both sides. That's why the Stiffs appear to be "well adjusted," able to "cope," and conform to what society expects of them. Betraying both parents gives them enough resiliency to develop the necessary talents required for success, for being of the world. That's why the guards are so strong. They are resilient, they are hard to break, and they hide behind an idealized self of being well adjusted, and being successful. However, the idealized self must be broken and the crisis experienced in order for this person to make it in the Kingdom of God.

3) So, we see here the relationships that exist in the Will Rays—Ray I corresponding to the Apollo, in Ray V. Cinderella, Venus in Ray V, with her pseudo-love and her purism, corresponds to Ray II. Indeed, the exaggerated love in her corresponds to the withholding of love in Ray II. The

withholding of sexuality in Ray II corresponds to the using of sexuality in Ray V. Thus, many Cinderellas would very much want to be Ray II, Love/Wisdom types. If, in a typological workshop, you were to ask them to determine their Rays, most of them will instantly say Ray II, being blind to the calculative, seductiveness of the Fifth Ray.

Ray III corresponds to Dionysus, and to Diana/Athene of Ray VII. We can also see how the Ray I and Ray III types have one single betrayal to contend with, whereas, in the Rays of Attributes, we have two betrayals, making the problem that much more difficult.

Perhaps the saddest aspect of the Stiff types in Ray V and Ray VII is the wholesale closing of the heart. For all of their skill, proficiency, knowledge, capacity to cope, it is all done and developed in contradistinction to, as a protection from, and therefore, as a betrayal of love. Those people who are so impeccably healthy and who suddenly succumb to a heart attack, live most of their lives in a broken-hearted state. What is sad is that the destruction of the heart is continuously affected through the development of everything else in them. Thus, every success, every achievement, every victory is a blow to the heart. The only way out is either death or the destruction of what heretofore meant success and achievement. In midlife crisis many of them completely reverse themselves. Some experience this reversal earlier. The astonishing cases of muscular dystrophy and other "inexplicable" diseases that seem to destroy everything they have built is actually a great relief since finally they can experience and express love. Indeed, the great renewal that occurs is always accompanied by great outbursts of needing or loving/giving or both.

The same can be experienced when these people do serious cleansing of themselves. For example, when they realize their betrayal and they feel the pain of it they bring on a crisis harmlessly. Instead of contracting muscular dystrophy or having a heart attack in order to finally open their hearts, this can be achieved through total honesty and total willingness to experience the betrayal and the pain that comes from it.

That's why, when teaching somebody of these types in a method such as this one, they must be attacked relentlessly. Their type/guards must be broken. The total honesty must be brutal in order for it to work. Not to worry, like Humpty Dumpty, they will know how to put themselves all back together again. It is the breaking of the type that is difficult, not the mending of it. The former, they resist tooth and toenail; the latter, they know how to do very well.

Their pretense that they will die, that it will be the end of the world if their type is broken, is a travesty. Don't believe it. Invite them to disbelieve it as well. Their only hope to salvation must come through the brutal dynamiting of their defensive positions, through the relentless attack of truth which sometimes must be forcefully expressed to them. The worst that can happen is that they will leave, accusing you of brutality and bias. Do not be glamoured by this reaction. It comes from the petulant child that wants to remain a child. If they can't stand the heat, indeed, they should get out of the kitchen and go be pampered somewhere by some other pseudo-system of work that will collude with them. The sooner they do this the better since the collusion will accelerate the crisis, which will be, unfortunately, a harmful one now. But, harmful as it is, it will bring them to their senses. Perhaps then they will come back here and do some good cleansing.

4) If we now consider the Love Rays, we will see a) the antithetical relationship between Ray II, the withholder, and Ray IV, the over-giver. Essentially, they both reacted to the actively giving parent in opposite ways. Ray II withheld from

him. Ray IV held in what was given to him and developed a pattern of over-giving to others in adulthood.

What about Ray VI? Well, Ray VI disconnected from the giving, interpreting the giving as an intrusive threat, which by the way it may have been.

In essence, true to form, the Love Rays, II, IV and VI, have betrayed the active love as expressed by the Will Rays in three different ways.

### *Ray VI from the Point of View of Betrayal*

Ray VI also betrays both parents by disconnecting from both. However, let's not forget that at the core of Ray VI is to be found rigidity. Within this rigidity, the double betrayal of the Stiff Rays is discovered. So, we are dealing here with a **triple betrayal**, first a betrayal of both parents in the rigid core, and on top of that, an overlay of disconnection, i.e., a betrayal of that rigid core, betrayal of the whole world, betrayal of the whole enchilada. That's why here we have the most disturbed of all types, the closest to psychosis. That's why also here we have the type who is the closest to connection with the infinite. The last shall be first and the first shall be last, said the Christ. So, beware of judgement, Stiffs. Your contempt for the Ray VI type discounts the fact that they have an ability to contact their inmost self which is a lot greater than yours. The fact that their guards are continuously shattered makes them a lot more open than you.

At the same time, the reverse warning should be given to the Ray VI's, reminding them that their "openness" and feigned vulnerability is after all a hypocritical and dishonest game that betrays the truth for the third time.

✛✛✛

The method suggested in the last chapter concerning the healing of these problems is the same here. It focuses basically on the experience of the act of betrayal perpetrated against the loving parent or against the loving aspect of both parents. The goodness of the Universe is demonstrated in the very fact that the mere willingness to experience the pain of our betrayal releases the long lost love, forgiveness, healing and atonement with God.

# Chapter 32
## *The Spiritual Citizen*

---

In this faith, and in any respectable faith or form of government, any occurrence, inner or outer, must be interpreted as an out picturing of an inner condition. Everyone has the responsibility to find out how they have contributed to this situation, no matter how remote it seems to be. The present political crisis is such an event. In this Church, we will use it in this manner, seeing in it a cleansing tool, an opportunity for greater freedom and closeness to God.

The privilege of voting, just as it is for the privilege of freedom, is earned. Being earned, it can be abused, betrayed and, eventually, in that manner, lost.

These privileges are earned through the evolution of individuals when they follow a cleansing path, the Path of Purification, as Buddhagosa called it. This Path abundantly exists in all religions at their healthy beginning.

The following of this Path by individuals magnetically influences their environment, thus creating a group, then a nation of self-responsible individuals. The group or the nation's soul is then ready for the highest form of government, democracy.

The Path of Purification consists in detecting, denouncing and dissolving all wrong associations of ideas, the Pavlovian conditioning that creates all problems in life.

I have said before that the deepest, the most difficult to

find, wrong associations are revealed in political opinions and religious fanaticism. It is in these areas that all the wrong and obsolete faithfulness manifest themselves.

Do you find yourself continuously adhering to a particular political or religious stance, regardless of natural needs and of change? Scan your life and find this type of perennial stubbornness. Ask yourself:

- Whose opinion is it? Is it one of my parent's? Is it a rebellion to one of my parents? What about substitute parents, such as teachers, glamourous actors, etc.?
- Was it adopted because of a glamour, for or against one of my parents? Or substitutes?
- Do I maintain it for other reasons than the truth?
- How do I persist in it in spite of the fact that it proves to be wrong?

> Cicero:
> *Being so devoted to some preconceived opinions, they are compelled to defend that which they disapprove.*

- How have I felt compelled to defend that which I knew was wrong simply to maintain my seeking of approval? Of what am I afraid?

> Job 22:3:
> *What do you profit by trying to make it seem that your ways are perfect because you are afraid?* —Lamsa Bible

- To what extent have I created my identity around these preconceptions?
- Am I afraid of humiliation if I change my mind? How far does that fear go? Does it go as far as impairing my

capacity to freely think? Am I afraid to think lest I be humiliated?

**This is how I have destroyed my own freedom. Consequently, this is how I am a carrier of the slavery virus, creating around me an atmosphere of tyranny, injustice, destroying democracy and freedom for others.**

I am a teacher to others. I influence those around me—my children, my wife, my friends, my superiors and my subordinates. I am responsible for my own thoughts and for their influence on others.

Am I aware of the degree to which others seek my approval? How about those who honestly seek my guidance, who emulate me for ethical reasons? My responsibility to be fair is not just for myself. It involves everyone with whom I come in contact.

It, therefore, becomes extremely important for myself and for others to cleanse myself of the harmful and obsolete influences emanating from my Pavlovian conditioning.

**My cleansing, therefore, becomes my primary duty as a citizen.**

### *Parting the Waters; Right Discrimination*

Parting the waters is a symbol of discrimination. In this faith, we teach cleansing through two phases of discrimination. When Moses parts the waters to reach Sinai, he compels the Chosen People to effect the first step of discrimination.

Exodus 14:21-22:
> [21] *And Moses stretched out his hand over the sea; and the LORD caused the sea to go back by a strong east wind all that night, and made the sea dry land, and the waters were divided.* [22] *And the children of Israel went into the midst of the sea upon the dry ground: and the waters were a wall unto them on their right hand, and on their left.*

This consists in finding the Pavlovian conditioning, the early freezes that we have adopted for the sake of gaining our parents' approval. Thus, the first discrimination must be:

1) **Separating and clarifying the first vertical split, Mother/Father,** the Ray Type split, the one that erroneously associates particular Rays to a particular parent and the others to the other. We have dwelt extensively on this. However, it is an exercise that must constantly be revisited, particularly when holding intense opinions or perennial ones.

The debacle of this election is a consequence of the unwillingness, conscious or unconscious, to effect this exercise. When people, or a nation and its Supreme Court, vote strictly along party lines, it is a sure indication that they have not cleansed their Mother/Father Split. This is a nationwide disaster, blinding nations and individuals from knowing the truth; it perpetuates harmfulness and presages further outrages.

The intensity of reactions from you and others compounds the debacle. Your duty as a citizen and as a person on the Path of Purification is to urgently cleanse this level of distortion, these freezes, this Pavlovian conditioning.

Maintaining this conditioning constitutes regressing into the animal kingdom. Indeed, as self-conscious individuals, we have outgrown the level of association of ideas. We are concerned with finding the truth through reason.

For a quick refresher, ask yourself the questions that I gave you in the beginning. With whom do you associate the candidate of your choice? Why? What about his ideology? Do the same with the opposite candidate. What you are interested in is not rational answers, but the irrational ones, the ones that don't make sense anymore. **While analyzing this, you are still unfit to vote. Within yourself you live in tyranny. Your vote would impose this tyranny on others.**

The capacity to pass through the middle in different phases of life constitutes a newly earned faculty, symbolized in the Bible by the Chosen People's ability to go forward past the freezes that bogged them down in the past. The people become chosen and protected by following the Path of Purification. The way through the parted waters is the way through the distortions of the Pavlovian Mother/Father Split. The old status quo forces of the mighty pharaoh are pursuing them, intending to annihilate them.

Expect the same fate for yourself. You, too, will be pursued and persecuted by the status quo forces who expect you not to change and would rather annihilate you. You have hit too close to home for them. Your existence and progress constitutes a mortal threat to their way of life. However, since you have regained nature, nature will help you. The waters will close in on them.

---

Exodus 14:28:
> *And the waters returned, and covered the chariots, and the horsemen, and all the host of Pharaoh that came into the sea after them; there remained not so much as one of them.*

---

This represents the fact that since they are still in

confusion, the undifferentiated Mother/Father Split drowned them. Unless, of course, you collude with them. In which case, the waters will close in on you with them. Don't look back. Remember Lot's wife.

2) **The second split, an existential and ethical, horizontal split.** As you gradually dissolve the first split, a lengthy and painstaking process achieved by the Chosen People in Sinai for 40 years, you will start seeing the difference between right and wrong. Ethics will become important for you. You will see the choice of following God's nature and of abandoning the unnatural ways of the past. You will reach a point when you will have enough clarity to sustain inner justice.

This is achieved when you are able to differentiate within yourself between Higher Self and lower self, between idealized self and real self. The art—the skill—of doing this is taught by any right religion. It is the Path that runs through all religions and philosophies and cuts through all problems, resolving all conflicts.

You are gradually qualifying as a citizen in a democracy, having freed yourself of your inner tyranny. You can now be a citizen of the promised land. This is symbolized in the Bible by the crossing over from Sinai into Palestine.

**You can now vote.**

✝✝✝

Voting is exercising choice. How freely you do so depends on the extent of your inner freedom from your self-imposed tyranny. The way you vote is the way you live. Correct voting, for its own sake, takes you one step closer to at-onement and serenity in God.

## Chapter 33

# *Christmas, The Cross, Giving and Selling*

---

The completion of the vertical and horizontal splits forms the Crucifixion of the Ego. Again, we find here a religious symbol of self-actualization, freedom and completion of task.

This, of course, has everything to do with Christmas. Crucifixion means:

1) The dissolution of idolatry through the resolution of the vertical Mother/Father Split.

2) The arrival at the human and ethical level of the horizontal split between right and wrong, ethical and unethical.

It must be done in that order. As we have seen, the arrival of the second is a function of the resolution of the first. One must give up idols, glamours, capitulation and sell out, being a pet or making others into our pets. Only then will we find the freedom, the clarity of the existential level, the second level.

We will have then crucified our lower self and our idealized self. The real self is then freed to soar and accomplish its task.

## *Giving*
True giving can only come from the human and ethical

level. As long as we are still **subjects, pets,** to the idolatrous Mother/Father sell out self, no giving can be true. True giving only occurs when enough spiritual growth has been achieved to enable you to neutralize the idolatrous Mother/Father sell out.

Notice that you don't necessarily have to have totally resolved it. You must achieve enough growth to decide to neutralize it. **This is a choice that can be exercised at any time. At any time, you can know right and wrong. Certainly in this faith there is enough help and mirroring to make that available to you.**

Christmas giving, in order to be true, must be done in this spirit.

### *Needs*

Giving is not antithetical to the fulfillment of your needs. On the contrary, true giving is a need and true needing is a giving. Finding and revealing your true needs is a gift to yourself. Revealing these needs to others is a gift to others. Do you give your needs sincerely and totally? Consider the fact that this may be the greatest of all Christmas gifts.

Unify your giving and your needing and find in that true rebirth of the Christ within you.

There is a great need to give what you have received. If you don't, you clog up and become a hindrance, not a support. The revelation and the imparting of the truth is such a need and such a giving.

### *Imparting the Truth*

1) When revealing the truth, one must consider the principle of love, without which the truth can become a tool for harmfulness, serving the dark side of whoever imparts it.

2) Reciprocity should apply: if this truth pertained to you, would you have liked it imparted? Would it be right to do so?

3) Social responsibility should be respected: does imparting this truth help society? In what manner does it and how doesn't it?

4) The power hunger or money hunger of the entity imparting the truth will lead to sensationalizing it and thus doing harm by distorting it. With this motive, the truth becomes a weapon or bludgeon. It is no longer the truth.

5) Truth should not be imparted to whomever has no right to it. The right to privacy should be respected through the practice of discretion and proper silence.

6) The media should abide by the same laws, whether in imparting information, news, education, opinions, or, and particularly advertising. What is communicated should be:

- True and complete.
- Helpful and healing.
- Given in the spirit of love and caring; this by the way helps and does not hinder the making of money.
- Charitable and compassionate.
- In the spirit of justice.
- Ethical.
- Uphold the respect and dignity of everyone concerned.

7) Using half-truths, abusing the truth, concealing the truth, embellishing the truth, are all worse than blatant lies. They are more difficult, more manipulative than lies.

- They must be denounced precisely and publicly.
- We must look within to find how we are tempted to agree with them.

### *Imparting this Faith*

I would love to be your friend, but not at the expense of my beliefs. That would be dishonest and manipulative. I would be stealing your feelings.

The giving of this faith to others floods them with the

light. See where you believe that you can seduce them into it. Seducing them is inconsistent with the imparting of this faith. This is why you find yourself struggling in trying to talk about it and are ashamed of it.

Whenever you find yourself ashamed, reluctant or anxious in sharing this faith, it means that:

- You are enslaved by approval seeking forces within you.
- In the zone in which you interact with this other person, you still capitulate to the mundane, submitting to what you believe is expected of you by the other person.
- You are, therefore, still responding to the Pavlovian conditioning of the subhuman and sub-ethical part of yourself, the one that has not as yet sufficiently been cleansed and resolved of the Mother/Father Split.
- **You are, therefore, their pet, willingly responding to their training of you.**
- As their pet, **how can you possibly be seen and respected as a teacher, a bringer of a new faith, a life renewer?**
- In your relationship to this person you do not belong to our faith. Thus, presenting it to them is bound to be warped.

The correct imparting of our faith must, therefore, be done under the following conditions:

- You must confront yourself for being their pet, and them for maintaining you in that position.
- This means a challenge to someone whose approval you heretofore sought.
- It means the destruction of a contract, a petrified energy form in which you are both caught.
- It may mean the destruction of a false friendship; **this is where the imparting of this faith heals you—and them; it eliminates debilitating and regressive**

**relationships with bad influences.**

- Rather than seeing this as a problem, see it as a liberation.
- If you still feel that it is a problem, you are not of this faith. You belong to them, to the worldly world, as a dog is the property of his master
- The imparting of this faith means renewal. In the destruction of evil around you, through the imparting of this faith, you create protection and happiness for yourself.
- The imparting of this faith, far from being resisted, should be sought with loving eagerness, seeing it not only as a spreading of the light, but as a warding off of evil and of potential evil.

### *Link to Ethical Sales*

Selling is not selling out, nor seeking approval. On the contrary, it is the bringing of renewal, the shedding of light, the offering of goodness.

Anything less than that is dishonest, manipulative, and destructive. For instance, the belief that you have to make nice and capitulate to others in order to sell them is a shot in the foot. Why would you buy anything that you don't respect? Why would you buy anything from anyone that you don't respect? So, why do you expect others to buy from you in a context of lack of self-respect?

Besides, any selling that does not bring renewal, shed light or offer goodness creates guilt. It is that guilt that debilitates, making you afraid of rejection, and burns you out in your sales effort.

So, if you find yourself reluctant to sell, to make cold calls, to present your product and offer it, it means that you want to cheat, steal, be dishonest, capitulate and sell out. That's why you burn out, not the other way around. **Burn out is a consequence of destruction of integrity, not the other way around.**

The real test is found through the imparting of your faith. It is a form of selling. It will test you, in the clearest way, in the integrity with which you bring renewal to others, whether through your business selling, or through the selling of your faith.

Ethically sell, don't sell out. Sell from your zone of serenity in God.

# *Endnotes*

1. *Sensible* as in perceivable through the senses, a.k.a., 3-D reality, in contradistinction to intelligible, i.e., perceivable through the mind, inaccessible through the senses, belonging to the world of ideas, or to the Absolute. Sensible and intelligible are terminologies found in Augustine, who, himself, took them from Plato through Plotinus.

2. *Higher Self* and *lower self*: Found in the Aquarian Gospel of Jesus the Christ, copyrighted in 1907; in the Tibetan's A. A. Bailey's works (A. A. Bailey died in 1949); it is also to be found in many other writings of the 19th and the 20th Centuries.

3. Some have had the audacity to believe that they have exclusive rights to this word. They are ignorant fools. The word *path* is mentioned countless times in the Bible (61 times), in Augustin, where it is seen as a way to free the self of images, in early Christian terminology, in Moses Mendelssohn, in Descartes, not to mention the Koran and all Buddhist literature. It is mentioned in Alice A. Bailey 1810 times, and in Edgar Cayce 407 times. We can go on like this for a long time.

4. A *Ray* is defined in Chapter 3.

5. The *Rays of Aspect* are defined in Chapter 3.

6. The *line of least resistance* is found in Alice A. Bailey's books 124 times. (She died in 1949.)

7. *Higher Self* and *lower self*: Found in *The Aquarian Gospel of Jesus the Christ*, copyrighted in 1907; in the Tibetan's A. A. Bailey's works (A. A. Bailey died in 1949); it is also to be found in many other writings of the 19th and the 20th Centuries.

8. See endnote #7.

9. —*Esoteric Psychology*, Volume II, Page 267: *When the soul influences the personality and pervades all the lower manifestation, then and only then, does the personality measure up to its true significance, which is to constitute the* **mask** *of the soul, that which is the outer appearance of inner spiritual forces.*
—*From Intellect to Intuition*, Alice A. Bailey: Page 51: *Secondly: The sum total of these lower aspects, when developed and co-ordinated we call the Personality. This unity is composed of the mental and emotional states of being, the vital energy and the physical response apparatus, and these "mask" or hide the soul. These aspects develop sequentially and progressively, according to the eastern philosophy, and only on reaching a relatively high state of unfoldment does it become possible for man to [Page 52] coordinate them and later to unify them, in consciousness, with the indwelling soul.*
—*Esoteric Psychology*, Volume I, Page 49: *But potentially every human unit is all these three, and some day the appearances which were called personalities, that* **mask** *or veil reality, will fully reveal the qualities of Deity.*
—*Esoteric Healing*, Page 147: *It corresponds to the physical sun and is the expression of the personality, integrated and functioning—first of all as the disciple, and finally as the initiate. This is the true persona or* **mask.**
—*The Rays and the Initiations*, Page 51: *It is the "true* **mask**, *hiding the radiant light and the dynamic energy of a revealed Son of God."*

10. *Person*: The word comes from *persona* in Latin, which itself comes from the Greek *prosopon*. Both the Greek and the Latin terminologies mean **the mask** worn by actors on state. The meaning goes further into signifying the part played in an individual's life story. (From William Reese, under person.)

11. In C. G. Jung, the persona is what the individual wants to appear as, vis a vis, the world. (From William Reese, Carl Gustav Jung, (3)). So the *mask* concept is an adaptation of the persona concept, returned to its ancient meaning.

12. *Man's Search for Meaning*, by Viktor Frenkl, first published in Austria, 1946; then translated and, apparently first copyrighted in English in 1959, WSP Non-fiction books, p. 129: "moreover, there are various *masks* and guises under which the existential vacuum appears."

13. *A Practical Guide to Qabalistic Symbolism*, Volume I by Gareth Knight, copyright 1965, First Edition, page 13, . . . *the true is masked by the clamour and exhibitionism of the false*.

14. —1223-4
    —254-107
    —1208-1
    —2123-1

15. *Feelings mask the soul*, a chapter in *Divine Romance* by Yogananda, page 218 (1942).

16. Shelley: *The loathsome mask has fallen from* ..., from his work, *Prometheus Unbound*.

17. *Life Application Study Bible*, (Zondavan) p. 253; under Balaam: *Who and what we are will somehow come to the surface, destroying any masks we may have put on to cover up our real selves.*

18. As **cloak** in the Bible: 1 Peter 2:16: *As free, and not using your liberty for a cloak of maliciousness, but as the servants of God.*

19. Intention, intentionality:
   • From *Dictionary of Philosophy and Religion*, William Reese, page 345:
      —Aquinas distinguishes first and second **intention** following Avicenna's concept of first and second understanding.
      —Franz Brentano (1838-1917) appears to have coined the term *intentionality*.
      —Edmund Husserl(1859-1938) makes it one of the most important concepts in his philosophy. For him, all meaning and all consciousness have **intentionality.**
      —**Intentionality** also treated by other philosophers such as Donald Davidson (1917-) and John Searle (1932-) who wrote *Intentionality* in 1983.
   • The fundamental characteristic of humans is **intentionality**. It is to be found on the psychic level. **Intentionality** leads us to the spiritual level where we belong. This is according to Francisco Romero (1891-1962), Argentine philosopher. *Dictionary of Philosophy and Religion*, William Reese, page 658.

20. Sensible world, in Augustin, Plato and other philosophers, means the world that is perceived through the physical senses. Some have called it "three-dimensional reality." It is to be distinguished from the intelligible world, which is perceived outside the physical senses and which has been called by some "metaphysical reality," or "spiritual reality."

21. It is better in French: *Dieu me l'a donnée; gare à qui la touche.*

22. See the chapters on inferior functions and on the switch at puberty.

23. Plato originates the idea that before birth we knew the Absolute. The *shock of birth* created amnesia in us. Now we have a vague longing and recollection of this knowledge. These are our innate ideas and they explain reincarnation. Plato in *Parmenides Dialogue. Dictionary of Philosophy and Religion,* William Reese, page 585.

24. *Compliant:* Karen Horney speaks about three "solutions," not resolutions: *aggressive, compliant* and *detached,* in her book *Our Inner Conflicts.*

25. This is an old philosophical concept investigated since Aristotle under the Greek name *diallelus.* For Latin speaking philosophies, it has been later known as *circulus vitiosus.* The term is to be found in Bertrand Russell, in the first half of this century, in Alfred North Whitehead (1861-1947) and in Hermann Weyl (1885-1955). It was also used by Henri Poincaré (1854-1912). A.k.a. begging the question, *petitio principii* in Latin. In addition, it is many times commented on in Alice A. Bailey's books. It is also used abundantly by Karen Horney.

26. This material has been copyrighted by me in October 17, 1979 with copyright registration number TXu 37-758.

27. This portion of the book was written in the nineties.

28. From Titus 3:5: *He saved us through the washing of rebirth and renewal by the Holy Spirit.* We are, therefore, *renewers.* So are those on the Path of Purification, or on any other spiritual path. There are narrow- minded people who believe that their path is the only one. They are bigoted fanatics.

29. This is taken from a sermon written at Christmas time.

30. *Imageless* thought, i.e., thought free of images is a notion to which the Wurzburg School of Psychology devoted itself to proving in the beginning of the 20th Century.

31. The concept of *emanation* is particularly wonderful in Plotinus. For him, everything emanates from the One. In terms of Higher Self, the One is then its center.

32. The notions of *being* and *becoming* are abundantly explored in Plato. For Buddha, *becoming* is a temporary state—the wheel of becoming—which is repeated through reincarnation. *Non-being,* negated by Plato seems to refer to being devoid of consciousness.

33. *Idealized self* is a term and concept by Karen Horney, found in many of her writings.

34. It is interesting to note that Plutarch knew two of the *Rays of Aspect.* Indeed, in his *Lives* is to be found the phrase ...*pride, and self-will, the consort, as Plato calls it, of solitude, made him insufferable.* (Plutarch *Lives,* "Comparison of Alcibiades with Coriolanus," pg. 188, Collier, copyright 1909.)

35. I differentiate between *cowardice* and *fear*, the former being a distortion of the latter. Indeed, there is natural and useful fear that protects and prevents harm. The difference with cowardice occurs when the individual perennially protects himself against a possible danger, hardening himself on a permanent basis. Thus, cowardice becomes a permanent state in that individual.

36. *Daily Review* is found in *Discipleship in the New Age I* by Alice A. Bailey, page 196. The concept is developed by the Tibetan between pages 196-200.

37. As found in Alice A. Bailey, *Discipleship in the New Age II*, page 461; . . .*but do not identify yourself with them.*

38. Buddhaghosa, a Buddhist teacher early in the first millennium, wrote a book by the same title, stressing the primordial importance of self-purification.

39. This terminology and expression is abundantly found in Edgar Cayce's readings, of which here are some: T528-16; T793-2; T1917-1; T4028-1; R345-3. It has been subsequently taken up by others.

40. This terminology and expression is found in Edgar Cayce's readings: 1940-2. "He won't **own up** being as bad as he is."

41. *Webster's New World College Dictionary*, Fourth Edition: **act out:** *Psychiatry* to behave in a way that unconsciously expresses (feelings that were repressed in an earlier situation) .

42. This material has been copyrighted by me in October 17, 1979 with copyright registration number TXu 37-758.

43. This material has been copyrighted by me in October 17, 1979 with copyright registration number TXu 37-758.

44. Diana fell in love with Endymion, according to Jean Humbert, in *Mythologie, Grecque et Romaine*, 20th Edition, page 42. Other versions give a different story.

# Index

*—N—*

Nailing
    the lower self, 264
Natural state
    openness, 188
Need
    true giving is a, 368
Needs
    fulfillment of, 368
    habit of transforming
        demands into, 255
    is great to give what you
        have received, 368
    revealing is a gift, 368
Neuroses
    product of the lower self,
        270
Nixon, Richard
    after lost his identity
        through leaving the
        political scene, 301
    crisis due to holding on to
        particular trait, 301

*—O—*

Obsessive Penetrator
    doesn't like to be
        challenged, 344
    double betrayal, 344
Occurrence, inner or outer
    out picturing of an inner
        condition, 361
Oedipus
    becomes Dionysus/Hermes,
        92
    started off as Apollo male,
        92
Oppression of compliance
    difficult for Ray III to admit,
        261
O'Toole, Peter
    a Ray VI Type, 107

*—P—*

Pain
    for events of life, 164
    today's extent of, 164
Paradise
    as state of blissful
        ignorance, 253
    as state with full
        consciousness, 253
Parent
    becoming like our, 210
    hatred of a, 210
    once our role model, 210
Parent A
    of Ray IV, 341
    child betrays, 333
    child has early stimulation
        through the seduction of,
        334
    perceived as always there,
        123
Parent B
    of Ray IV, 341
    desirable, 123
    perceived as not always
        there, 123
Parents
    as role models, 229
    child doesn't perceive reality
        of, 122
    children emulate their good
        and bad habits, 229
    reality is falsified with
        freezes, 122
    try to assuage the pain of
        child's birth, 120
Parroting
    becomes, 209
    creates freezes, 210
    harbours a negative intent,
        210
    limit themselves, 210